Traction Recognition

Colin J. Marsden

Ian Allan
PUBLISHING

First published 2007

ISBN (10) 0 7110 3277 7
ISBN (13) 978 0 7110 3277 4

© Ian Allan Publishing Ltd 2007

Published by Ian Allan Publishing

an imprint of Ian Allan Publishing Ltd, Hersham, Surrey KT12 4RG.
Printed in England by Ian Allan Printing Ltd, Hersham, Surrey KT12 4RG.

Code: 0801/D

Visit the Ian Allan Publishing website at www.ianallanpublishing.com

Above: *One of the most impressive recent line-ups of modern traction was staged at Alstom Wembley on 8 January 2007, when brand new Electro-Motive Canada Class 66/7s Nos 66723, 66724, 66725, 66726 and 66727 were lined up in numeric order and staggered outside the depot's heavy repair shop. This was a joint event staged by GB Railfreight and Alstom, to show off to the media the application of full FirstGroup livery to the locomotive fleet. The line-up is seen with the new Wembley Stadium as a backdrop.* **Author**

Welcome to *Traction Recognition*, the enthusiast's guide to the present fleet of locomotives, diesel multiple-units and electric multiple-units operating over the main-line rail network in the UK.

It does not seem possible that it is now 27 years since I authored the predecessor volumes of this title, 'Motive Power Recognition', with one entire book covering each of the three basic traction principles. In the intervening years the entire UK rolling stock fleet has changed beyond belief, with a huge amount of standardisation in both locomotive and multiple unit classes, a massive reduction in the number of locomotives and a substantial increase in the number of multiple-unit trains.

The procurement of new train types has also largely altered; in the previous volumes, most 'modern' trains came from established UK builders or the erstwhile British Railways' own workshops. Today we see the vast majority of new power built by overseas companies; General Motors, now Electro-Motive Diesel have supplied locomotives, with Siemens, Bombardier and Alstom the principal multiple-unit builders. During the course of production of this title the first Japanese-built trains commenced delivery to the UK with the Class 395 'Javelin' sets for domestic HS1 services arriving in a 'ready to run' condition.

Traction Recognition has been arranged in three main chapters, colour-coded for your convenience; blue for locomotives, red for diesel multiple-units and green for electric multiple-units. Each of these chapters is divided up in TOPS class order. Each class has a full technical description giving the basic dimensions, capacities, outputs and, if passenger-carrying, the number of seats. The technical information has been supplied by the lease owners and train operators, supported by visual checks where possible. As with all such works, some conflicts of information exist, especially in terms of local modifications. In the main, the information provided is for the core fleet.

Unlike the days of British Rail, where just a handful of exterior liveries was to be found, today hundreds of different colour schemes are prevalent. *Traction Recognition* has tried to show the majority of these colours, but it goes without saying that a number of local schemes will be found, especially in the application of branding and signage on some of the older classes.

For most classes or types enumerated, illustrations are included, showing position and identity of cab-end, underside or in the case of locomotives, internal equipment positions. For some classes, cab views have been included detailing equipment; generally, equipment is the same or very similar on all types.

It is sad to record that in the UK we no longer have any factory offering a new build of diesel or electric locomotives, with fleet owners now having to look to overseas suppliers for all needs. In terms of diesel locomotives, General Motors, now Electro-Motive Diesels, based in the USA with production facilities in Canada, dominate the field of new build. Their introduction into the UK came in 1985 when Foster Yeoman purchased a handful of locomotives for aggregate traffic. Due to unparalleled levels of reliability, follow-on orders from other private operators were placed, as large industrial companies would not accept the levels of reliability offered by the then BR traction fleet.

Under privatisation the new 'owners' of the UK railway soon required new locomotives. As no British builders could meet the specifications stipulated, and as the main customer, the newly-formed English Welsh and Scottish Railway (EWS) had parentage in the US, General Motors was contracted to supply a sizeable fleet. The choice of supplier and design was very limited as only General Motors had a design accepted by the UK safety authorities, and tight delivery timescales meant no time existed for others to validate a new design. Thus General Motors modified its original Class 59 design, used a newer series power unit, incorporated other Group Standard features and introduced the Class 66 to the company catalogue.

Such was the success of the EWS build that all subsequent new-build freight locomotives for the UK have been of the same design and are now operated by Freightliner, GB Railfreight and Direct Rail Services, as well as by mainland European operators.

On the passenger market, following privatisation most operators sought to replace their inherited traction fleets, improving the travelling environment for passengers; this was hastened by the Government's demand that slam-door passenger stock be phased out as quickly as possible.

A number of builders bid for these very lucrative contracts with German-owned Bombardier Transportation and Siemens being the principal winners, both producing huge numbers of new trains over the last 10-15 years. The Bombardier (*née* Adtranz/ABB) trains have been built mainly in the UK at Derby with some production in Belgium, while the Siemens products have been built in Germany or Austria.

When Virgin Trains re-equipped the West Coast Main Line, fixed-formation-unit trains were ordered in preference to locomotives and coaches; the winner here was another joint UK/European consortium involving Alstom and Fiat.

The compilation of *Traction Recognition* would not have been possible without the assistance of the train builders, lease companies and train operators, many of which have answered numerous e-mails about the technical specifications and details of their products. The acquisition of illustrations to show as many different types, modifications, liveries and parts has not been easy and I am very grateful for the assistance of John Wills, Kevin Wills, Brian Morrison, Derek Porter, Bill Wilson and Nathan Williamson who have made their photographic collections available to me.

I do hope you enjoy the pages of *Traction Recognition* and I welcome any updates or comments from readers. These should be addressed to me via the publishers or sent with an illustration by e-mail to cjmarsden@btinternet.com.

Colin J. Marsden
December 2007
Dawlish, Devon

Class 01.5

In winter 2007, some 55 small diesel locomotives operated under the Class 015xx numeric group. These are technically not Class 01 locos, this being a collection of private owner, industrial and ex-BR classes which are Network Rail certified to operate over small sections of the national infrastructure.

The largest user of the Class 01.5 number range is the MoD and Defence Rail, with locomotives of MoD origin operating at Marchwood, Caerwent, Ludgershall, Eastriggs, Bicester, Glen Douglas, Shoeburyness, Ashchurch, Kineton, Longtown and Long Marston.

Other operators with '01s' are Siemens, T. J. Thomson, Cleveland Potash, Barton Dock, Croft Quarry, Fastline Engineering, Victa Railfreight, Lafarge Aggregates and Imerys.

Some ex-BR locomotives, such as a Class 11 and 14, are allocated '01' numbers but in the main these come from industrial backgrounds. Their operation over the NR system is very restricted.

Left Top: Built by BR Derby in 1950, this ex-BR Class 11 0-6-0 diesel-electric shunter is now owned by Harry Needle Railroad Company and used for hire work. It is painted in HNRC yellow and grey livery and presently works at Long Marston, where it is frequently involved in shunting stored items of rolling stock. Carrying its BR number of 12082 as well as its '01' identity 01553, it is viewed from its nose end in September 2005. This locomotive is modified for air brake only operation. **Kevin Wills**

Left Middle: Ministry of Defence-operated, Thomas Hill-built 0-4-0 diesel hydraulic No 265 is allocated the Network Rail identity 01526. It is usually operated within the Defence Munitions base at MoD Kineton. The locomotive is air brake fitted and can operate in multiple with other MoD shunters of the same type. **Author**

Below: This larger 0-6-0 Ministry of Defence shunter, originally MoD631, is now black-liveried 01506. It usually operates at MoD Ashchurch but is seen on public display at Old Oak Common, London. **John Wills**

Above: *The mid-1960s built Class 14 diesel-hydraulic locomotives, authorised to operate over National Network tracks are classified as 01. During the construction of the Channel Tunnel Rail Link, two Class 14s, Nos D9504 and D9529 (14029) were used, and for the duration of work were deemed as Class 01.5. Painted in mock BR blue livery and devoid of its four-character route display, No 14029 is viewed on the CTRL in mid-2006.* **Kevin Wills**

Below: *One of the more unusual locomotives to be allocated an '01' identity is Blue John, a purpose-built B-B diesel-hydraulic introduced in 1990, constructed by Hunslet Barclay for use at the Blue Circle Industries works at Hope in Derbyshire. The twin-cabbed locomotive operates the industrial connection between the Blue Circle works and the National Network transfer yard. It is air braked and has verandah-type cab ends.* **Richard Tuplin**

TOPS number range:	03001-03399 (only 03179 operational)
BR 1957 number ranges:	11187-11211 (allocated not carried)
	D2000-D2199, D2370-D2399
Former class codes:	DJ15, later D2/2, 2/1
Built by:	BR Swindon and Doncaster
Introduced:	1957-61
Wheel arrangement:	0-6-0
Weight (operational):	30.3 tonnes
Height:	12ft 7^7/$_{16}$in (3.72m)
Width:	8ft 6in (2.59m)
Length:	26ft (7.92m)
Min curve negotiable:	2 chains (40.23m)
Maximum speed:	28^1/$_2$ mph (42km/h)
Wheelbase:	9ft (2.74m)
Wheel diameter:	3ft 7in (1.09m)
Brake type:	Originally Vacuum, modified to Dual
Sanding equipment:	Pneumatic
Heating type:	Not fitted
Route availability:	1
Multiple coupling restriction:	Not fitted
Brake force:	13 tonnes
Engine type:	Gardner 8L3
Engine horsepower:	204hp (1,490kW)
Power at rail:	152hp (113kW)
Tractive effort:	15,300lb (68kN)
Cylinder bore:	5^1/$_2$in (0.13m)
Cylinder stroke:	7^3/$_4$in (0.19m)
Transmission (engine-gearbox):	Fluidrive Type 23 HYD
Transmission (gearbox):	Wilson-Drewry CA5 R7
Transmission (final drive):	SCG Type RF11
Gear ratio:	1st 4.07:1, 2nd 2.33:1, 3rd 1.55:1,
	4th 1:1, 5th 1:1.87
Fuel tank capacity:	300 gal (1,364lit)
Cooling water capacity:	40 gal (182lit)
Lub oil capacity:	8 gal (36lit)
Operator:	First Capital Connect

Fact File

The sole example of the standard BR 'small' diesel shunter is No 03179, working for First Capital Connect at its Hornsey depot in North London.

More than 120 of this design of small 'go anywhere' diesel-mechanical shunter were built between 1957-61 to replace steam shunting locos from numerous location with restricted curvature tracks or light freight operations.

The majority of the fleet was withdrawn in the 1970s-80s as smaller yards were closed in favour of larger marshalling yards. One or two members were retained for specific duties, such as working in the Isle of Wight; when operations here were replaced by track machine based vehicles, one of the class returned to the mainland and was allocated to Hornsey for depot pilot work, first with WAGN and more recently with First Capital Connect.

Below: *The sole member of Class 03, No 03179, is seen at Hornsey Depot in June 2007, displaying First Capital Connect livery.* **Author**

Locomotives

Sub class:	08/0	08/9
TOPS number range:	08001 - 08958	08993-08995
Previous number ranges:	13000-13366, D3000-D4192	(From main fleet)
Former class codes:	DEJ4, then D3/2, 3/1	08/0
Built by:	BR workshops Derby, Crewe, Darlington, Doncaster, Horwich	BR Landore
Years introduced:	1953-59	1985-87
Wheel arrangement:	0-6-0	0-6-0
Weight:	49.6 - 50.4 tonnes	49.8 tonnes
Height:	12ft 8⁵/₈in (3.87m)	11ft 10in (3.60m)
Length:	29ft 3in (8.91m)	29ft 3in (8.91m)
Width:	8ft 6in (2.59m)	8ft 6in (2.59m)
Wheelbase:	11ft 6in (3.50m)	11ft 6in (3.50m)
Wheel diameter:	4ft 6in (1.37m)	4ft 6in (1.37m)
Min curve negotiable:	3 chains (60.35m)	3 chains (60.35m)
Engine type:	English Electric 6KT	English Electric 6KT
Engine output:	400hp (298kW)	400hp (298kW)
Power at rail:	260hp (194kW)	260hp (194kW)
Tractive effort:	35,000lb (156kN)	35,000lb (156kN)
Cylinder bore:	10in (0.25m)	10in (0.25m)
Cylinder stroke:	12in (0.30m)	12in (0.30m)
Maximum speed:	15mph (25km/h)	15mph (25km/h)
Brake type:	Originally Vacuum, some modified to Dual or Air	Dual
Brake force:	19 tonnes	19 tonnes
Route availability:	5	5
Heating type:	Not fitted	Not fitted
Multiple coupling type:	Not fitted (See notes)	Not fitted
Main generator type:	EE801-8E or E801-14E	EE801-8E or E801-14E
Aux generator type:	90V locos - EE736-2D or EE736-4E 110V locos - EE906-3D	EE736-2D or EE736-4E
Traction motor type:	EE506-6A or EE506-7C	EE506-6A
No of traction motors:	2	2
Gear ratio:	Overall - 23.9:1, First train - 82:15, Second train - 70:16	Overall - 23.9:1, First train - 82:15 Second train - 70:16
Fuel tank capacity:	668gal (3,036lit)	668gal (3,036lit)
Lub oil capacity:	45gal (204lit)	45gal (204lit)
Sanding equipment:	Pneumatic	Pneumatic
Present owners:	Various	EWS Finance
Present operators:	EWS, Freightliner, RT Rail, Wabtec FGW, Serco, Alstom, HNRC, Maintrain, Bombardier, Victa/ Westlink Rail, Cotswold, Eurostar UK	EWS
Special fittings:	Some locos - Radio, TPWS, Buck-eye couplers, high-level air pipes 08948 - Scharfenberg coupler 08466/596/752/854/886/921/951 - remote control equipment	Some locos - Radio
Sub-class variations:	Standard loco, a direct descendant of LMS prewar design	Locomotives modified from Class 08/0 with reduced cab height for use on BPGV line in West Wales
Notes:	08738/939 fitted with multiple control for EuroCargo Rail	

Based on the pre-war LMS-design of 0-6-0 diesel-electric shunting locomotive, 1,193 locomotives of this design were built for British Railways in a ten-year period from 1952. The design was the 'standard' heavy shunting locomotive for the UK and operated in all areas, except where limited clearance or axle restrictions were imposed.

The class was gradually reduced in size over the years as yards and the need for pilot locomotives reduced; today, around 240 remain active for the mainstream operators, with fewer than 180 authorised for Network Rail use.

A number of the fleet are now owned by the private sector and used within industry, while others have been preserved. Originally all were painted in BR black or green, adopting BR blue from the late 1960s. After privatisation many new liveries were applied to reflect ownership.

Above: *A number of Class 08s were fitted over the years with high-level brake and main reservoir pipes; these were a direct 'spur' from the buffer-beam connections. They were used to couple to EMU and DEMU stock fitted with waist height pipes. No 08830 is a dual air/vacuum brake locomotive, operated by LNWR, Crewe.* **John Wills**

Left Middle: *Following the 1990s privatisation of the rail industry, a number of businesses were formed to hire locomotives to operators. One such company was RT Rail, who supply quality shunting power. Air brake only fitted No 08762 is seen at Dagenham, painted in RT Rail black livery with 'wasp' colours on the nose end and front flat surfaces.* **Author**

Left Bottom: *Freightliner operate a small fleet of Class 08s, mainly fitted for air brake-only operation. Some are painted in Freightliner's house colours of green and yellow, as shown here on No 08624 at Midland Road, Leeds. With a top speed of only 15mph, the Class 08s are seldom allowed onto main line tracks, and are usually confined to marshalling yards or private terminals. However, it is increasingly common for train locomotives to perform depot pilot duties.* **John Wills**

Above: *One of the principal suppliers of hire traction, mainly of the main line type, is Cotswold Rail, a company which has a number of ongoing contracts to supply TOCs with pilot and standby traction. One of the first locomotives to go under the Cotswold banner was Class 08 No 08871, which was refurbished to main-line certified condition by Wabtec of Doncaster. It is seen here in the works yard at Wabtec after completion, painted in Cotswold Rail silver livery offset by wasp ends which are also applied to the cab front, fuel tank front and exhauster box. This example has two nose-end marker lights and sports the last three digits of its number on the buffer beam.* **Author**

Below: *Standard Class 08/0 No 08804, viewed from the left side. Main equipment areas are: A-radiator/cooler group with fan on front, B-engine compartment, C-generator compartment, D-driving cab, E-vacuum exhauster compartment (if fitted), F-battery box, G-air compressor compartment, H-fuel tank, I-removable roof section, J-sand boxes, K-fuel filler port. These are the standard equipment positions for all members of Class 08 and 09. No. 08804 displays standard EWS livery, the cab end has been modified to have only two marker/tail lights.* **John Wills**

Left: *Maintrain, the depot facility operator at Leeds Neville Hill and Derby Etches Park, maintains a small fleet of Class 08s for pilot work. These are air brake-fitted machines, painted in Maintrain blue livery and are usually maintained to a high standard. No 08525 also sports a standard headlight, mounted centrally on the cab end. It is seen at Leeds Neville Hill.* **John Wills**

Left Middle: *Doncaster-based Wabtec is another of the main hire companies maintaining a spot-hire Class 08 fleet for TOC or industrial use. Most are painted in Wabtec black livery with the company logo on the engine compartment side doors. No 08669 is seen at Plymouth during a hire contract with First Great Western. Note the detachable buck-eye coupling attached to the front draw hook, used for connection to HST stock. This air brake-only example carries an instanter coupling hanging over the far lamp iron.* **John Wills**

Below: *Operator Midland Mainline (now East Midland Trains) applied turquoise livery to Derby-based yard pilot No 08899, complete with wasp ends on the front, back and on forward-facing flat surfaces. The fully-branded locomotive is seen shunting stock at Derby. Today the vast majority of the Class 08 fleet is prevented from main-line operation by the omission of TPWS and OTMR equipment.* **John Wills**

Right: *One specialist locomotive within the Class 08 fleet is No 08948, owned by Eurostar UK and based at Temple Mills Eurostar depot for shunting Class 373 Eurostar stock. To facilitate this work, BREL Crewe installed a drop-head Scharfenberg coupling in 1993 and associated air brake and control equipment, in the process increasing the locomotive's length to 31ft 2in. It is painted in double-grey livery and never strays from the Eurostar facility.* **Author**

Right Middle: *EWS has three reduced cab-height Class 08/9s on roster; these were converted for use on the restricted-gauge Burry Port & Gwendraeth Valley (BPGV) line in west Wales, but are now part of the core fleet. No 08994, complete with cast number and nameplate* Gwendraeth *stands at Swindon. Note the integral front-end headlight and combination coupler.* **Kevin Wills**

Below: *Alstom, which operates a number of depot and works facilities, has a fleet of Class 08s for depot pilot duties. A number of inherited liveries are carried, but gradually the operator's black colours are being applied following overhaul. No 08454 is shown shunting Class 325 Royal Mail stock at Wembley depot in January 2007. This locomotive retains dual brake equipment. In recent years a number of Class 08s have been fitted with cab radio equipment, enabling a more clear understanding of shunt moves to be made between control staff and drivers.* **Author**

Sub class:	09/0	09/1	09/2
TOPS number range:	09001-09026	09101-09107	09201-09205
Previous number range:	D3665-71, D3719-21, D4099-114	Rebuilt from Class 08	Rebuilt from Class 08
Former class codes:	DEJ4, then 3/1	Class 08	Class 08
Built by:	BR Darlington/ Horwich	RFS Kilnhurst	RFS Kilnhurst
Years introduced:	1959-62	1992-93	1992-93
Wheel arrangement:	0-6-0	0-6-0	0-6-0
Weight:	50 tonnes	50 tonnes	50 tonnes
Height:	12ft 8⁵/₈in (3.87m)	12ft 8⁵/₈in (3.87m)	12ft 8⁵/₈in (3.87m)
Length:	29t 3in (8.91m)	29t 3in (8.91m)	29t 3in (8.91m)
Width:	8ft 6in (2.59m)	8ft 6in (2.59m)	8ft 6in (2.59m)
Wheelbase:	11ft 6in (3.50m)	11ft 6in (3.50m)	11ft 6in (3.50m)
Wheel diameter:	4ft 6in (1.37m)	4ft 6in (1.37m)	4ft 6in (1.37m)
Min curve negotiable:	3 chains (60.35m)	3 chains (60.35m)	3 chains (60.35m)
Engine type:	English Electric 6KT	English Electric 6KT	English Electric 6KT
Engine output:	400hp (298kW)	400hp (298kW)	400hp (298kW)
Power at rail:	269hp (201kW)	269hp (201kW)	269hp (201kW)
Tractive effort:	25,000lb (111kN)	25,000lb (111kN)	25,000lb (111kN)
Cylinder bore:	10in (0.25m)	10in (0.25m)	10in (0.25m)
Cylinder stroke:	12in (0.30m)	12in (0.30m)	12in (0.30m)
Maximum speed:	27¹/₂ mph (34km/h)	27¹/₂ mph (34km/h)	27¹/₂ mph (34km/h)
Brake type:	Dual	Dual	Dual
Brake force:	19 tonnes	19 tonnes	19 tonnes
Route availability:	5	5	5
Heating type:	Not fitted	Not fitted	Not fitted
Multiple coupling type:	Not fitted	Not fitted	Not fitted
Main generator type:	EE801-13E or EE801-14E	EE801-13E or EE801-14E	EE801-13E or EE801-14E
Aux generator type:	EE906-3D	EE906-3D	EE906-3D
Traction motor type:	EE506-10C	EE506-10C	EE506-10C
No of traction motors:	2	2	2
Gear ratio:	Overall - 23.9:1 First train - 82:15 Second train - 70:16	Overall - 23.9:1 First train - 82:15 Second train - 70:16	Overall - 23.9:1 First train - 82:15 Second train - 70:16
Fuel tank capacity:	668gal (3,037lit)	668gal (3,037lit)	668gal (3,037lit)
Cooling water capacity:	140gal (636lit)	140gal (636lit)	140gal (636lit)
Lub oil capacity:	45gal (204lit)	45gal (204lit)	45gal (204lit)
Sanding equipment:	Pneumatic	Pneumatic	Pneumatic
Present operators:	EWS, Southern	EWS	EWS
Present owner:	EWS Finance, Southern	EWS Finance	EWS Finance
Special fittings:	Some locos - Radio, Headlight, TPWS	Some locos - Radio, Headlight, TPWS	Some locos - Radio Headlight, TPWS
Sub class variations:	Higher-speed version of standard Class 08 originally allocated to the former BR Southern Region	Modified from standard Class 08, using 110V electrical equipment	Modified from standard Class 08, using 90V electrical equipment

Left: *Class 09 cab layout, also applicable to Class 08. The cab layout of these machines was little altered from the pre-war LMS design and is very spartan by today's standards. The main 'driving' position is on the right side in this view, taken looking towards the nose of engine section. The main items of equipment are: A-master switch, which when rotated against a spring resistance starts the locomotive (no driver's key is used on these locomotives), B-direction controller (forward, engine only, reverse), C-power controller, D-direct air brake valve, E-whistle valve, F-automatic brake valve, air, vacuum on train and air on loco, G-sand valve. The cab shown is of No 09026.* **Author**

The 26 members of the original Class 09 fleet were built for BR Southern Region use and had a higher top speed of 27.5mph. The fleet also incorporated waist height air connections for coupling to Southern Region EMU and DEMU stock. After the need for '09s' diminished on the Southern Region, the fleet found deployment around the entire network.

In 1992-93, when modernisation of the shunter fleet was on the cards, two batches of Class 09 were modified from Class 08s with new equipment and a higher top speed of 27mph. These conversions did not have waist-height air connections.

Above left/right: *Cab/nose end layout, also applicable to Class 08. A-main reservoir pipe, B-position for vacuum pipe, C-air brake pipe, D-main reservoir pipe, E-waist height dual air pipes, F-marker/tail light, G-coupling. Equipment is the same at both ends. The above-right view shows No 09026 also fitted with depot third-rail de-icing equipment.* **Author**

Right middle: *Standard Class 09/0 painted in all over 'general' grey livery, viewed from the cab end. Originally cab doors on the Class 08 and 09 fleet were metal-framed wood; however, over the years standard metal doors with an upper and lower opening handle have been fitted. No 09016 at Plymouth is a dual air/vacuum brake example; most are now air brake only.* **Author**

Right bottom: *The twelve Class 08-09 conversions by RFS Kilnhurst in 1992-93 were part of a project to modernise the 0-6-0 fleet, and saw a total rebuild with much new and reconditioned equipment. The higher maximum speed of 27mph was incorporated, together with electric fuel-transfer pumps and cab radios. The fleet is now operated by EWS and can be found throughout the UK rail network. No 09103 is seen at Aberdeen.* **Author**

Sub class:	20/0	20/3	20/9
TOPS number range:	20001-20228	20301-20315	20901-20906
1957 BR number range:	D8000-D8199, D8300-D8327 series	20047/084/127/120/095/ 131/128/187/075/190/ 102/042/194/117/104	20101/060/083/041/ 225/219
Former class codes:	D10/3, then 10/3	20/0	20/0
Built by:	English Electric, Vulcan Foundry or Robert Stephenson & Hawthorn	Rebuilt: Brush Traction or RFS Doncaster	Rebuilt: Hunslet Barclay
Years introduced:	1957-1968	1995-1998 (as 20/3)	1989 (as 20/9)
Wheel arrangement:	Bo-Bo	Bo-Bo	Bo-Bo
Weight:	73 tonnes	73 tonnes	73 tonnes
Height:	12ft 7⅝in (3.84m)	12ft 7⅝in (3.84m)	12ft 7⅝in (3.84m)
Length:	46ft 9¼in (14.26m)	46ft 9¼in (14.26m)	46ft 9¼in (14.26m)
Width:	8ft 9in (2.66m)	8ft 9in (2.66m)	8ft 9in (2.66m)
Wheelbase:	32ft 6in (9.90m)	32ft 6in (9.90m)	32ft 6in (9.90m)
Bogie wheelbase:	8ft 6in (2.59m)	8ft 6in (2.59m)	8ft 6in (2.59m)
Bogie pivot centres:	24ft 0in (7.31m)	24ft 0in (7.31m)	24ft 0in (7.31m)
Wheel diameter:	3ft 7in (1.09m)	3ft 7in (1.09m)	3ft 7in (1.09m)
Min curve negotiable:	3.5 chains (70.40m)	3.5 chains (70.40m)	3.5 chains (70.40m)
Engine type:	English Electric 8SVT Mk2	English Electric 8SVT Mk2	English Electric 8SVT Mk2
Engine output:	1,000hp (745kW)	1,000hp (745kW)	1,000hp (745kW)
Power at rail:	770hp (574kW)	770hp (574kW)	770hp (574kW)
Tractive effort:	42,000lb (187kN)	42,000lb (187kN)	42,000lb (187kN)
Cylinder bore:	10in (0.25m)	10in (0.25m)	10in (0.25m)
Cylinder stroke:	12in (0.35m)	12in (0.35m)	12in (0.35m)
Maximum speed:	75mph (121km/h)	75mph (121km/h)	60mph (97km/h)
Brake type:	Vacuum, later dual	Air	Air
Brake force:	35 tonnes	31 tonnes	35 tonnes
Route availability:	5	5	5
Heating type:	Not fitted(through piped)	Not fitted	Not fitted
Multiple coupling type:	Blue star	DRS system	Blue star
Main generator type:	EE819-3C	EE819-3C	EE819-3C
Aux generator type:	EE911-2B	EE911-2B	EE911-2B
ETS generator type:	Not fitted	Not fitted	Not fitted
Traction motor type:	EE526-5D or EE526-8D	EE526-8D	EE526-8D
No of traction motors:	4	4	4
Gear ratio:	63:17	63:17	63:17
Fuel tank capacity:	380gal (1,727lit)	1,080gal (4,909lit)	380-1,040gal (1,727-4,727lit)
Cooling water capacity:	130gal (591lit)	130gal (591lit)	130gal (591lit)
Lub oil capacity:	100gal (455lit)	100gal (455lit)	100gal (455lit)
Sanding equipment:	Pneumatic	Pneumatic	Pneumatic
Special fittings:	Snowplough brackets	Snowplough brackets,	Snowplough brackets,
Present operator:	HNRC	DRS	HNRC
Sub class variations:	Standard as built locos	DRS-owned/operated locos fitted with modified cab equipment and fully + 640gal (2,909lit)	Modified from Class 20/0 sold to Hunslet-Barclay, then DRS, now HNRC
Notes:			

Fact File

The BR Standard Type 1, later Class 20 fleet, built as a direct result of the BTC's 1955 Modernisation Plan and introduced in 1957, is one of the most robust and reliable diesel-electric fleets ever built.

A total of 228 locomotives of the design was built over an eleven-year period, with members operating principally on the Eastern, London Midland and Scottish Regions.

With the run-down of diesel classes from the late 1970s, the vast majority of Class 20s was withdrawn, however the 1990s expansion into the private sector saw a large number of locomotives pass to further operational ownership; at first six were sold to Hunslet Barclay of Kilmarnock to operate weed-control trains. Private ownership expanded when BNSF's rail division Direct Rail Services purchased a fleet and refurbished them for flask and general freight traffic.

Today, 50 years after their first introduction, a number of Class 20s are still in daily operation, working for DRS and several 'spot-hire' companies such as Harry Needle Railroad Company (HNRC). A large number of the fleet has also been saved by the preservation movement as ideal power for small branch-line operations.

All examples now operating for DRS have been fully refurbished.

Above and Below: *Views of both ends of a standard DRS Class 20/3; these locomotives have been heavily rebuilt from their past BR days and brought up to modern operating standards. The main equipment areas/items are: A-No 2 end, B-No 1 end, C-compressor and traction motor fan compartment, D-radiator unit, E-engine compartment, F-generator compartment, G-traction motor blower compartment, H-secondary fuel tank, I-battery box and air reservoirs behind, J-fuel filler port, K-group standard light cluster, (head, marker and tail lights), L-headlight, M-horns behind grille, N-sandbox, O-engine control air pipe, P-main reservoir pipe, Q-air brake pipe, R-DRS multiple control jumper socket. As will be seen in the above illustration, the cab-end equipment is the same as on the nose end. It will be noted that during refurbishment for DRS, new cab front and side windows were installed and a number of revisions made to the cab controls, including the fitting of TPWS and OTMR equipment. During the course of DRS rebuilding, the traditional blue-star multiple control jumper equipment was removed. Locomotives operated by HNRC and the preservation sector differ in equipment positions, especially the retention of vacuum brakes and blue-star jumpers. Also secondary fuel tanks to extend operating range are not fitted. No 20307 is seen at Wabtec Doncaster.* **Author**

Class 21

Sub class:	21/5	21/6
Number range:	21544-21547 (not carried)	21610-21611 (not carried)
Class type:	G1206	G1000
Built by:	Vossloh	Vossloh
Introduced:	2005-2006	2006
Wheel arrangement:	B-B	B-B
Weight (operational):	87.3 tonnes	80 tonnes
Height:	13ft 8in (4.22m)	13ft 9in (4.25m)
Width:	10ft 10in (3.08m)	10ft 10in (3.08m)
Length:	48ft 2in (14.70m)	46ft 3in (14.13m)
Min curve negotiable:	197ft (60m)	262ft (80m)
Maximum speed:	62mph (100km/h)	62mph (100km/h)
Wheelbase:	31ft 5in (9.6m)	
Bogie wheelbase:	7ft 9in (2.4m)	
Bogie pivot centres:	23ft	
Wheel diameter:	3ft 3in (1m)	3ft 3in (1m)
Brake type:	Air (disk)	Air (disk)
Sanding equipment:	Pneumatic	Pneumatic
Route availability:	Not UK issued	Not UK issued
Heating type:	Not fitted	Not fitted
Multiple restriction:	Within type (up to three locos)	Within type (up to three locos)
Brake force:	?? tonnes	?? tonnes
Engine type:	Caterpiller 3512B DI-TA	MTU 8V 4000 R41L
Engine horsepower:	2,011hp (1,500kW)	1,475hp (1,100kW)
Power at rail:	1,700 hp (1,268kW)	1,150hp (857kW)
Tractive effort:	57,101lb (254kN)	58,225lb (259kN)
Cylinder bore:	6.7in (.17m)	6.49in (0.165m)
Cylinder stroke:	7.5i n (.19m)	7.48in (0.190m)
Transmission type:	Hydraulic Voith L5r4zU2	Hydraulic Voith L4R4
Fuel tank capacity:	770Gal (3,500 Lit)	660gal (3,000lit)
Owner:	Angel Trains	Angel Trains
Operator:	Euro Cargo Rail (EWS-I)	Euro Cargo Rail (EWS-I)

Fact File

In October 2005 the French Minister of Transport authorised EWS to operate services in France. Until Class 66s could be modified for this role, Angel Trains hired EWS International, through a new operating arm Euro Cargo Rail (ERC) using firstly four and then six Vossloh single-cab locomotives of Class G1206 and G1000. ERC also operates a sizeable wagon fleet.

The locomotives are painted in maroon livery and do not carry UK TOPS identification, as they are used exclusively in Mainland Europe.

Allocated to Dollands Moor, the fleet does not have a UK Safety Case, but are authorised to be hauled through the Channel Tunnel.

Below: *Painted in EWS International maroon livery, Vossloh G1206 No 1544 (UK No 21544) is seen at Dollands Moor depot in December 2005.* **A. M. Denny**

Fact File

Built as the second main order for the BR standard Type 2, following the Class 24 design off the production line. The Class 25 fleet became the third most numerous BR class of diesel-electric locomotive.

Used over all parts of the BR network, these were of the mixed traffic design used for both passenger and freight operations. The main fleet was withdrawn in between the 1970s-90s as traffic declined and more modern locomotives were introduced.

A number entered the world of preservation and are now fully restored to original body conditions and liveries.

The North Yorkshire Moors Railway-based No D7628 is certified for Network Rail operation (limited routes) and has been used on through services between the NYMR and Whitby. It is presently in 1960s BR green livery.

Below: *The only Network Rail certified Class 25, No D7628 (25278) stands at Pickering on the North Yorkshire Moors Railway. As can be seen from the buffer beam, this locomotive does not retain train heating.* **Author**

TOPS number range:	25001-25327 - only 25278 (D7628) certified for main line use
BR 1957 number range:	D5151-D5299, D7500-D7677
Former class codes:	D12/1, later 12/1
Built by:	BR Derby, Darlington, Crewe and Beyer Peacock, Gorton
Introduced:	1961-1967
Wheel arrangement:	Bo-Bo
Weight (operational):	73.9 tonnes
Height:	12ft 8in (3.86m)
Width:	9ft 1in (2.76m)
Length:	50ft 6in (15.39m)
Min curve negotiable:	$4^{1}/_{2}$ chains (90.52m)
Maximum speed:	90mph (145km/h)
Wheelbase:	36ft 6in (11.12m)
Bogie wheelbase:	8 ft 6in (2.59m)
Bogie pivot centres:	28ft (8.53m)
Wheel diameter:	3ft 9in (1.14m)
Brake type:	Originally Vacuum, modified to Dual
Sanding equipment:	Pneumatic
Heating type:	Steam - Stones L 4610 (if fitted)
Route availability:	5
Multiple coupling restriction:	Blue Star
Brake force:	38 tonnes
Engine type:	Sulzer 6LDA28B
Engine horsepower:	1,250hp (931kW)
Power at rail:	1,000hp (746kW)
Tractive effort:	45,000lb (200kN)
Cylinder bore:	11in (0.27m)
Cylinder stroke:	14in (0.35m)
Main generator type:	AEI RTB 15656
Aux generator type:	AEI RTB 7440
Number of traction motors:	4
Traction motor type:	AEI 253AY or AEI 137BK
Gear ratio:	18:67
Fuel tank capacity:	500 gal (2,273lit)
Cooling water capacity:	187 gal (850lit)
Boiler water capacity:	580 gal (2,651lit) - if fitted
Lub oil capacity:	100 gal (455lit)
Operator:	North Yorkshire Moors Railway
Authorised for main line use:	25278 (D7628)

Sub Class:	31/1	31/4	31/5
TOPS Number range:	31101-31327	31400-31469	31507-31569
1957 BR number range:	D5518-D5862	From Class 31/1 fleet	From Class 31/4 fleet
Former class codes:	D14/2, then 14/2	31/1	31/4
Built by:	Brush, Loughborough	Modified by BR	Modified by BR
Years introduced:	1958-1962	As 31/4 1970-1985	As 31/5 1990-1994
Wheel arrangement:	A1A-A1A	A1A-A1A	A1A-A1A
Weight:	107-111 tonnes	107-111 tonnes	107-111 tonnes
Height:	12ft 7in (3.83m)	12ft 7in (3.83m)	12ft 7in (3.83m)
Length:	56ft 9in (17.29m)	56ft 9in (17.29m)	56ft 9in (17.29m)
Width:	8ft 9in (2.66m)	8ft 9in (2.66m)	8ft 9in (2.66m)
Wheelbase:	42ft 10in (13.05m)	42ft 10in (13.05m)	42ft 10in (13.05m)
Bogie wheelbase:	14ft 0in (4.26m)	14ft 0in (4.26m)	14ft 0in (4.26m)
Bogie pivot centres:	28ft 10in (8.78m)	28ft 10in (8.78m)	28ft 10in (8.78m)
Wheel diameter:	Powered - 3ft 7in (1.09m) Pony - 3ft 3^1/2in (1m)	Powered - 3ft 7in (1.09m) Pony - 3ft 3^1/2in (1m)	Powered - 3ft 7in (1.09m) Pony - 3ft 3^1/2in (1m)
Min curve negotiable:	4.5 chains (90.52m)	4.5 chains (90.52m)	4.5 chains (90.52m)
Engine type:	English Electric 12SVT	English Electric 12SVT	English Electric 12SVT
Engine output:	1,470hp (1,097kW)	1,470hp (1,097kW)	1,470hp (1,097kW)
Power at rail:	1,170hp (872kW)	1,170hp (872kW)	1,170hp (872kW)
Tractive effort:	31102-110 42,000lb (190kN) 31128-319 35,900lb (160kN)	35,900lb (160kN)	35,900lb (160kN)
Cylinder bore:	10in (0.25m)	10in (0.25m)	10in (0.25m)
Cylinder stroke:	12in (0.30m)	12in (0.30m)	12in (0.30m)
Maximum speed:	31102-110 80mph (129km/h) 31128-319 90mph (145km/h)	90mph (145km/h)	90mph (145km/h)
Brake type:	Vacuum, modified to Dual	Dual	Dual
Brake force:	49 tonnes	49 tonnes	49 tonnes
Route availability:	5	6	6
Heating type:	Steam - Spanner Mk 1 (removed)	Electric, index 66, dual heat Spanner Mk 1	Electric – isolated
Multiple coupling type:	Blue star	Blue star	Blue star
Main generator type:	Brush TG160-48	Brush TG160-48	Brush TG160-48
Aux generator type:	Brush TG69-42	-	-
Aux ETS alternator type:	-	Brush BL100-30	Brush BL100-30
Traction motor type:	Brush TM73-68	Brush TM73-68	Brush TM73-68
No of traction motors:	4	4	4
Gear ratio:	31101-31116 - 64:17 31117-31327 - 60:19	60:19	60:19
Fuel tank capacity:	530gal (2,409lit)	530gal (2,409lit)	530gal (2,409lit)
Cooling water capacity:	156gal (709lit)	156gal (709lit)	156gal (709lit)
Lub oil capacity:	110gal (500lit)	110gal (500lit)	110gal (500lit)
Boiler water capacity:	600gal (2,727lit) (if fitted)	600gal (2,727lit) (if fitted)	-
Boiler fuel capacity:	100gal (454lit) (if fitted)	100gal (454lit) (if fitted)	-
Sanding equipment:	Pneumatic	Pneumatic	Pneumatic
Present operators:	Network Rail, Nemesis Rail, private owners	Mainline Rail, Network Rail, RVE	Rail Vehicle Engineering (RVE)
Sub class variations:	Basic locomotives	Locos fitted with electric train supply	31/4s with ETS isolated

Note: Locomotives numbered lower than D5530 (31112) and selectively between D5531-5561 (31113-31143) had disc train reporting equipment. All other locomotives had roof-mounted headcode/marker light boxes.

Fact File

This is another of the classes built as a direct result of the 1955 Modernisation Plan, the Brush Type 2, or BR Class 31. Over the years various derivatives have been introduced with the provision of electric train supply.

Following withdrawal from BR and the main private freight operators, a number of class members were sold to Fragonset (later FM Rail and now Mainline Rail and Nemesis Rail), and Network Rail. The latter's locomotives are painted in yellow livery and power track-test trains, while the Mainline and Nemesis Rail locomotives can be found virtually anywhere on the rail network powering freight, charter or 'spot-hire' services.

The Class 31s are also popular with preservation groups and a number are to be found fully restored and in frequent use on the larger preserved lines.

31/6
31601-31602
From Class 31/1 fleet
31/1
Modified by Fragonset
As 31/6 1999
A1A-A1A
107-111 tonnes
12ft 7in (3.83m)
56ft 9in (17.29m)
8ft 9in (2.66m)
42ft 10in (13.05m)
14ft 0in (4.26m)
28ft 10in (8.78m)
Powered - 3ft 7in (1.09m)
Pony - 3ft 3½in (1m)
4.5 chains (90.52m)
English Electric 12SVT
1,470hp (1,097kW)
1,170hp (872kW)
35,900lb (160kN)

10in (0.25m)
12in (0.30m)
60mph (97km/h)

Dual
49 tonnes
5
Through wired

Blue star
Brush TG160-48
Brush TG69-42
-
Brush TM73-68
4
60:19

530gal (2,409lit)
156gal (709lit)
110gal (500lit)
-
-

Pneumatic
Mainline Rail,
Rail Vehicle Engineering
Class 31/1 fitted with through
ETS control and cabling to enable
operation at remote end of trains

Above: *Standard Class 31/1 viewed from the No 2 end. Originally all members had front communicating doors, but these have now all been sealed. This locomotive, No 31128 is painted in FM Rail black livery, is dual brake fitted and has a central headlight.* **Author**

Below: *Between 1970 and 1985 around 70 Class 31s were fitted with electric train supply to enable passenger operation; these locomotives were recognisable by the ETS jumper and socket on the front end. ETS-fitted locomotives became Class 31/4 under the TOPS notation system. No 31468 is illustrated.* **Author**

Right: *Two locomotives are classified as Class 31/6; these are standard Class 31/1s fitted with ETS jumper cables and control equipment, allowing remote control of a Class 31/4 at the rear end of a train. No provision for ETS is fitted. No 31602 is illustrated.* **Author**

Above: *Class 31 equipment positions, applicable to all sub-classes. A-No 1 end, B-No 2 end, C-radiator compartment, fan on roof, D-engine compartment, E-electrical control equipment compartment, F-battery box, G-sandbox, H-fire extinguisher hand pull. No 31190, then painted in West Coast maroon livery, is seen stabled on Exeter shed.* **Author**

Left Middle: *While operated under the FM Rail banner, Class 31/6 No 31601 was repainted into Wessex Trains pink/maroon livery to power summer relief services on the Bristol-Westbury-Weymouth and Bristol-Brighton routes. The livery did not particularly suit the body profile of the '31' and was hard to keep clean. No 31601 is viewed from its No 1 end at Exeter.* **Author**

Left Bottom: *Network Rail has a major need for motive power to operate track test trains throughout the UK network. In addition to the HST and multiple unit formed trains a number of locomotive-hauled sets operate each week. These are frequently powered by hired-in traction from DRS or EWS, but the company does own a fleet of five Class 31s, of which four, Nos 31105/233/285/465 are operational and painted in NR yellow livery. In most cases these have extra lights, sockets and equipment fitted depending on the type of test or inspection service being operated. On many occasions the 'NR '31s' are used for drivers' route training in preparation for test train use. No 31285 is seen passing Dawlish.* **Author**

Above: *An offshoot of the defunct FM Rail operation to emerge in 2007 was Rail Vehicle Engineering which owns and operates Class 31 No 31190, which operates with its original number D5613 and is painted in immaculate 1960s BR green and grey livery with a small yellow warning panel. The locomotive has been brought up to the latest Group Standards and is frequently used to power Network Rail test trains. It is seen here at Taunton with one of the NR test formations.* **Nathan Williamson**

Right: *Class 31 front end layout. Major equipment is found in the same positions for all sub'classes, with the exception of ETS and jumper equipment on 31/4s and 31/6s. A-front marker lights, B-headlight, C-tail lights, D-windscreen washers (behind shield), E-electric train supply jumper, F-electric train supply jumper receptacle, G-blue-star multiple control jumper socket, H-blue-star multiple control jumper cable, I-engine control air pipe (white), J-main reservoir pipe (yellow), K-air brake pipe (red), L-vacuum brake pipe, M-coupling. On some locomotives the headlight has been positioned towards the driving side, while some locomotives have two of the original footholes in the central gangway door plated over. No 31465 is illustrated.* **Author**

Class 33

Sub Class:	33/0	33/1	33/2
TOPS Number range:	33001-33065	33101-33119	33201-33212
BR 1957 number range:	D6500-D6585	Random from 33/0 fleet	D6586-D6597
Former class codes:	D15/1, later 15/6	-	D15/2, later 15/6A
Southern Region code:	KA	KB	KA-4C
Built by:	Birmingham RC&W	Birmingham RC&W	Birmingham RC&W
Years introduced:	1960-1962	1965-1966	1962
Wheel arrangement:	Bo-Bo	Bo-Bo	Bo-Bo
Weight:	77 tonnes	78 tonnes	77 tonnes
Height:	12ft 8in (3.86m)	12ft 8in (3.86m)	12ft 8in (3.86m)
Length:	50ft 9in (15.47m)	50ft 9in (15.47m)	50ft 9in (15.47m)
Width:	9ft 3in (2.81m)	9ft 3in (2.81m)	8ft 8in (2.64m)
Wheelbase:	39ft 0in (11.88m)	39ft 0in (11.88m)	39ft 0in (11.88m)
Bogie wheelbase:	10ft 0in (3.04m)	10ft 0in (3.04m)	10ft 0in (3.04m)
Bogie pivot centres:	29ft 0in (8.83m)	29ft 0in (8.83m)	29ft 0in (8.83m)
Wheel diameter:	3ft 7in (1.09m)	3ft 7in (1.09m)	3ft 7in (1.09m)
Min curve negotiable:	4 chains (80.46m)	4 chains (80.46m)	4 chains (80.46m)
Engine type:	Sulzer 8LDA28A	Sulzer 8LDA28A	Sulzer 8LDA28A
Engine output:	1,550hp (1,154kW)	1,550hp (1,154kW)	1,550hp (1,154kW)
Power at rail:	1,215hp (906kW)	1,215hp (906kW)	1,215hp (906kW)
Tractive effort:	45,000lb (200kN)	45,000lb (200kN)	45,000lb (200kN)
Cylinder bore:	11.02in (0.27m)	11.02in (0.27m)	11.02in (0.27m)
Cylinder stroke:	14.17in (0.36m)	14.17in (0.36m)	14.17in (0.36m)
Maximum speed:	85mph (137km/h)	85mph (137km/h)	85mph (137km/h)
Brake type:	Dual	Dual	Dual
Brake force:	35 tonnes	35 tonnes	35 tonnes
Route availability:	6	6	6
Heating type:	Electric - index 48	Electric - index 48	Electric - index 48
Multiple coupling type:	Blue star	Blue star, 27 way 1951-66 EMU jumpers	Blue star
Main generator type:	Crompton Parkinson CG391-B1	Crompton Parkinson CG391-B1	Crompton Parkinson CG391-B1
Aux generator type:	Crompton Parkinson CAG193-A1	Crompton Parkinson CAG193-A1	Crompton Parkinson CAG193-A1
ETS generator type:	Crompton Parkinson CAG392-A1	Crompton Parkinson CAG392-A1	Crompton Parkinson CAG392-A1
Traction motor type:	Crompton Parkinson C171-C2	Crompton Parkinson C171-C2	Crompton Parkinson C171-C2
No of traction motors:	4	4	4
Gear ratio:	62:17	62:17	62:17
Fuel tank capacity:	750gal (3,410lit)	750gal (3,410lit)	750gal (3,410lit)
Cooling water capacity:	230gal (1,046lit)	230gal (1,046lit)	230gal (1,046lit)
Lub oil capacity:	108gal (491lit)	108gal (491lit)	108gal (491lit)
Sanding equipment:	Pneumatic	Pneumatic	Pneumatic
Special fittings:		Buck-eye couplers, Waist height connections, Weymouth tramway light socket	Slow Speed Control
Owner/Operator:	West Coast Railway Co	Nemesis Rail, Private	Cotswold Rail, WCRC
Sub class variations:	Basic locomotive	Fitted with push-pull control equipment to operate with post-1951 EP EMU stock	Locos built to narrower Hastings profile

Fact File

One of the most versatile locomotives ever built was the BRCW Type 3, designed for the BR Southern Region to replace steam traction from the main lines.

The fleet of 98 was fitted from new with electric train supply, the last 12 being constructed to the narrower 'Hastings' gauge to allow operation over the Tonbridge-Hastings line.

In 1965-66, when electrification of the Waterloo-Bournemouth line was progressing, 19 members of the standard fleet were modified to allow push-pull operation with post-1951-built EMU stock. these locomotives constituted the highly sought-after Class 33/1 fleet.

By the time of privatisation the majority of the fleet had been withdrawn. Several entered preservation and others continue to operate for Nemesis Rail, Cotswold Rail and West Coast Railways. All operational locomotives now have TPWS and OTMR.

Right: *A small number of Class 33/0s remain active; these are the basic locomotives fitted with dual brakes, ETS and blue-star multiple control. The cab design with a driving position on either side proved to be very useful in shunting yards over the years, but these were the only diesels apart from shunting power fitted with the arrangement. No 33021 is seen painted in a non-standard red livery. In the times of Group Standard fittings, standard high-power headlights were installed; prior to this the only frontal illumination was the two-character headcode display.*
John Wills

Above: *The 19 push-pull 'bagpipe'-fitted locomotives (so-called from the pipes on the front) were able to multiple with 1951, 57, 63 and 1966 BR/SR EMU designs and were the backbone of the Waterloo-Weymouth line after electrification to Bournemouth. The main equipment positions are: A-No 1 end, B-No.2 end, C-cooler group with fan in roof, D-engine compartment, E-generator compartment, F-electrical compartment, G-fuel tank, H-battery box, I-roof aerial. No 33103 in FM Rail black is shown.* **Author**

Right: *The 12 narrow-profile locomotives for the Hastings Line were immediately recognisable from the side or end profile, as shown by No 33202 at Bournemouth. All equipment was the same as on Class 33/0 except that slow-speed control equipment was installed.* **Author**

METEOR

Left: *Several Class 33s were named in BR days, a policy that continued with private ownership, especially when operated by FM Rail. The Meteor nameplate carried by No 33202 is shown.* **Author**

Locomotives

	37/0	37/3	37/4
Sub class:	37/0	37/3	37/4
TOPS number range:	37001-37308	37330-37383	37401-37431
1957 BR number range	D6600-D6999	From main fleet	From main fleet
Former class codes:	D17/1, then 17/3	37/0	37/0
Built by:	English Electric, Vulcan Foundry or Robert Stephenson & Hawthorn	-	-
Refurbished by:	-	BR Depots	BREL Crewe
Years introduced:	1960-1965	1988-1995	1985-1986
Wheel arrangement:	Co-Co	Co-Co	Co-Co
Weight:	102-108 tonnes	102-108 tonnes	107 tonnes
Height:	Between 12ft 9^1/$_{16}$in and 13ft 0^3/$_4$in (3.96m) (3.89m-3.96m) #	Between 12ft 9^1/$_{16}$in and 13ft 0^3/$_4$in (3.96m) (3.89m-3.96m) #	13ft 0^3/$_4$in (3.96m)
Length:	61ft 6in (18.74m)	61ft 6in (18.74m)	61ft 6in (18.74m)
Width:	8ft 11^5/$_8$in (2.73m)	8ft 11^5/$_8$in (2.73m)	8ft 11^5/$_8$in (2.73m)
Wheelbase:	50ft 8in (15.44m)	50ft 8in (15.44m)	50ft 8in (15.44m)
Bogie wheelbase:	13ft 6in (4.11m)	13ft 6in (4.11m)	13ft 6in (4.11m)
Bogie pivot centres:	37ft 2in (11.32m)	37ft 2in (11.32m)	37ft 2in (11.32m)
Wheel diameter:	3ft 7in (1.14m)	3ft 7in (1.14m)	3ft 7in (1.14m)
Min curve negotiable:	4 chains (80.46m)	4 chains (80.46m)	4 chains (80.46m)
Engine type:	English Electric 12CSVT	English Electric 12CSVT	English Electric 12CSVT
Engine output:	1,750hp (1,304kW)	1,750hp (1,304kW)	1,750hp (1,304kW)
Power at rail:	1,250hp (932kW)	1,250hp (932kW)	1,254hp (935kW)
Tractive effort:	55,500lb (245kN)	56,180lb (250kN)	57,440lb (256kN)
Cylinder bore:	10in (0.25m)	10in (0.25m)	10in (0.25m)
Cylinder stroke:	12in (0.30m)	12in (0.30m)	12in (0.30m)
Maximum speed:	As built 90mph (145km/h) Modified 80mph (129km/h)	80mph (129km/h)	90mph (145km/h)
Brake type:	Vacuum, later dual	Dual	Dual
Brake force:	50 tonnes	50 tonnes	50 tonnes
Route availability:	5	5	5
Heating type:	Steam, later removed	Not fitted	Electric, index 30
Multiple coupling type:	Blue star	Blue star	Blue star
Main generator type:	EE822-10G, EE822-13G or EE822-16J	EE822-10G	-
Main alternator type:	-	-	Brush BA1005A
Aux generator type:	EE911/5C	EE911/5C	-
Aux alternator type:	-	-	Brush BA606A
ETS alternator type:	-	-	Brush BAH701
Traction motor type:	EE538-1A	EE538-1A	EE538-5A
No of traction motors:	6	6	6
Gear ratio:	53:18	53:18	59:16
Fuel tank capacity:	890gal (4,046lit)	890gal (4,046lit)	1,690gal (7,682lit)
Cooling water capacity:	160gal (727lit)	160gal (727lit)	160gal (727lit)
Lub oil capacity:	120gal (545lit)	120gal (545lit)	120gal (545lit)
Sanding equipment:	Pneumatic	Pneumatic	Pneumatic
Special fittings:		CP7 bogies	Some locos - RETB OTMR
Operator:	DRS, WCRC	-	EWS, DRS
Sub class variations:	Basic locomotive, fitted with steam heating, now removed	Fitted CP7 bogies	Refurbished loco fitted with electric train supply and CP7 bogies

Notes:

37/5	37/6	37/7	37/9
37503-37521, 37667-37699	37601-37612	37701-37899	37901-37906
From main fleet 37/0	From main fleet 37/5	From main fleet 37/0	From main fleet 37/0
-		-	-
BREL Crewe	BRML Doncaster	BREL Crewe	BREL Crewe
1986-1987	1994-1996	1986-1987	1986-1987
Co-Co	Co-Co	Co-Co	Co-Co
107 tonnes	106 tonnes	120 tonnes	120 tonnes
13ft 0³/₄in (3.96m)	13ft 0³/₄in (3.96m)	13ft 0³/₄in (3.96m)	13ft 0³/₄in (3.96m)
61ft 6in (18.74m)	61ft 6in (18.74m)	61ft 6in (18.74m)	61ft 6in (18.74m)
8ft 11⁵/₈in (2.73m)	8ft 11⁵/₈in (2.73m)	8ft 11⁵/₈in (2.73m)	8ft 11⁵/₈in (2.73m)
50ft 8in (15.44m)	50ft 8in (15.44m)	50ft 8in (15.44m)	50ft 8in (15.44m)
13ft 6in (4.11m)	13ft 6in (4.11m)	13ft 6in (4.11m)	13ft 6in (4.11m)
37ft 2in (11.32m)	37ft 2in (11.32m)	37ft 2in (11.32m)	37ft 2in (11.32m)
3ft 7in (1.14m)	3ft 7in (1.14m)	3ft 7in (1.14m)	3ft 7in (1.14m)
4 chains (80.46m)	4 chains (80.46m)	4 chains (80.46m)	4 chains (80.46m)
English Electric 12CSVT	English Electric 12CSVT	English Electric 12CSVT	Mirrlees MB275T §
1,750hp (1,304kW)	1,750hp (1,304kW)	1,750hp (1,304kW)	1,800hp (1,340kW)
1,250hp (932kW)	1,250hp (932kW)	1,250hp (932kW)	1,300hp (940kW)
55,590lb (248kN)	55,500lb (245kN)	62,000lb (276kN)	62,680lb (279kN)
10in (0.25m)	10in (0.25m)	10in (0.25m)	10¹/₄in (0.275m)
12in (0.30m)	12in (0.30m)	12in (0.30m)	12¹/₄in (0.305m)
80mph (129km/h)	90mph (145km/h)	80mph (129km/h)	80mph (129km/h)
Dual	Air	Dual	Dual
50 tonnes	50 tonnes	50 tonnes	50 tonnes
5	5	7	7
Not fitted	Through wired	Not fitted	Not fitted
Blue star	Blue star, plus DRS	Blue star	Blue star system
-	-	-	-
Brush BA1005A	Brush BA1005A	Brush BA1005A@	Brush BA1005A
-	-	-	-
Brush BA606A	Brush BA606A	Brush BA606A	Brush BA606A
-	-	-	-
EE538-5A	EE538-5A	EE538-5A	EE538-5A
6	6	6	7
59:16	59:16	59:16	59:16
1,690gal (7,682lit)	1,690gal (7,682lit)	1,690gal (7,682lit)	1,690gal (7,682lit)
160gal (727lit)	160gal (727lit)	160gal (727lit)	160gal (727lit)
120gal (545lit)	120gal (545lit)	120gal (545lit)	120gal (545lit)
Pneumatic	Pneumatic OTMR	Pneumatic	Pneumatic
DRS	DRS	-	-
Refurbished standard freight locos	Refurbished locos, for Nightstar and Eurostar tractor use. Fitted with special jumpers. All sold to DRS.	Refurbished heavy weight freight locos	Refurbished heavy weight freight locos, fitted with experimental power units
		@ 37796-37803 have GEC G564AZ	§ 37905-906 fitted with Ruston RK270T

Above: *Few of the original Class 37/0 locomotives are still in capital stock and authorised for Network Rail operation, West Coast and DRS being the main operators. No 37248* Loch Arkaig *is seen painted in West Coast Railway maroon at Rugby.*
John Wills

Left: *Class 37 front end layout. Main equipment is in the same place on all types (except 37/6). This example is a Class 37/4 with electric train supply. A-warning horns, B-radio aerial, C-marker lights x 2, D-tail light x 2, E-sandbox filler, F-manual fire bottle pull, G-electric train supply jumper socket, H-electric train supply jumper, I-headlight, J-blue star multiple control jumper cable (socket hidden behind left buffer), K-vacuum pipe, L-coupling, M-main reservoir pipe (yellow), air brake pipe (red) and engine control air pipe (white), N-main reservoir pipe (yellow), engine control air pipe (white). No 37415 is illustrated.*
Author

Fact File

Over 300 Class 37s were built by English Electric between 1960-65 and allocated to all BR regions except the Southern. As time progressed the fleet reached all parts of the network and became one of the most reliable classes ever built.

By the mid-1980s, major refurbishment commenced, with 31 examples fitted with electric train supply for passenger operations and a significant number refurbished for freight service with an alternator replacing the original generator.

After privatisation, EWS took over the majority of locomotives, and still operates a very small number today.

Direct Rail Services and the smaller private-sector operators now maintain a sizeable fleet for freight and charter and spot hire use.

The preservation movement has managed to save a large number of locomotives from the cutter's torch, with many superbly restored in various contemporary liveries.

Above: *Class 37 equipment positions, applicable for all sub-classes. A-No 1 end, B-No 2 end, C-nose section housing traction motor blower and air compressor, D-cooler group with fan assembly on roof, E-engine and generator/alternator compartment, F-electrical compartment, G-nose section housing traction motor blower and vacuum exhauster, H-fuel tanks. Class 37/4 No 37418 is illustrated at Chester. Note the older EW&S branding.* **Author**

Right Middle: *The refurbished freight examples of Class 37/5 and 37/7 introduced from the mid-1980s followed the same body style as the 37/4; in most cases the area of skirt below the buffer beam was removed, while a slight revision was made to the nose-end grilles. Painted in the very attractive Railfreight Speedlink triple-grey livery offset by red/yellow bodyside logos, Class 37/5 No 37675 is seen at Plymouth Laira.* **Author**

Right Bottom: *The 12 Class 37/6s converted for Eurostar UK are now operated by DRS. Some have been modified in recent years and now sport two large headlights in the original gangway door position. Some Nightstar jumpers remain. No 37604 is seen at Clapham Junction. Note the Channel Tunnel bodyside logos.* **Author**

Left Top: *Direct Rail Services in Carlisle operates two Class 37/5 locomotives (Nos 37510 and 37515). They sport air brake-only equipment and blue-star multiple control, but are not fitted with DRS multiple control jumpers. No 37510 is seen from its No 1 end.* **Derek Porter**

Left Middle: *The Class 37/6s are now operated by Direct Rail Services and deployed on flask and general freight traffic. Most carry DRS blue livery and modifications have been made to incorporate Group Standard light clusters and DRS multiple-control jumpers. Nos. 37610 and 37606 pass Bristol Temple Meads on 11 April 2006 powering a Bridgwater-Crewe flask working.* **Author**

Left Bottom: *Front end arrangement of rebuilt DRS Class 37/6, showing an originally modified 'split-box' example. A-high-level markerlight, B-warning horn grilles, C-former markerlight positions, D-Group Standard light clusters (head, marker, tail lights), E-DRS multiple control jumper socket, F-RCH jumper cables, G-UIC jumper cable, H-train supply on/of switches and indicator, I-fire system activation handle, J-sandbox filler port, K-electric train supply jumper receptacle, L-electric train supply jumper cable. Buffer beam equipment as per Class 37/4 illustration.* **Author**

In 2001, 14 EWS Class 37s were exported to Spain to operate on construction trains for the new Spanish high speed line. The locomotives were repainted prior to departure into two-tone turquoise and branded GIF. After deployment in Spain, the operator was changed to Continental Rail.

Three of the locomotives have subsequently been withdrawn, while in late 2007 the others remain operational.

Now in poor external condition, it is unlikely that these machines will ever return to the UK.

Above: *The mid-1980s refurbishment of some Class 37s, saw six locomotives fitted experimentally with different power units, either a Mirrlees MB275T or a Ruston RK270T. These were installed for a possible squadron re-engining. The locomotives were reclassified as Class 37/9 and were operated by the freight sector. Although none are presently under Network Rail certification for main line use, it is quite possible that one will be used for main line operations in the future. No 37906 is illustrated.* **Author**

Right: *Class 37 cab layout. A-telephone handset, B-auto brake valve, C-straight air brake valve, D-windscreen wiper valve, E-windscreen wiper motor, F-OTMR, G-cab radio, H-warning lights (engine stop, wheelslip, fault), I-desk dimmer switch, J-speedometer, K-ammeter, L-brake pipe gauge, M-vacuum gauge, N-brake cylinder pressure, O-train length button, P-AWS rest button, Q-Sand button, R-headlight switch, S-slave loco cut-out, T-main reservoir pressure gauge, U-slow speed control switch, V-engine start button (stop button below), W-switches (nose light, cab heat x 2), X-slow speed control speedometer, Y-master switch. key socket and power controller, Z-horn valve. The cab illustrated is from Class 37/7 'heavyweight' No 37718.* **Author**

Locomotives

TOPS number range:	40001-40199
BR 1957 number range:	D200-D399
Former class codes:	D20/1, later 20/3
Built by:	English Electric, Vulcan Foundry and Robert Stephenson & Hawthorn
Introduced:	1958-62
Wheel arrangement:	1Co-Co1
Weight (operational):	136 tonnes
Height:	12ft 10^3/sin (3.92m)
Width:	9ft (2.74m)
Length:	69ft 6in (21.18m)
Min curve negotiable:	4^1/2 chains (90.52m)
Maximum speed:	90mph (145km/h)
Wheelbase:	61ft 3in (18.66m)
Bogie wheelbase:	21 ft 6in (6.55m)
Bogie pivot centres:	34ft 4in (10.46m)
Wheel diameter (driving):	3ft 9in (1.14m)
Wheel diameter (pony):	3ft (0.91m)
Brake type:	Originally Vacuum, modified to Dual
Sanding equipment:	Pneumatic
Heating type:	Steam - Stones OK 4625 (if fitted)
Route availability:	6
Multiple coupling restriction:	Blue Star, then removed
Brake force:	51 tonnes
Engine type:	English Electric 16SVT Mk11
Engine horsepower:	2,000hp (1,490kW)
Power at rail:	1,550hp (1,160kW)
Tractive effort:	52,000lb (231kN)
Cylinder bore:	10in (0.25m)
Cylinder stroke:	12in (0.30m)
Main generator type:	EE822
Aux generator type:	EE911-2B
Number of traction motors:	6
Traction motor type:	EE 526-5D
Gear ratio:	61:19
Fuel tank capacity:	710 gal (3,250lit)
Cooling water capacity:	200 gal (909lit)
Boiler water capacity:	800 gal (3,637lit)
Lub oil capacity:	140 gal (636lit)
Operator:	Private
Authorised for main line use:	40145

Fact File

This is another of the classes which owes its existence to the 1955 Modernisation Plan. This build of 200 Type 4s, later classified as Class 40, were the standard main-line 'heavy' diesel on the London Midland and Eastern Regions until the mid-1960s built Class 47s emerged.

This design is the production derivative of the late 1940s 'prototype' 1Co-Co1 locomotives used on the Southern and London Midland Regions, and incorporate English Electric 16-cylinder SVT Mk2 power unit set to develop 2,000hp. Construction, to three slightly different body designs, was carried out at English Electric Vulcan Foundry and Robert Stephenson and Hawthorn Works. They were delivered between 1958 and 1962 and formed the backbone of main-line dieselisation.

The original body structure for Nos D200-D323 incorporated disk train reporting. Split route indicator boxes were fitted to Nos D324-D344. while solid four-character route displays were fitted to Nos D345-D399.

When built, locomotives were painted in BR green livery, which gave way to BR corporate rail blue from late 1966.

After withdrawal by BR, several members of the fleet were preserved, with No D345 (40145) now restored to full Network Rail standard and authorised for main line use. When not in use the locomotive is based on the East Lancs Railway, Bury.

All Class 40s were delivered with steam heating and vacuum brakes; many were modified for dual-brake operation.

Left: *Although only one Class 40 is presently authorised for operation on Network Rail, No 40145 (D345), a number of other examples are preserved and operational on light railways. One such is No D212, seen here at Exeter. This locomotive shows the original front-end layout using the disc train reporting system and the structure incorporating nose-end doors, enabling train crews to move between locomotives while on the move.* **Author**

Above: *The restoration of No 40145 (D345) to main-line condition can only be described as one of the masterpieces of modern preservation. Main equipment positions are: A- No 1 end, B-No 2 end, C-traction motor blower, fire bottles, D-radiator with fan on roof, E-engine and generator group, F-boiler compartment (if fitted) and electrical frame, G-traction motor blower and vacuum exhauster, H-boiler water tank. Front-end equipment follows the same style as the standard Class 37. This locomotive has an additional Group Standard headlight.* **John Wills**

Below: *No 40145 is frequently requested to power main line charter services, as it is very popular with haulage enthusiasts and in recent years has visited many parts of the UK rail network, several off the traditional stamping ground for the class. In 2007 it was repainted into mock 'large-logo' rail blue, prior to being named* East Lancashire Railway. *Here No 40145 passes Dawlish Warren in Devon, powering a charter to Kingswear on 8 September 2007.* **Author**

TOPS number range:	43002-43198, 43206-43367
Built by:	BREL Crewe
Refurbished:	Brush Traction, Loughborough
Years introduced:	1976-82
Refurbished:	2006-2008
Wheel arrangement:	Bo-Bo
Weight:	70.25 tonnes
Height:	12ft 10in (3.90m)
Length:	58ft 5in (17.80m)
Width:	8ft 11in (2.73m)
Wheelbase:	42ft 4in (12.90m)
Bogie wheelbase:	8ft 7in (2.60m)
Bogie pivot centres:	33ft 9in (10.28m)
Wheel diameter:	3ft 4in (1.02m)
Min curve negotiable:	4 chains (80.46m)
Brake Force:	35 tonnes
Engine type:	As built: Paxman Valenta 12RP200L
	Refurbished: MTU 16V4000
Engine output:	Paxman Valenta 12RP200L - 2,250hp (1,680kW) at 1,500rpm
	MTU 16V4000 - 2,700hp (2,010kW) at 1,500rpm (derated to 2,250hp (1,680kW))
Power at rail:	1,770hp (1,320kW)
Tractive effort:	17,980lb (80kN)
Cont Tractive effort:	10,340lb (46kN)
Cylinder bore:	Valenta - $7^3/_4$in (196mm)
	MTU4000 $6^1/_2$in (165mm)
Cylinder stroke:	Valenta - $7^1/_2$in (190mm)
	MTU4000 $7^1/_2$in (190mm)
Maximum speed:	125mph (201km/h)
Brake type:	Air
Route availability:	5
Bogie type:	BP16
Heating type:	Electric - three phase 415V
Multiple coupling type:	Within type
Main alternator type:	Brush BA1001B
Aux ETS alternator:	43002-123/153-198 -Brush TMH68-46
	43124-152 - GECG417AZ
No of traction motors:	4
Gear ratio:	59:23
Fuel tank capacity:	1,030gal (4,680lit)
Cooling water capacity:	163gal (741lit)
Lub oil capacity:	75gal (341lit)
Sanding equipment:	Not fitted
Luggage capacity:	1.5 tonnes, increased to 2.5 tonnes
Special fittings:	ATP on all FGW powercars
	43013/014/065/067/068/080/084/123 fitted with nose end buffing gear
Owners:	Porterbrook, Angel Trains, FirstGroup
Operators:	First Great Western, East Midlands Trains, National Express East Coast, Grand Central, Network Rail

Left: *Standard unrefurbished First Great Western Class 43 power car. Vehicle No 43169 is illustrated from the cab end at Bristol and shows the original design of light clusters and early FirstGroup 'Barbie' livery. This power car was one of a small batch fitted with a Paxman VP185 engine, a type which is being removed during the current round of refurbishments. All FGW power cars were MTU fitted by January 2008.* **Author**

Fact File

The High Speed Train or HST is without doubt the most successful high-speed diesel-powered passenger train in the world. Built in the mid-1970s as a 'stop-gap' until advanced passenger trains were introduced, the 196 power cars soon formed the backbone of InterCity power.

Operated on the Western, Eastern, Scottish and London Midland Regions, the sets passed into the private sector, working for (First) Great Western, GNER (now National Express), Virgin Trains and Midland Mainline (now East Midlands Trains).

Eight vehicles were modified with conventional nose-end draw gear and several trial re-engining projects have been undertaken.

Today, all Class 43s operated by FGW and National Express are being refurbished with German MTU power units.

In 2007 a new era opens for the HST with six of the buffer-fitted powercars operated by 'new' train operator Grand Central on North East–London services.

Since introduction just three Class 43s have been withdrawn following collisions.

Above: *Painted in First Great Western's latest livery, a refurbished Class 43 is viewed from the nose end. The main electrical, alternator and power unit is located directly behind the driving cab, with the radiator group at the two-thirds point. The inner end of the vehicle is a luggage van. Between the bogies is the fuel tank and battery box. No 43098 is viewed at Dawlish.* **Author**

Below left and right: *The two ends of a refurbished First Great Western power car in detail. On unrefurbished vehicles separate marker and tail lights are provided on the outer end. A-LED style combined marker and tail light (able to show white or red light), B-headlight, C-warning horns (behind grille), D-emergency coupling (behind cover plate). E- emergency end powercar door, F-HST control jumper, G-main reservoir pipe, H-air brake pipe, I-central door locking jumper, J-buck-eye auto coupler. When originally built, power cars had a window to the right of the emergency end door. Both:* **Author**

Above: *The ex-BR Eastern Region route from London King's Cross to Leeds, Newcastle and Scotland was the second InterCity route to be taken over by HSTs in the mid-1970s. From privatisation until late 2007, services were operated by Great North Eastern Railway, and their house colours of dark blue were applied. From December 2007 the east coast route has been operated by National Express East Coast and the new company house colours have been applied, shown here on refurbished power car No 43300 at Edinburgh Craigentinny.* **NEG**

Below: *In common with First Great Western, the desire to improve the reliability of the ageing HST fleet saw a contract for wholesale refurbishment of the entire GNER fleet authorised in 2006. Work is being undertaken at Brush Traction and includes a total rebuild, with the latest MTU4000 power unit fitted. A number of other refinements to electrical, pneumatic and cooler systems are being incorporated during the work. Refurbished cars also sport a revised front end with the two-light-group style. Vehicles also carry a 'Rebuilt by Brush' works plate on the bodyside and some carry a blue and red MTU logo to the left of the GNER fleet name. To identify refurbished MTU-fitted vehicles GNER have renumbered powercars on release from works, with 200 being added to the original number, i.e. No 43300 illustrated below was previously No 43100.* **Richard Tuplin**

Right Top: *The passenger seating area of the HST fleet has seen a number of changes from the original, rather stark orange (first class) and turquoise blue (standard class) offered when the trains entered service. Under the BR banner two refurbishment projects were undertaken when upgraded seating and internal furniture was incorporated, this seeing the use of 'airline' or 'uni-directional' seating in place of four-seat groups in standard class, in the quest to cram more people into each vehicle. In first class the standard 2+1 style has been retained with many different seating styles. This view shows a Midland Mainline refurbished first-class vehicle, incorporating the traditional 2+1 seating style but having modified saloon lighting.* Author

Right Middle: *By far the most radical alteration to the HST interior has occurred from late 2006, when First Great Western started to roll out their refurbished train sets. This work, undertaken by Bombardier Derby (the same factory which built the trains 30 years before) and Bombardier Ilford, saw the cars taken back to their basic frame members and a totally new interior fitted. To meet the aspirations of FirstGroup's FGW franchise, many extra seats per coach were needed and this has been achieved by using predominantly airline seating in standard class and taking out tables. The seating is now high-backed, has hinged armrests and with bright lighting reflecting off the light wall panels, gives an overall cramped sensation. FGW standard class coaches are being refurbished in low and high density modes.* **Author**

Right Bottom: *The most radical part of the FGW refurbishment has been in first class, where the 2+1 style has been retained but new luxurious leather seats have been fitted, sporting grey and blue, together with revised tables and improved lighting. Hinged armrests are fitted throughout, and as in standard class, three-pin power sockets have been provided by each seat for the charging of laptop computers and mobile phones. During the course of this latest refurbishment, which covers by far the largest number of HST vehicles, the buffet cars have been totally rebuilt to a 'cafe' standard and new toilets have been installed in both first and standard class.* **Author**

Left Top: *Midland Mainline, part of the National Express Group, operated InterCity services from St Pancras to Derby, Sheffield and Nottingham until November 2007 when East Midlands Trains took over. Their traction fleet is a mix of HSTs and Class 222 stock. Most of the HSTs are powered by the original Paxman engines and sport deep turquoise livery offset by 'blocks' of white and graphite grey. The passenger stock is a mix of white, deep turquoise and grey. The Class 43s are to be refurbished with MTU engines from 2008. As Midland Mainline had some spare capacity in its fleet, one or two sets were offered on 'spot-hire' to other operators. Here a MML set operates for Virgin Trains on the Derby-Plymouth route near Teignmouth.* **Author**

Left Middle: *In the autumn of 2007 operator Grand Central took delivery of six Class 43s for its new Sunderland–London King's Cross service. The powercars have been refurbished by DML at Devonport Dockyard, while EWS have rebuilt a mix of ex HST and loco-hauled Mk3s to provide passenger stock. The sets are painted in black and allocated to Heaton depot, Newcastle. Power car No 43080 leads a GC set along the Sunderland Coast Line on a pre-service trial run in November 2007.* **Ken Short**

Above: *Refurbished FGW Class 43 cab. A-main reservoir pressure gauge, B-bogie brake cylinder gauge, C-brake pipe gauge, D-Speedometer with ATP below, E-Notice clip, F-Engine output, G-Cab-train telephone, H-ATP isolation switch and data box below, I-TPWS, J-Windscreen wiper control, K-Switches - headlight flash, train supply on/off, DRA, fault, parking brake, fire alarm test, L-AWS, M-Switches - Engine start/stop, wheelslip, brake overcharge, buzzer, locked wheelset, cab ventilation, N-Brake test switch, O-Headlight switch, P-Switches - cab lights, demister, marker lights, tail lights, engine room lights, Q-emergency brake plunger, R-brake controller, S-power controller, T-master switch and master key socket, U-AWS reset button, V-warning horn switch, W-National Radio Network (NRN) telephone, X-screenwash filler, Y-drivers safety device (DSD) peddle. Cab of No. 43175 illustrated.* **Author**

Network Rail - New Measurement Train

The Network Rail New Measurement Train, or NMT, is formed of a modified HST. It is designed for assessing the condition of track and overhead power line infrastructure. The NMT is rostered to check the condition of most main line routes in the UK on a pre-programmed basis. In addition to test car recording data, the train captures video footage from the front end with cameras mounted in a box between the cab window and horn grille. The train also measures the contact between wheels and track and pantographs with the overhead power supply.

Lasers and other instruments are used to take measurements of the track geometry and other features such as overhead line height and stagger, as well as track gauge, twist and cant.

The train was launched in 2003 using rebuilt ex-HST vehicles.

The NMT operates with Class 43s Nos. 43013/014/062/089/160 allocated to the QCAR pool. Some powercars are fitted with nose cameras. Stock is modified Mk3.

Below left: *Modified front end showing recording camera equipment and standard draw gear.* **Kevin Wills**

Below: *The complete New Measurement Train, formed with Mk3 stock passing Dawlish while checking the Great Western section infrastructure.* **Author**

Hitachi, Brush, Porterbrook, Network Rail dual-power project

Europe's first hybrid energy-saving high-speed train was rolled out in May 2007. Developed and proven under test by Hitachi in Japan, the technology cuts fuel use by 20 per cent and emissions by up to 50 per cent. The test train uses a hybrid traction system consisting of a battery-assisted diesel-electric traction drive installed in power car No 43089 and modified TGS No 44062.

Hitachi, together with partners Porterbrook Leasing, Network Rail and Brush Traction, test ran the vehicles in mid-2007 with Paxman Valenta powercar No 43160 and other trailer vehicles. By September 2007 the hybrid powercar was operating within the New Measurement Train.

Below: *Dual power No 43089, TGS No 44062, test car No 977974 and blue-liveried PC No 43160 are seen under test on the Great Central Railway.* **Brian Morrison**

Class 45 'Peak'

Sub class:	45/0	45/1
TOPS number range:	45001-45077	45101-45150
1957 BR number range:	D11-D137	D11-D137
Former class codes:	D25/1, later 25/1	D25/1, later 25/1
Built by:	BR Derby and Crewe	Rebuilt BREL Derby
Introduced:	1960-1962	1973-1975
Wheel arrangement:	1Co-Co1	1Co-Co1
Weight (operational):	138 tonnes	135 tonnes
Height:	12ft 10^1/2in (3.91m)	12ft 10^1/2in (3.91m)
Length:	67ft 11 in (20.70m)	67ft 11in (20.70m)
Width:	9ft 1^9/16in (2.78m)	9ft 1^9/16in (2.78m)
Wheelbase:	59ft 8in (18.18m)	59ft 8in (18.18m)
Bogie wheelbase:	21 ft 6 in (6.55m)	21 ft 6in (6.55m)
Bogie pivot centres:	32ft 8in (9.95m)	32ft 8in (9.95m)
Wheel diameter (driving):	3ft 9in (1.14m)	3ft 9in (1.14m)
Wheel diameter (pony):	3ft (0.91m)	3ft (0.91m)
Min curve negotiable:	As built - 5 chains	As built - 5 chains
	Modified - 3 chains	Modified - 3 chains
Engine type:	Sulzer 12LDA28 B	Sulzer 12LDA28 B
Engine output:	2,500hp (1,862kW)	2,500hp (1,862kW)
Power at rail:	2,000hp (1,490kW)	2,000hp (1,490kW)
Tractive effort:	55,000lb (245kN)	55,000lb (245kN)
Cylinder bore:	11in (0.27m)	11in (0.27m)
Cylinder stroke:	14in (0.35m)	14in (0.35m)
Maximum speed:	90mph (145km/h)	90mph (145km/h)
Brake type:	Originally Vacuum,	Dual
	modified to Dual	
Brake force:	63 tonnes	63 tonnes
Route availability:	7	6
Heating type:	Steam - Stones OK 4625	Electric - Index 66
Multiple restriction:	Blue Star, later removed	Not fitted
Main generator type:	Crompton CG426A1	Crompton CG426A1
Aux generator type:	Crompton CAG252A1	Crompton CAG252A1
ETS alternator:	Not fitted	Brush BL 100-30 Mk II
Traction motor type:	Crompton C172A1	Crompton C172A1
No of traction motors:	6	6
Gear ratio:	62:17	62:17
Fuel tank capacity:	840gal (3,819lit)	840gal (3,819lit)
Cooling water capacity:	346gal (1,572lit)	346gal (1,572lit)
Lub oil capacity:	190gal (864lit)	190gal (864lit)
Boiler water capacity:	1,040gal (4,727lit)	Not fitted
Boiler fuel capacity:	From main supply	Not fitted
Sanding equipment:	Pneumatic	Pneumatic
Present operator:	Private sector	Private sector
Sub class variations:	As built locos with	Modified locos fitted
	steam heat	with electric heat

Fact File

In 1957 the BTC ordered post 'Pilot' scheme locomotives and 127 'Peak' Type 4s were ordered, similar to 'Pilot' scheme Nos D1-D10.

These were fitted with a Sulzer 2,500hp power unit and assembled at either BR Derby or Crewe Works. Deliveries ran from 1960 to late 1962 with locomotives allocated to the Midland and Eastern Regions. Originally all were fitted with steam heat equipment, but by the early 1970s, after BR decided to opt for electric train heating, a batch of 50 was modified at the then BREL Works in Derby to provide electric train heating, at the same time the steam heat boilers were removed. Under the TOPS classification system, locomotives which retained steam heating (77 in total) were classified as Class 45/0, while the electric train supply fitted locomotives became Class 45/1.

The main stamping ground for the Class 45s was always on the Midland route from London St Pancras to Derby, Sheffield and Nottingham, as well as North East and North West passenger and freight duties. The class also ventured to the West Country, primarily on CrossCountry passenger and long distance freight services.

The class was progressively withdrawn in the 1980s, mainly following the introduction of HSTs. Thankfully a number have been preserved and in 2007 one locomotive, No 45112, was certified under the Cotswold banner to operate on the main line.

Left: *Privately-owned No 45112 The Royal Army Ordnance Corps, is painted in 1970s BR rail blue livery; it is seen from its No 1 end. This example of the Class 45 has a two-section four-character route indicator, some members of the class had a solid route box, as fitted to the Class 46 No 46035. A total of eight Class 45s still remain, but only No 45112 has a main line certificate.* **Author**

Fact File

The final batch of 76 'Peaks' was ordered in 1959 from BR Derby Works, with equipment supplied by Brush. However, only 56 locomotives of the order were built, the balance of electrical equipment going into the first 20 Brush Type 4s.

These locomotives became classified under TOPS as Class 46. The first one emerged in October 1961, and was allocated to Derby. External appearance was almost identical to the Class 45s, except for minor grille and battery box ribbing detail.

The locomotives originally operated on the Midland and North Eastern Region, but after withdrawal of diesel-hydraulics from the Western Region, a batch of '46's went to both Bristol and Plymouth Laira depots.

Due to 'non-standard' equipment, the Class 46 fleet was set for early withdrawal between 1977 and 1984. Departmental duties saved some from immediate disposal. Three Class 46s are in preservation, of which No 46035 is certified for main-line use but is presently under overhaul.

Below: *Displaying BR rail-blue livery, 'Peak' No 46035 is seen powering a main-line charter in February 2003 at Powderham, Devon. It boasts dual brake and steam heating.* **Author**

TOPS number range:	46001-46056
1957 BR number range:	D138-D193
Former class codes:	25/1A
Built by:	BR Derby
Introduced:	1961-1963
Wheel arrangement:	1Co-Co1
Weight (operational):	138 tonnes
Height:	12ft 10^{1}/$_{2}$in (3.91m)
Length:	67ft 11 in (20.70m)
Width:	9ft 1^{9}/$_{16}$in (2.78m)
Wheelbase:	59ft 8in (18.18m)
Bogie wheelbase:	21 ft 6in (6.55m)
Bogie pivot centres:	32ft 8in (9.95m)
Wheel diameter (driving):	3ft 9in (1.14m)
Wheel diameter (pony):	3ft (0.91m)
Min curve negotiable:	As built - 5 chains
	Modified - 3 chains
Engine type:	SuIzer 12LDA28 B
Engine output:	2,500hp (1,862kW))
Power at rail:	1,960hp (1,460kW)
Tractive effort:	55,000lb (245kN)
Cylinder bore:	11 in (0.27m)
Cylinder stroke:	14 in (0.35m)
Maximum speed:	90mph (145km/h)
Brake type:	Vacuum, later Dual
Brake force:	63 tonnes
Route availability:	7
Heating type:	Steam - Stones OK 4625
	or Spanner Mk111
Multiple restriction:	Not fitted
Main generator type:	Brush TG160-60
Aux generator type:	Brush TG69-28
Traction motor type:	Brush TM73-68
No of traction motors:	6
Gear ratio:	62:19
Fuel tank capacity:	840gal (3,819lit)
Cooling water capacity:	346gal (1,572lit)
Lub oil capacity:	190gal (864lit)
Boiler water capacity:	1,040gal (4,727lit)
Boiler fuel capacity:	From main supply
Sanding equipment:	Pneumatic
Present operator:	Private sector

Class 47

Sub class:	47/0	47/3	47/4
TOPS number range:	47001-47299	47300-47381, 47981	47401-47665, 47971-47976
1957 BR number range:	D1521-D1998	D1782-D1900	Random from fleet
Former class code:	27/2	27/2	27/2
Built by:	Brush, Loughborough and BR Crewe Works	Brush, Loughborough and BR Crewe Works	Brush, Loughborough and BR Crewe Works
Years introduced:	1962-65	1964-65	1962-1987
Wheel arrangement:	Co-Co	Co-Co	Co-Co
Weight:	111-121 tonnes	114 tonnes	120-125 tonnes
Height:	12ft 10³/sin (3.91m)	12ft 10³/sin (3.91m)	12ft 10³/sin (3.91m)
Length:	63ft 6in (19.38m)	63ft 6in (19.38m)	63ft 6in (19.38m)
Width:	9ft 2in (2.79m)	9ft 2in (2.79m)	9ft 2in (2.79m)
Wheelbase:	51ft 6in (15.69m)	51ft 6in (15.69m)	51ft 6in (15.69m)
Bogie wheelbase:	14ft 6in (4.41m)	14ft 6in (4.41m)	14ft 6in (4.41m)
Bogie pivot centres:	37ft 0in (11.27m)	37ft 0in (11.27m)	37ft 0in (11.27m)
Wheel diameter:	3ft 9in (1.14m)	3ft 9in (1.14m)	3ft 9in (1.14m)
Min curve negotiable:	4 chains (80.46m)	4 chains (80.46m)	4 chains (80.46m)
Engine type:	Sulzer 12LDA28C	Sulzer 12LDA28C	Sulzer 12LDA28C
Engine output:	2,580hp (1,922kW)	2,580hp (1,922kW)	2,580hp (1,922kW)
Power at rail:	2,080hp (1,550kW)	2,080hp (1,550kW)	2,080hp (1,550kW)
Tractive effort:	60,000lb (267kN)	60,000lb (267kN)	60,000lb (267kN)
Cylinder bore:	11in (0.27m)	11in (0.27m)	11in (0.27m)
Cylinder stroke:	14in (0.35m)	14in (0.35m)	14in (0.35m)
Maximum speed:	95mph (153km/h) later 75mph (121km/h)	95mph (153km/h) later 75mph (121km/h)	95mph (153km/h)
Brake type:	Dual or air	Dual or air	Dual or air
Brake force:	61 tonnes	61 tonnes	61 tonnes
Route availability:	6	6	7
Heating type:	Steam, later removed	Not fitted	Electric - index 66, some fitted with dual heating
Multiple coupling type:	Not fitted, some later with DRS system	Not fitted	Not fitted, some later with DRS system
Main generator type:	Brush TG160-60 Mk2, TG160-60 Mk4 or TG172-50 Mk1	Brush TM172-50 Mk1A	Brush TG160-60 Mk2, TG160-60 Mk4 or TG172-50 Mk1
Aux generator type:	Brush TG69-20 or Brush TG69-28Mk2	Brush TG69-20	Brush TG69-20 or Brush TG69-28Mk2
ETS Alternator type:	-	-	Brush BL100-30
Traction motor type:	Brush TM64-68	Brush TM64-68 Mk1	Brush TM64-68
No of traction motors:	6	6	6
Gear ratio:	66:17	66:17	66:17
Fuel tank capacity:	720-1,221gal (3,273-5,550lit)	720-1,221gal (3,273-5,550lit)	720-1,295gal (3,273-5,887lit)
Cooling water capacity:	300gal (1,364lit)	300gal (1,364lit)	300gal (1,364lit)
Lub oil capacity:	190gal (864lit)	190gal (864lit)	190gal (864lit)
Sanding equipment:	Not fitted	Not fitted	Not fitted
Owners:	Various	Various	Various
Operators:	Cotswold Rail, DRS, WCRC	Cotswold Rail	DRS
Sub class variations:	Original locomotives built with steam train heating, many later converted to electric heating, all remaining are devoid of train heat equipment. (Some classified as 47/2 with air brakes only)	Locomotives built without provision for train heat - Freight-only locos. (Some classified as 47/2 fitted with air brakes)	Constructed with either dual (steam and electric) or just electric train heating
Notes:	Engine output originally 2,750hp		

47/7	47/7	47/4 (47/8)
47701-47717	47721-47793	47798-47799, 47801-47854
From Class 47/4 fleet	From Class 47/4 fleet	From Class 47/4 fleet
-	-	-
Rebuilt BREL Crewe	Modified by BR depots	Rebuilt BREL Crewe or BR depots
-	-	-
1979-1984	1993-1995	1989-1995
Co-Co	Co-Co	Co-Co
119 tonnes	119-121 tonnes	124 tonnes
12ft 10³/sin (3.91m)	12ft 10³/sin (3.91m)	12ft 10³/sin (3.91m)
63ft 6in (19.38m)	63ft 6in (19.38m)	63ft 6in (19.38m)
9ft 2in (2.79m)	9ft 2in (2.79m)	9ft 2in (2.79m)
51ft 6in (15.69m)	51ft 6in (15.69m)	51ft 6in (15.69m)
14ft 6in (4.41m)	14ft 6in (4.41m)	14ft 6in (4.41m)
37ft 0in (11.27m)	37ft 0in (11.27m)	37ft 0in (11.27m)
3ft 9in (1.14m)	3ft 9in (1.14m)	3ft 9in (1.14m)
4 chains (80.46m)	4 chains (80.46m)	4 chains (80.46m)
Sulzer 12LDA28C	Sulzer 12LDA28C	Sulzer 12LDA28C
2,580hp (1,922kW)	2,580hp (1,922kW)	2,580hp (1,922kW)
2,080hp (1,550kW)	2,080hp (1,550kW)	2,080hp (1,550kW)
60,000lb (267kN)	60,000lb (267kN)	60,000lb (267kN)
11in (0.27m)	11in (0.27m)	11in (0.27m)
14in (0.35m)	14in (0.35m)	14in (0.35m)
95mph (153km/h)	95mph (153km/h)	95mph (153km/h)
Dual or air	Dual or air	Dual or air
61 tonnes	61 tonnes	61 tonnes
7	6	6
Electric - index 66	Electric - index 66	Electric - index 66
Not fitted - TDM wired (47714 green circle system)	Not fitted - TDM wired	Not fitted (47971-47976 fitted with Blue star system)
Brush TM172-50 Mk1A	Brush TM172-50 Mk1A	Brush TG160-60 Mk2, TG160-60 Mk4 or TG172-50 Mk1
Brush TG69-20 or Brush TG69-28Mk2	Brush TG69-20 or Brush TG69-28Mk2	Brush TG69-20 or Brush TG69-28Mk2
Brush BL100-30	Brush BL100-30	Brush BL100-30
Brush TM64-68 Mk1	Brush TM64-68	Brush TM64-68
6	6	6
66:17	66:17	66:17
1,295gal (5,887lit)	1,295gal (5,887lit)	1,295gal (5,887lit)
300gal (1,364lit)	300gal (1,364lit)	300gal (1,364lit)
190gal (864lit)	190gal (864lit)	190gal (864lit)
Not fitted	Not fitted	Not fitted
Various	Various	Various
Cotswold Rail, DRS	Colas Rail, DRS, WCRC, Riviera Trains	DRS, Riviera, Cotswold Rail, WCRC
Converted Class 47/4s with an early RCH (Railway Clearing House) push-pull system for use on the Edinburgh-Glasgow high speed service	Modified Class 47/4s with RCH Time Division Multiplex push-pull equipment for use with trains formed of PCV sets on Royal Mail duties under the 'Railnet' scheme	Locomotives refurbished for passenger services, fitted with ETS, refurbished from 47/4 fleet

Fact File

The Class 47 or Brush Type 4 fleet was the single largest class of diesel ever built, with 512 examples being constructed between 1962-65 as the second generation of main-line UK diesel power.

The fleet has operated to all corners of the UK network powering passenger and freight services and over the years has become one of the most reliable fleets to operate the BR/National Network.

Many locomotives have now been withdrawn, but upon privatisation a large number passed to the passenger and freight operators and today a number of the smaller operators and 'spot-hire' companies use the fleet.

Many modifications have been carried out to the design over the years, these being reflected in the sub-classes. Several sub-classes have now been withdrawn and are not included in this technical data.

The class is set to remain in service for many years to come.

Left: *Viewed from its No 1 end, the Class 47/0 derivative of the Brush Type 4 fleet is depicted by No 47145. This locomotive, viewed at Tonbridge, was operated by FM Rail and sports a refurbished (cut-back) front bodyside, a standard headlight and a more recently fitted green-dot multiple control system; without the fitting of vacuum brakes this technically renders the locomotive a Class 47/2. No 47145 is sporting early-design grommeted white marker lights and recessed headcode panel.* **Author**

Left Middle: *This Class 47/0 (47/2) is also viewed from the No 1 end, but shows the opposite side of the locomotive to the above view. No 47150 is operated by Freightliner and sports the later style filled-in route indicator box with sealed beam marker lights. Standard draw-gear connections are provided, with an additional control air pipe (white) to the left of the coupling. No 47150 is seen at Dawlish.* **Author**

Below: *Gloucester-based Cotswold Rail operated a sizeable fleet of Class 47s for 'spot hire' and contract work; several are painted in Cotswold Rail silver livery as shown on No 47200, viewed from its No 2 end. As will be seen from the buffer beam, this locomotive has had its vacuum brake equipment removed and 'green-dot' multiple control fitted. The space on the underframe between the battery boxes shows the boiler water tank has also been removed.* **Author**

Above: *Some members of the Class 47 fleet are fitted with three-piece miniature snowploughs, as shown on Cotswold Rail No 47318. This equipment is not intended to shift major snow drifts, but can shift accumulations of up to 8-10in above rail height. The ploughs also act as excellent obstacle deflectors. No 47318 is shown from its No 2 end, with the different style of the roof clearly visible. The locomotive is operating with Anglia-liveried Class 47/7 No 47714. All Class 47s sport a central 'lamp iron' on the nose end just below cab window height; however, only small headboards can be carried, otherwise the driver's forward vision could be impaired.* **Author**

Right and Below: *Class 47 equipment positions (same for all sub-classes). A-No 1 end, B-No 2 end, C-radiator fans, D-hinged roof inspection hatches over engine, E-radiator/cooler group, F-former steps to roof boiler water filler point, G-power unit compartment, H-main generator/alternator compartment, I-electrical compartment, position for steam heat boiler/generator, J-Original boiler compartment, K-battery box, L-fuel gauge, M-marker lights, N-tail lights O-Time Division Multiplex (TDM) jumpers, P-headlight, Q-electric train supply (ETS) jumper, R-air brake pipe (red), S-main reservoir pipe (yellow), T-vacuum brake pipe, U-coupling, V-electric train supply (ETS) jumper socket, W-radio aerial. Locomotive illustrated is Class 47/7 No 47737* **Author**

Above: *The Class 478xx group of Class 47s, which are officially Class 47/4s refurbished and fitted with long range fuel tanks, are by far the most versatile machines of the fleet. A large number of these are still operational for the national operators and smaller businesses including 'spot-hire' companies. Although a diverse selection of modifications are applied, many examples still retain dual (air/vacuum) brake equipment. Viewed from its No 2 end, No 47802 is illustrated in DRS 'compass' livery. In keeping with most DRS traction, a unique DRS-style multiple-jumper system is fitted (to the left of the headlight.)* **Bill Wilson**

Left Middle: *West Coast Railways operates a small fleet of Class 47s, painted in its maroon house colours. No 47854 is illustrated at Crewe. These locomotives are used for charter and spot hire work.* **Chris Perkins**

Left Below: *A significant number of the 17 original Class 47/7 locomotives now operates with the private sector, including two painted in 1960s Blue 'Pullman' livery for charter train use. The '47/7s' are modified from standard Class 47/4s in having bodyside air cooling pipes, extra fuel capacity and revised electrics. All have nose mounted TDM jumpers. No 47712, painted in Nankin Blue, is shown.* **Author**

Above: *Colas Rail, a new operator formed by a partnership of Seco Rail and Amec Spie Rail, entered the rail scene in late 2007, providing Class 47s for use on Network Rail 'Rail Head Treatment Train' (RHTT) services. Overhauled at Eastleigh and painted into a green, black and orange livery, four locomotives are presently in traffic. Nos. 47727 and 47749 are seen with the NR RHTT train passing Dawlish.* **Kevin Wills**

Below: *Class 47 cab layout. A-train brake valve, B-Straight air brake valve, C-Automatic Warning System (AWS) reset button, D-horn valve, E-master switch and power controller and key socket, F-headlight switch, G-main reservoir gauge, H-bogie brake cylinder gauge, I-speedometer, J-brake pipe pressure gauge, K-traction ammeter, L-switches/lights (anti-slip brake, engine stopped, wheel slip, general alarm, engine start, engine stop, train heat and fire alarm test), M-switches (tail light, demister, panel lights, marker lights, cab heat, foot rest warmer and compartment lights), N-National Radio Network (NRN) radio, O-Drivers Safety Device (DSD) pedal. The locomotive illustrated is No 47815.* **Author**

TOPS number range:	50001-50050 (50149)
1957 BR number range:	D400-D449
Former class codes:	27/3
Built by:	English Electric, Vulcan Foundry
Years introduced:	1967-68
Wheel arrangement:	Co-Co
Weight:	117 tonnes
Height:	12ft 10^1/2in (3.95m)
Length:	68ft 6in (20.87m)
Width:	9ft 1^1/4in (2.77m)
Wheelbase:	56ft 2in (17.11m)
Bogie wheelbase:	13ft 6in (4.11m)
Bogie pivot centres:	42ft 8in (13.00m)
Wheel diameter:	3ft 7in (1.09m)
Min curve negotiable:	4 chains (80.46m)
Engine type:	English Electric 16CSVT
Engine output:	2,700hp (2,014kW)
Power at rail:	2,070hp (1,540kW)
Tractive effort:	48,500lb (216kN)
Cylinder bore:	10in (0.25m)
Cylinder stroke:	12in (0.30m)
Maximum speed:	100mph (161km/h)
Brake type:	Dual
Brake force:	59 tonnes
Route availability:	6
Heating type:	Electric - index 66
Multiple coupling type:	Orange square
Main generator type:	EE840-4B
Aux generator type:	EE911-5C
ETS generator type:	EE915-1B
Traction motor type:	EE538-5A
No of traction motors:	6
Gear ratio:	53:18
Fuel tank capacity:	1,055gal (4,797lit)
Cooling water capacity:	280gal (1,272lit)
Lub oil capacity:	130gal (591lit)
Sanding equipment:	Electro-pneumatic, then isolated
Present operator:	Class 50 Alliance
Authorised for main line use:	50031, 50049

Fact File

Built by English Electric in 1967-68 and initially owned by the company and hired to BR, these 50 locomotives were later sold to the BRB. Originally working on the West Coast main line between Crewe/Preston and Glasgow, they were displaced by the mid 1970s and transferred to the Western Region, taking over the West of England routes to both Waterloo and Paddington.

The class found favour with enthusiasts and had an almost cult following in their declining years of main line operation.

Withdrawn in the 1990s, a staggering 19 locomotives (38%) of the original fleet were preserved. Great effort was expended by preservation groups to keep the locomotives operational on light railways, and one is currently authorised for National Network operation.

When first introduced, the fleet was painted in corporate BR rail blue; this gave way to 'large logo' blue/yellow livery in the 1980s. Network SouthEast colours were applied to many locomotives when the fleet operated Waterloo-Exeter and Paddington commuter services, while a number of 'one-off' colour schemes were applied, including Railfreight, Civil Engineers and Great Western green.

Thankfully, with the number in preservation, the distinctive sound of a 'dubbing' 50 will be heard for many years to come.

Left: *Painted in 'Large Logo' wrap-around yellow livery, the two locomotives authorised for main line use, Nos 50031 and 50049, are seen light at Dawlish Warren. The leading locomotive has its No 2 end leading, with the cooler group and radiator at the far end. The rear locomotive has its No 1 end leading, thus showing the two different body styles of the locomotives. After deployment on the Western Region, all 50 were named with a Royal Navy theme.* **Author**

Above: *No 50033, restored to full working condition by Laira depot before withdrawal, was presented to the National Railway Museum for retention by the nation; however, the authorities at York saw fit to remove the locomotive from public display, where it was a major attraction, in favour of such exhibits as Thomas the Tank Engine, sending the '50' to the Steam Museum at Swindon, where it was dumped in an outbuilding for some time. In late 2007 the locomotive was transferred to Railschool at North Woolwich, where it will again be made operational and used for training purposes.* **Author**

Right: *Class 50 front end layout, showing refurbished condition. A-marker lights, B-horns (behind grille), C-headlight, D-orange square multiple jumper cable, E-orange square multiple jumper socket, F-tail light, G-electric train supply (ETS) jumper, H-vacuum pipe, I-engine control air pipe (white), J-main reservoir pipe (yellow), K-coupling, L-air brake pipe (red), M-electric train supply jumper socket. No D400 (50050) is illustrated.* **Author**

Class 52 'Western'

1957 BR number range:	D1000-D1073
Former class codes:	D27/1, later 27/1
Built by:	BR Swindon & Crewe
Introduced:	1961-1964
Wheel arrangement:	C-C
Weight (operational):	108 tonnes
Height:	12ft 11⁷/₈in (3.95m)
Width:	9ft (2.74m)
Length:	68ft (20.73m)
Min curve negotiable:	4¹/₂ chains (90.52m)
Maximum speed:	90mph (145km/h)
Wheelbase:	54ft 8in (16.66m)
Bogie Wheelbase:	12ft 2in (3.70m)
Bogie pivot centres:	42ft 6in (12.95m)
Wheel diameter:	3ft 7in (1.09m)
Brake type:	Originally - Vacuum, most later Dual
Sanding equipment:	Pneumatic
Route availability:	6
Heating type:	Steam - Spanner Mk 111
Multiple coupling restriction:	Not Multiple Fitted
Brake force:	82 tonnes
Engine type:	2 x Maybach MD655
Engine horsepower:	Total - 2,700hp (2,013kW)
Power at rail:	2,350hp (1,760kW)
Tractive effort:	72,600lb, later reduced to 70,000lb
Cylinder bore:	7¹/₄in (0.18m)
Cylinder stroke:	8¹/₄in (0.21m)
Transmission type:	Voith L630rU
Fuel tank capacity:	850gal (3,864lit)
Lub oil capacity:	100gal (455lit)
Boiler water capacity:	800gal (3,637lit)
Boiler fuel supply:	From main supply
Present owner/operator:	Diesel Traction Group
Authorised for main line use:	D1015

Fact File

Probably the most loved of all the diesel classes were the 74 C-C 'Western' diesel-hydraulics built for the Western Region between 1961-64 for main line service. In the mid-1970s, thousands of enthusiasts followed every move the final members of the class made up to 1977, and it was this class that really formed the 'modern traction' enthusiasm we see today.

The locomotives were born into a growing diesel-electric world and thus had a very short life span. All were allocated to the Western Region and operated passenger and freight services.

After withdrawal by BR, a small number were purchased for private preservation and one example passed to the National Railway Museum, York to be saved for the Nation. Of the preserved locomotives, No D1015 *Western Champion*, owned by the Diesel Traction Group, has been totally rebuilt and now returned to the main line, powering charter services a few times each year at speeds up to 90mph.

Below: *Painted in early 1960s 'golden ochre' livery, No D1015* Western Champion *skirts the River Teign at Shaldon bridge on 26 October 2006 with a charter service from Crewe to Plymouth. This locomotive now sports 'dot' marker lights and a headlight hidden in the original third character position of the headcode box, to avoid an unsightly headlight mounted on the front end.* **Author**

Above: *The Diesel Traction Group keeps 'Western' No D1015 at Old Oak Common depot in West London, where suitable facilities for its maintenance are available. From 2006 the locomotive was repainted into 1960s maroon livery, offset by a small yellow warning end. To conform with present-day Group Standards a headlight has to be fitted, but rather than spoil the lines of the locomotive, this has been located in what would have been the third position of the route indicator display. A National Radio Network phone is also installed and the pick-up for this is bolted to the front handrail just in front of the non-driving window. No D1015 is seen in Cornwall.* **Sam Felce**

Below: *From time to time filming contracts are offered to private owners, when locomotives might be repainted or renumbered for short periods. One was in early 2007 when No D1015 Western Champion was renumbered D1046 Western Marquis and used for filming at London Paddington. After the filming was complete, it retained its non-authentic identity for a short period and was used to power the 30th anniversary special marking the end of the 'Western' in everyday BR service on 24 February 2007; this is viewed near Exeter en route to Meldon Quarry.* **Author**

Class 55 'Deltic'

TOPS number range:	55001-55022
1957 BR number range:	D9000-D9021
Former class codes:	D33/1, later 33/2
Built by:	English Electric, Vulcan Foundry
Years introduced:	1961-62
Wheel arrangement:	Co-Co
Weight:	100 tonnes
Height:	12ft 11in (3.94m)
Length:	69ft 6in (21.18m)
Width:	8ft 9½in (2.68m)
Wheelbase:	59ft 6in (18.14m)
Bogie wheelbase:	13ft 6in (4.11m)
Bogie pivot centres:	45ft 0in (13.72m)
Wheel diameter:	3ft 7in (1.09m)
Min curve negotiable:	4 chains (80.46)
Engine type:	2 x Napier D18.25 'Deltic'
Engine output:	Total - 3,300hp (2,460kW)
Power at rail:	2,460hp (1,969kW)
Tractive effort:	50,000lb (222kN)
Cylinder bore:	7in (0.18m)
Cylinder stroke:	3¾in (0.095m)
Maximum speed:	100mph (161km/h)
Brake type:	Vacuum, later Dual
Brake force:	51 tonnes
Route availability:	5
Heating type:	Dual, steam later isolated
ETS index:	66
Multiple coupling type:	Not fitted
Main generator type:	2 x English Electric EE829-1A
Aux generator type:	2 x English Electric EE913-1A
Traction motor type:	English Electric EE538A
No of traction motors:	6
Gear ratio:	59:21
Fuel tank capacity:	826gal (3,755lit)
Cooling water capacity:	33gal (150lit)
Lub oil capacity:	50gal (227lit)
Sanding equipment:	Pneumatic
Present operator:	Private sector
Authorised for main line use:	55009, 55016, 55019, 55022

Fact File

Another of the very popular early main line diesel classes was the Co-Co 'Deltic' fleet, allocated Class 55 under the TOPS system. These 22 locomotives formed the backbone of the East Coast main line from the end of steam until the introduction of HSTs in the 1970s. These twin-power-unit 3,300hp machines were, and indeed still are, an impressive sight when seen at speed.

Built by English Electric Vulcan Foundry in Newton-le-Willows, the locomotives were allocated to Finsbury Park (London), Gateshead (Newcastle) and Haymarket (Edinburgh).

After withdrawal from BR several '55s' passed into preservation and it was always a desire of their owners to return them to main line operation. It was D9000 (55022) that became the first official 'preserved' diesel to operate on BR metals in preservation.

When delivered all were finished in BR green livery; this was later offset by yellow warning ends. BR standard rail blue was applied from the late 1960s.

Four locomotives are currently certified for main line operation and power occasional charters.

Below: *Owned by the Deltic Preservation Society and usually kept at Barrow Hill, No D9009 (55009) is superbly restored to 1960s BR green livery. It is seen here at the head of a charter service at York. In its preservation main-line days, to meet Group Standards headlights have been installed; these have been carefully fitted above the front-end foot hole and thus blend in well with the original design.* **Author**

Above: *The first main-line preserved diesel to be allowed to operate back on the National Network was 'Deltic' No 55022 Royal Scots Grey, superbly restored with many thousands of hours of work. Funding issues eventually saw the locomotive sold and after a period of light railway running it returned to the main line in 2006, only to have a serious power unit failure. Repairs progressed during 2007 and 'RSG' has now returned to the main line. The locomotive is seen on the East Lancs Railway, its home base.* **Nathan Williamson**

Below: *When in use on the main line the 'Deltic' fleet always sees a huge turn out of observers and photographers. Looking their best when working on the East Coast Main Line, the twin-engined machines with the distinctive engine sound are always popular at Doncaster, where this view of No 55019 Royal Highland Fusilier was captured on 30 April 2002 powering 'The Silver Jubilee' tour from London King's Cross to Edinburgh.* **Richard Tuplin**

Locomotives

	Sub Class:	56/0	56/3
	TOPS number range:	56001-56135	56301-56303
	Former Nos:	-	56045/124/125
	Built by:	56001-56030 - Electroputere at Craiova in Romania 56031-56135 - BREL Doncaster and Crewe	BREL Doncaster and Crewe
	Refurbished by:	-	Brush Traction/FM Rail
	Years introduced New:	1976-84	1976-84
	Year introduced Refurbished:	-	2006
	Wheel arrangement:	Co-Co	Co-Co
	Weight:	126 tonnes	126 tonnes
	Height:	13ft 0in (3.96m)	13ft 0in (3.96m)
	Length:	63ft 6in (19.39m)	63ft 6in (19.39m)
	Width:	9ft 2in (2.79m)	9ft 2in (2.79m)
	Wheelbase:	47ft 10in (14.58m)	47ft 10in (14.58m)
	Bogie wheelbase:	13ft 5^7/sin (4.10m)	13ft 5^7/sin (4.10m)
	Bogie pivot centres:	37ft 8in (11.48m)	37ft 8in (11.48m)
	Wheel diameter:	3ft 9in (1.14m)	3ft 9in (1.14m)
	Min curve negotiable:	4 chains (80.46m)	4 chains (80.46m)
	Engine type:	Ruston Paxman 16RK3CT	Ruston Paxman 16RK3CT
	Engine output:	3,250hp (2,420kW)	3,250hp (2,420kW)
	Power at rail:	2,400hp (1,790kW)	2,400hp (1,790kW)
	Tractive effort:	61,800lb (277kN)	61,800lb (277kN)
	Cylinder bore:	10in (0.25m)	10in (0.25m)
	Cylinder stroke:	12in (0.30m)	12in (0.30m)
	Maximum speed:	80mph (129km/h)	80mph (129km/h)
	Brake type:	Air	Air
	Brake force:	60 tonnes	60 tonnes
	Route availability:	7	7
	Heating type:	Not fitted	Not fitted
	Multiple coupling type:	Red diamond	Red diamond
	Main alternator type:	Brush BA1101A	Brush BA1101A
	Aux alternator type:	Brush BAA602A	Brush BAA602A
	Traction motor type:	Brush TMH73-62	Brush TMH73-62
	No of traction motors:	6	6
	Gear ratio:	63:16	63:16
	Fuel tank capacity:	1,150gal (5,228lit)	1,150gal (5,228lit)
	Cooling water capacity:	308gal (1,400lit)	308gal (1,400lit)
	Lub oil capacity:	120gal (545lit)	120gal (545lit)
	Sanding equipment:	Pneumatic	Pneumatic
	Special fittings:	-	OTMR
	Present operators:	EWS (out of use)	Fastline Freight
	Sub class variations:	As built locos	Rebuilt locos for Fastline Freight

Fact File

After a gap of some nine years in new diesel-locomotive construction in the UK, the BRB sought tenders for new high-power freight locomotives, following a belief that there would be a major upturn in coal demand due to an oil crisis.

A fleet of 135 locomotives was eventually built, the first 30 constructed under a contract through Brush Traction with Electroputere in Romania, with the balance built by British Rail Engineering Ltd (BREL) at their plants in Doncaster and Crewe.

The design was broadly based on the Class 47, but incorporated state-of-the-art electronics and featured a 3,250hp Ruston Paxman 16RF3CT power unit.

After a troublesome entry into service the fleet settled down well, powering all kinds of freight services and became a very reliable locomotive design. Under the BR banner the fleet was operated by Railfreight and upon privatisation passed to shadow freight operators and eventually to EWS.

In terms of standardisation, EWS decided to phase the fleet out of service in favour of Canadian-built Class 66s and the '56' fleet was gradually run down, being withdrawn in 2005.

With the expanding private freight market, three '56s' have returned to front-line use for Fastline Freight. The locomotives operated by this company were overhauled and form a new sub-class 56/3.

EWS still retain a number of locomotives which are available for spot hire; in the early years of the decade this saw a large number work in France on high speed line construction.

The preservation movement has saved several locomotives from the cutter's torch.

Above & Right: *Class 56 equipment positions: A- No 1 end, B-No 2 end, C-radiator compartment with fans on roof, D-engine compartment, E-alternator compartment, F-electrical compartment, G-hinged and removable roof sections, H-battery box, I-fuel tank, J-air compressor, K-fire pull handle, L-sand box, M-radio telephone aerial, N-headlight, O-red diamond multiple control jumper socket, P-red diamond multiple control jumper cable, Q-marker and tail light group, R-horns behind grille, S-main reservoir air pipe (yellow), T-engine control air pipe (white), U-air brake pipe (red), V-coupling. The side view is of Fastline Freight No 56302, the front end is of No 56027 in the short-lived Loadhaul livery, showing some of the earlier equipment styles. Items are in the same place today.* **John Wills/Author**

Below: *Fastline Freight operates the three main-line-certified Class 56s, which are usually used on container traffic from either Doncaster or the Midlands to Kent and can usually be found operating over the southern section of the West Coast Main Line. All three are painted in two-tone grey, offset by yellow and white stripes and the company name on the bodyside. No 56303 is officially owned by Railway Vehicle Engineering Ltd and on hire to Fastline Freight, while the other two are owned by the operator. No 56303 is seen at Rugby.* **John Wills**

Class 57

Sub class:	57/0	57/3	57/6
TOPS number range:	57001-57012	57301-57316	57601
Rebuilt by:	Brush Traction	Brush Traction	Brush Traction
Originally built by:	Brush	Brush	Brush
Years introduced – as Class 47:	1962-64	1962-64	1962-64
Years introduced – as Class 57:	1998-2000	2002-2005	2001
Wheel arrangement:	Co-Co	Co-Co	Co-Co
Weight:	120.6 tonnes	117 tonnes	121 tonnes
Height:	12ft 10³/₈in (3.91m)	12ft 10³/₈in (3.91m)	12ft 10³/₈in (3.91m)
Length:	63ft 6in (19.38m)	63ft 6in (19.38m)	63ft 6in (19.38m)
Width:	9ft 2in (2.79m)	9ft 2in (2.79m)	9ft 2in (2.79m)
Wheelbase:	51ft 6in (15.69m)	51ft 6in (15.69m)	51ft 6in (15.69m)
Bogie wheelbase:	14ft 6in (4.41m)	14ft 6in (4.41m)	14ft 6in (4.41m)
Bogie pivot centres:	37ft 0in (11.27m)	37ft 0in (11.27m)	37ft 0in (11.27m)
Wheel diameter:	3ft 9in (1.14m)	3ft 9in (1.14m)	3ft 9in (1.14m)
Min curve negotiable:	4 chains (80.46m)	4 chains (80.46m)	4 chains (80.46m)
Engine type:	General Motors 645-12E3	General Motors 645-12F3B	General Motors 645-12E3
Engine output:	2,500hp (1,860kW)	2,750hp (2,051kW)	2,500hp (1,860kW)
Power at rail:	2,025hp (1,507kW)	2,200hp (1,640kW)	2,025hp (1,507kW)
Tractive effort:	55,000lb (244.5kN)	55,000lb (244.5kN)	55,000lb (244.5kN)
Cylinder bore:	9¹/₁₆in (0.23m)	9¹/₁₆in (0.23m)	9¹/₁₆in (0.23m)
Cylinder stroke:	10in (0.25m)	10in (0.25m)	10in (0.25m)
Maximum speed:	75mph (121 km/h)	95mph (153 km/h)	95mph (153 km/h)
Brake type:	Air	Air	Air
Brake force:	80 tonnes	60 tonnes	60 tonnes
Route availability:	6	6	6
Heating type:	Not fitted	Electric - index- 100	Electric - index- 100
Multiple coupling type:	Not fitted	Not fitted	Not fitted
Main alternator type:	Brush BA1101A	Brush BA1101A	Brush BA1101A
Aux alternator type:	Brush BAA602A	Brush BAA602A	Brush BAA602A
ETS alternator type:	-	Brush BAA	Brush
Traction motor type:	Brush TM68-46	Brush TM68-46	Brush TM68-46
No of traction motors:	6	6	6
Gear ratio:	66:17	66:17	66:17
Fuel tank capacity:	1,221 gal (5,551lit)	1,295gal (5,887lit)	720gal (3,273lit)
Cooling water capacity:	298gal (1,360lit)	298gal (1,360lit)	298gal (1,360lit)
Lub oil capacity:	190gal (864lit)	190gal (864lit)	190gal (864lit)
Sanding equipment:	Pneumatic	Pneumatic	Pneumatic
Special fittings:		Hinged Dellner coupler	
Owner:	Porterbrook	Porterbrook	WCRC
Operator:	Freightliner, DRS	Virgin Trains	WCRC
Sub class variations:	Porterbrook sponsored rebuild of Class 47 using secondhand/rebuilt GM power units supplied by VMV	Porterbrook/Virgin funded Class 47 rebuilds to act as 'Thunderbirds' for 220, 221 and 390 stock. Fitted with air dryers	Revised specification with electric train supply

Fact File

The Class 57 was the brainchild of Porterbrook Leasing in conjunction with Freightliner to provide a low-cost replacement for the ageing fleet of Class 47s. The project used the bodyshell of a Class 47, which was totally gutted to its main frame members and then rebuilt using refurbished equipment.

The original Sulzer power unit was deemed unsuitable for the new era and a 12-cylinder General Motors 645-series engine was incorporated, these were purchased second (or third) hand from US rebuild companies and fully refurbished for their UK role. Electrical equipment was provided by Brush Traction in the form of an alternator group of the same design as used on the Class 56. New cooler groups and control equipment was fitted and the cabs fully refurbished. Vacuum brakes were removed.

Following conversion of 12 locomotives for Freightliner, Porterbrook/Brush developed a version with electric train supply; a trial example (57601) was built and operated on Great Western.

When Virgin Trains sought 'Thunderbird' traction for the West Coast and CrossCountry operations, a fleet of 16 ETS-fitted Class 57/3s were ordered, which now sport drop-head Dellner couplers.

First Great Western later invested in four Class 57/6 ETS-fitted locomotives for use on the Paddington-Penzance sleeper operation. These retain conventional drawgear, but sport three-piece miniature snowploughs.

In 2007 half the Freightliner Class 57/0 fleet were returned to Porterbrook for re-lease to DRS.

57/6
57602-57605
Brush Traction
Brush
1962-64
2002-2003
Co-Co
117 tonnes
12ft 10³/₈in (3.91m)
63ft 6in (19.38m)
9ft 2in (2.79m)
51ft 6in (15.69m)
14ft 6in (4.41m)
37ft 0in (11.27m)
3ft 9in (1.14m)
4 chains (80.46m)
General Motors 645-F3B-12
2,750hp (2,051kW)
2,200hp (1,640kW)
55,000lb (244.5kN)
9¹/₁₆in (0.23m)
10in (0.25m)
95mph (153 km/h)
Air
60 tonnes
6
Electric - index- 100
Not fitted
Brush BA1101A
Brush BAA602A
Brush
Brush TM68-46
6
66:17
1,295gal (5,887lit)
298gal (1,360lit)
190gal (864lit)
Pneumatic

Porterbrook
First Great Western
Rebuilt for use on FGW
sleeper services

Above & Below: *Class 57 equipment positions: A- National Radio Network radio aerial, B-marker lights (white), C-tail lights (red), D-headlight, E-air brake pipe (red), F-main reservoir pipe (yellow), G-coupling, H-No 1 end, I-No.2 end, J-electrical compartment, K-power unit compartment, L-cooler group compartment with fans on roof, M-battery box, N-fuel tank, O-sandbox. No 57001 is illustrated. Both:* **Author**

Above: *In mid-2007, following the introduction of further Freightliner Class 66/5s for deployment on container traffic, Freightliner decided to return the Class 57/0s to owners Porterbrook Leasing. Six of the fleet were taken over by Carlisle-based Direct Rail Services (DRS) and repainted in the company house colours of blue. The first to be repainted was No 57011 seen at Carlisle Kingmoor. These six locos are to receive standard DRS multiple control jumpers.* **Glen Flurry**

Below Right: *The 16 members of Class 57/3, owned by Porterbrook and hired to Virgin Trains, are usually known as 'Thunderbird' locomotives; they are used to rescue or pilot Class 220 and 221 'Voyager' or 390 'Pendolino' stock as required. Each is fitted with drop-head Dellner couplers and air dryers to allow easy coupling to the passenger stock. All are painted in Virgin silver and red livery and named after characters from the TV programme 'Thunderbirds'. The view below shows No 57301 with its Dellner coupling in the upright or stowed position. The coupler is lowered to an operational position by air controls in the driving cab. The rebuild of the 57/3 and 57/6 locomotives saw major revisions to the cooler system with new roof-mounted ventilation grilles and fans. Group standard headlights and marker/tail lights were also fitted. One Class 57/3 is usually hired to AMEC for log traffic use between Scotland and Wales. At the time of writing a small number of Class 57/3s had their Dellner coupling removed due to an equipment failure.* **Author**

Left: *The first 10 Class 57/3s were released to traffic without drop-head 'Dellner' couplers; these were retro-fitted when the design specification was agreed. The fitting required a recess to be made in the front end, to house the coupler when retracted to the rear of the draw-gear line. The coupler on No 57309 is illustrated in the retracted position. Note the main reservoir and brake pipes are connected to the coupler.* **Author**

Above: *The four members of Class 57/6 are operated by First Great Western on the Paddington-Penzance sleeper service. The main conversion followed the 57/3 style but did not include the drop-head Dellner couplers. The locomotives retain a slab front end. No 57603, complete with cast numbers and nameplates in true Great Western style, passes Dawlish with a powercar move bound for Laira.* **Author**

Right Middle: *Viewed from its No 1 end at Plymouth, No 57604 Pendennis Castle shows a modification made in early 2006 - the fitting of two- or three-piece miniature snowploughs. In addition to powering the overnight sleeper services, if capacity exists the fleet can be used for stock moves between FGW depots.* **Sam Felce**

Right Bottom: *Class 57 cab layout (57/3). A-brake timing indicator, B-de-rate indicator, C-direct brake valve (loco only), D- automatic brake valve (loco and train), E-engine start/stop buttons, F-cab radio, G-fire alarm test button, H-Automatic Warning System 'sunflower' indicator, I-windscreen wiper control, J-Automatic Warning System reset button, K-warning horn, L-screenwash button, M-main reservoir gauge, N-brake cylinder gauge, O-brake pipe gauge, P-Driver's Reminder Appliance (DRA) button, Q-speedometer, R-alternator ammeter, S-master switch key, T-master switch (for/eo/rev), U-power controller, V-driver's safety device foot pedal. No 57305's cab is illustrated.* **Author**

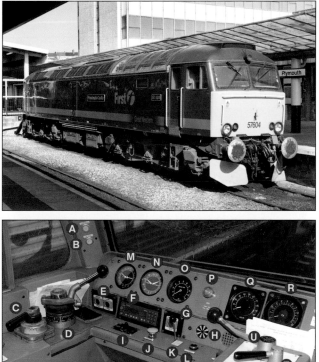

TOPS number range:	58001-58050
Design Code:	58-0AA
Built by:	BREL Doncaster
Years introduced:	1983-1987
Wheel arrangement:	Co-Co
Weight:	130 tonnes
Height:	12t 10in (3.91m)
Length:	62ft 9¹/₂in (19.13m)
Width:	9ft 1in (2.72m)
Wheelbase:	48ft 9in (14.85m)
Bogie wheelbase:	13ft 8¹/₂in (4.18m)
Bogie pivot centres:	35ft 5¹/₂in (10.80m)
Wheel diameter:	3ft 8in (1.12m)
Min curve negotiable:	4 chains (80.46m)
Engine type:	Ruston Paxman 12RK3ACT
Engine output:	3,300hp (2,460kW)
Power at rail:	2,387hp (1,780kW)
Tractive effort:	61,800lb (275kN)
Cylinder bore:	10in (0.25m)
Cylinder stroke:	12in (0.30m)
Maximum speed:	80mph (129km/h)
Brake type:	Air
Brake force:	60 tonnes
Route availability:	7
Heating type:	Not fitted
Multiple coupling type:	Red diamond
Main alternator type:	Brush BA1101B
Aux alternator type:	Brush BAA602B
Traction motor type:	Brush TM73-62
No of traction motors:	6
Gear ratio:	63:16
Fuel tank capacity:	927gal (4,214lit)
Cooling water capacity:	264gal (1,200lit)
Lub oil capacity:	110gal (416lit)
Sanding equipment:	Pneumatic
Special fittings:	OTMR
Owner:	EWS Finance
Present operators:	EWS (used as hire locos), ACTS (Netherlands), GIF (Spain)

Fact File

Following close behind the Class 56 order for UK freight motive power came various orders for 50 Class 58s, a modular-designed heavy freight locomotive which the BRB and its international arm Transmark thought would take BREL into the European locomotive construction business.

The design was a break from previous designs in having full width cabs but a narrow body section.

The 50 Class 58s emerged between 1983-87 and were initially allocated to coal traffic in the Midlands, later the fleet ventured onto all types of freight workings.

Under privatisation the fleet passed to EWS, who were not keen on keeping such a small non-standard class. The fleet were therefore withdrawn but retained by EWS.

EWS later entered the hire business offering the Class 58s to European operators. ACTS in the Netherlands now use three locomotives, while GIF in Spain operate eight. 19 have also operated in France for Fertis, Seco Rail and TSO on construction trains of the TGV line between Paris and Strasbourg. All of these have now returned to the UK and are available for further hire.

Below: *During the construction of the LGV Est route in France, The construction consortium hired a number of UK Class 56 and 58 locos to power engineering trains. These were operated by three companies Seco Rail, Fertis and TSO - all were painted in the liveries of the respective operators. Here Seco Rail-liveried No 58-027 is seen at the site of the new TGV Lorraine station. From the autumn of 2006 the locomotives all returned to the UK for store pending further Mainland European hire contracts.* **Brian Stephenson**

Right Top: *The first company to operate Class 58s in mainland Europe, after the design became spare in the UK, was ACTS in Holland. This mainly container haulier now hires three locomotives; two are painted in ACTS blue and one in a customer's black livery. The fleet operates in and around the Rotterdam and Antwerp area. On 21 November 2006 No 5811 (58039) passes Gilze-Rijen near Tilburg with a westbound container service.* **Author**

Right Middle: *The Class 58s hired to ACTS were fully overhauled by EWS at Toton depot prior to export, this included the installation of some European equipment, the balance being fitted by NedTrains in Holland after arrival. All were repainted into corporate livery in the Toton paint facility. The first to be exported, No 5811 (58039), is seen at Toton on 24 June 2003.* **Author**

Right Bottom: *Eight Class 58s are presently operated by Continental Rail and controlled by ADIF, the Spanish Administration of Rail Infrastructure. They are painted in two-tone blue and based at Bobadilla for high speed line engineering and construction trains. As the locomotives are UK gauge and much of Spain is 'broad gauge', some movements between worksites have to be made by road. Three locomotives are illustrated at Bobadilla, led by No L42 (58024). Originally they operated under the GIF banner but this operator is now part of ADIF. A few external modifications have been carried out, including the fitting of a central headlight and radio aerial on the front end.* **Enrique Dopico**

Mainland European Class 58s

The following Class 58s are currently working in mainland Europe. Present number in brackets.

ACTS Netherlands
58038 (5814)
58039 (5811)
58044 (5812)

GIF Spain
58020 (L43)
58024 (L42)
58025 (L41)
58029 (L44)
58030 (L46)
58031 (L45)
58041 (L38)
58043 (L37)

Class 58s which have operated overseas and now returned to the UK for store (former operator in brackets)

58004 (Fertis)
58007 (Seco)
58009 (Seco)
58010 (Fertis)
58011 (Fertis)
58015 (Fertis)
58016 (Fertis)
58018 (Fertis)
58021 (Fertis)
58027 (Seco)
58032 (Fertis)
58033 (TSO)
58034 (Fertis)
58035 (Fertis)
58040 (Seco)
58046 (Fertis)
58047 (TSO)
58049 (TSO)
58050 (TSO)

Class 59

Sub class:	59/0	59/1	59/2
TOPS number range:	59001-59005	59101-59104	59201-59206
GM Model:	JT26CW-SS	JT26CW-SS	JT26CW-SS
Built by:	GM-EMD, La Grange, Illinois, USA	GM-DD, London, Ontario, Canada	GM-DD, London, Ontario, Canada
Years introduced:	1985 - 1989	1990	1994-1995
Wheel arrangement:	Co-Co	Co-Co	Co-Co
Weight:	121 tonnes	121 tonnes	121 tonnes
Height:	12ft 10in (3.91m)	12ft 10in (3.91m)	12ft 10in (3.91m)
Length:	70ft 0^1/₂in (21.40m)	70ft 0^1/₂in (21.40m)	70ft 0^1/₂in (21.40m)
Width:	8ft 8^1/₄in (2.65m)	8ft 8^1/₄in (2.65m)	8ft 8^1/₄in (2.65m)
Wheelbase:	56ft 9in (17.29m)	56ft 9in (17.29m)	56ft 9in (17.29m)
Bogie wheelbase:	13ft 7in (4.15m)	13ft 7in (4.15m)	13ft 7in (4.15m)
Bogie pivot centres:	43ft 6in (13.25m)	43ft 6in (13.25m)	43ft 6in (13.25m)
Wheel diameter:	3ft 6in (1.06m)	3ft 6in (1.06m)	3ft 6in (1.06m)
Min curve negotiable:	4 chains (80.46m)	4 chains (80.46m)	4 chains (80.46m)
Engine type:	EMD 16-645E3C	EMD 16-645E3C	EMD 16-645E3C
Engine output:	3,000hp (2,238kW)	3,000hp (2,238kW)	3,000hp (2,238kW)
Power at rail:	2,533hp (1,889kW)	2,533hp (1,889kW)	2,533hp (1,889kW)
Tractive effort:	122,000lb (573kN)	122,000lb (573kN)	122,000lb (573kN)
Cylinder bore:	9^1/₁₆in (0.23m)	9^1/₁₆in (0.23m)	9^1/₁₆in (0.23m)
Cylinder stroke:	10in (0.25m)	10in (0.25m)	10in (0.25m)
Maximum speed:	60mph (97km/h)	60mph (97km/h)	75mph (121km/h)
Brake type:	Air	Air	Air
Brake force:	69 tonnes	69 tonnes	69 tonnes
Route availability:	7	7	7
Heating type:	Not fitted	Not fitted	Not fitted
Multiple coupling type:	AAR	AAR	AAR
Traction alternator:	EMD AR11	EMD AR11	EMD AR11
Companion alternator:	EMD D14A	EMD D14A	EMD D14A
Auxiliary alternator:	EMD 3A8147	EMD 3A8147	EMD 3A8147
Traction motor type:	EMD D77B	EMD D77B	EMD D77B
No of traction motors:	6	6	6
Gear ratio:	62:15	62:15	62:15
Fuel tank capacity:	1,000gal (4,546lit)	1,000gal (4,546lit)	1,000gal (4,546lit)
Cooling water capacity:	212gal (962lit)	212gal (962lit)	212gal (962lit)
Lub oil capacity:	202gal (920lit)	202gal (920lit)	202gal (920lit)
Sanding equipment:	Pneumatic	Pneumatic	Pneumatic
Present operator:	Mendip Rail	Mendip Rail	EWS
Sub class variations:	Original loco fleet of five locos owned and operated by Foster Yeoman	Second batch of GM locos ordered for UK for use by ARC Southern Slight modification to original design in front end area	Ordered and delivered to National Power and later sold to EWS. Modified technical and structural design to earlier '59s' to meet new Group Standards. Originally fitted with drop-head buck-eye couplers, now removed

Nobody could ever have imagined that in 1984 when the first four Class 59s were ordered from General Motors that the same structural design would still be in production some 23 years later in the form of the Class 66.

Mendip stone operator Foster Yeoman was the brave private company to demand higher availability from traction and wagons and entered the self owning market, firstly with wagons and then locomotives. As no UK builder could offer the levels of reliability sought, FY went to General Motors who, jointly with the BRB, designed the Class 59, broadly based on the Western front-end style, but incorporating proven North American technology - namely the 645E3C power unit.

The first order for four locomotives was quickly followed by a single follow-on order. ARC Southern was the next operator to see the huge benefits of private ownership and purchased four locomotives. The next on the ladder was National Power which eventually purchased six examples. All three breeds are slightly different, and the later two batches were built at the GM plant in Ontario, Canada.

Today the Foster Yeoman and ARC locomotives operate as one pool under the Mendip Rail banner, while the National Power fleet was later sold to EWS and is now deployed on London/Mendip area freight work, operating alongside the Mendip Rail fleet.

Above: *Class 59 equipment positions. A-No 1 end, B-No 2 end, C-internal air filtration group, D-engine/ alternator compartment, E-cooling system air intakes, F-cooling system air outlets, G-inspection hatches above power unit, H-fuel tank, I-batterybox, J-warning horns behind grille, K-marker/tail light cluster, L-twin headlights, M-multiple working control socket (cable kept in engine room), N-air brake pipe (red) and main reservoir pipe (yellow), O coupling. Locomotive shown is No 59005.* **Author**

Right Middle: *Class 59 driving cab layout. Although based on the Class 58 in terms of equipment position, the power pedestal on the right is standard North American, using a removable brass direction key and a push for power style controller. The brake controls are on the left side, while all the usual displays are on the angled front panel.* **Author**

Right Bottom: *In the summer of 1997 a new Foster Yeoman joint venture with German rail operator DB commenced, with one of the UK Class 59s being modified and shipped to Germany for freight use. No 59003 was repainted in a blue and red livery with a joint Yeoman/DB logo on the side and is seen here before departure. After a short time in mainland Europe, it became the property of Heavy Haul Power International (HHPI) and is still working in eastern Europe. It will not return to the UK.* **Author**

Above: *The second company to operate Class 59s in the UK was ARC Southern, later taken over by the Hanson Group. These locomotives are slightly different from the original Yeoman order, being built at the London plant in Ontario, Canada and incorporating a revised BRB-directed front-end design that moved the North American-style headlights from the centre of the cab to Group Standard clusters above each buffer. Body styling is the same as the 59/0s. No 59103 is seen from its No 1 end. All 59/0s and 59/1s have cast number, data panel and nameplates.* **Derek Porter**

Below: *When painted in Hanson silver, blue and red livery, designed to the same basic style as the Foster Yeoman fleet, the roof section is finished in red. This aerial view clearly shows the large exhaust module and silencer group carried in the roof at the No 1 end. The small black squares on the roof are the pick-up aerials for National Radio Network telephones, which were retro-fitted to both the Yeoman and Hanson fleets. Towards the centre of the locomotive, the hinged roof-inspection doors can be seen.* **Author**

Above: *The third and final company to operate Class 59s in the UK was National Power. Originally one locomotive was ordered, and as business flourished, five further examples followed. All were built in Canada and incorporated some modifications to the previous 59/1s, namely in external fire bottles and extra air piping. When delivered, drop-head knuckle couplers were fitted but these were later removed. After sale to EWS, No 59202, painted in full EWS livery (to a different style to the '66' in having a straight gold band), is seen on engineers' duty at Dawlish.* **Author**

Right Middle: *No 59201 is seen from its No 2 end, displaying EWS livery. These locomotives do not have cast numbers, but do carry cast nameplates, applied below the driver's side window. The EWS Class 59 and 66 can be immediately distinguished from the front end, with the '59' having its lamp iron centrally below the non-driving front window. On the '66' it is attached just above the lamp cluster.* **Author**

Right Bottom: *This view of No 59206 has been included to show the original and very distinctive National Power livery, as well as the now removed drop-head buck-eye coupler. The locomotive is seen 'on shed' at National Power's depot at Ferrybridge, which is now part of EWS.* **Author**

Locomotives

TOPS number range:	60001-60100, 60500
Built by:	Brush Traction, Loughborough
Years introduced:	1989-1993
Wheel arrangement:	Co-Co
Weight:	129 tonnes (131 tonnes*)
Height:	12ft 10³/₄in (3.95m)
Length:	70ft 0in (21.34m)
Width:	8ft 8in (2.64 m)
Wheelbase:	56ft 3¹/₈in (17.15m)
Bogie wheelbase:	13ft 6¹/₂in (4.13m)
Bogie pivot centres:	42ft 9³/₄in (13.02m)
Wheel diameter:	3ft 7in (1.18m)
Min curve negotiable:	4 chains (80.46m)
Engine type:	Mirrlees MB275T
Engine output:	3,100hp (2,240kW)
Power at rail:	2,415hp (1,800kW)
Tractive effort:	106,500lb (500kN)
Cylinder bore:	10¹/₄in (0.275m)
Cylinder stroke:	12¹/₄in (0.305m)
Maximum speed:	60mph (97km/h)
Brake type:	Air
Brake force:	74 tonnes (62 tonnes*)
Route availability:	7
Heating type:	Not fitted
Multiple coupling type:	Within class only
Main alternator type:	Brush BA1000
Aux alternator type:	Brush BAA700
Traction motor type:	Brush TM216
No of traction motors:	6
Gear ratio:	19:97
Fuel tank capacity:	990gal (4,500lit*)
Cooling water capacity:	125gal (567lit)
Lub oil capacity:	220gal (1,000lit)
Sanding equipment:	Pneumatic
Special fittings:	SSC

Note:
* 60002-05/07/09/10/12/15/17/20-28/30/37/38/41/42/46/
47/49-56/58/59/64/67/70/71/77/80/81/89-91/96-98
fitted with 1,150 gal (5,228 lit) fuel tanks, are heavier and have
reduced brake force.

Fact File

By the mid-1980s a need for new freight motive power was foreseen, and after much deliberation, an order for 100 state-of-the-art 3,100hp Co-Co locomotives was placed by the BRB with Brush Traction. The locomotives were assembled by Brush, Loughborough,with body shells produced by Procor Engineering, Wakefield.

The fleet started to enter service in 1989 but had a protracted launch, with the final example not taking to the road until 1993, numerous technical issues surrounding their deployment. However the fleet settled down well and returned good availability.

Under privatisation, the entire fleet passed to EWS, which originally favoured the design, incorporating the Mirrlees power unit. However, after introduction of Class 66s, compounded by a decline in EWS freight traffic, the '60s started to fall from favour and in recent years the fleet of 100 is frequently reduced in low traffic periods to around 40 in service, the balance being in 'warm store'.

When first introduced, the fleet was painted in Trainload triple-grey livery with 'sector' markings; under privatisation Loadhaul, Transrail and Mainline Freight colours were applied, and under EWS the corporate maroon and gold livery has been applied. All locomotives were named from new, some in recent years have been renamed in support of customers.

Left: *Viewed from its No 1 end, triple-grey-liveried No 60061 shows the Transrail logo on the side, acquired during the period of shadow privatisation. These locomotives have always given the appearance of being very spartan and business like. Few modifications have been carried out in their 18 years. The long-term retention of the fleet is uncertain with EWS, but private operators may well step in if and when the fleet is made redundant.*
Author

Above: *Class 60 equipment positions: A-No 1 end, B-No 2 end, C-radiator compartment, D-engine and alternator compartment, E-clean air compartment, F-cooler fans, G-exhaust and silencer group, H-air compressor, I-fuel tank, J-battery isolating switch, K-sand box. The locomotive illustrated is No 60085.* **Author**

Right: *Class 60 front end detail. A-warning horns, B-multiple control jumper socket (behind hinged door, cable kept in engine compartment), C-light cluster - marker, head and tail lights, D-air brake pipe (red), E-main reservoir pipe (yellow), F-coupling, G-sand box. Illustrated is No 60019 from its No 1 end.* **Author**

Below: *All Class 60s are fitted with a manually adjustable nose-end deflector plate, which in poor weather can be lowered to act as a plough for small snowdrifts. Viewed from its No 2 end and showing the 'B' side of the locomotive, the pioneer member of the fleet, No 60001, is seen at Carlisle. This one was originally named* Steadfast, *but this was changed in 2001 to* The Railway Observer *after the journal of the RCTS. Class 60s are allocated to Toton, Immingham, Thornaby and Margam depots.* **Author**

Sub class:	66/0	66/4	66/5
TOPS number range:	66001-66250	66401-66430	66501-66599
Built by:	General Motors, London, Canada	General Motors, London, Canada & EMCC London, Canada	General Motors London, Canada & EMCC London, Canada
GM model:	JT-42-CWR	JT-42-CWR	JT-42-CWR
Years introduced:	1998-2000	2003-2007	1999-2007
Wheel arrangement:	Co-Co	Co-Co	Co-Co
Weight:	126 tonnes	126 tonnes	126 tonnes
Height:	12ft 10in (3.91m)	12ft 10in (3.91m)	12ft 10in (3.91m)
Length:	70ft 0^1/2in (21.40m)	70ft 0^1/2in (21.40m)	70ft 0^1/2in (21.40m)
Width:	8ft 8^1/4in (2.65m)	8ft 8^1/4in (2.65m)	8ft 8^1/4in (2.65m)
Wheelbase:	56ft 9in (17.29m)	56ft 9in (17.29m)	56ft 9in (17.29m)
Bogie wheelbase:	13ft 7in (4.15m)	13ft 7in (4.15m)	13ft 7in (4.15m)
Bogie pivot centres:	43ft 6in (13.25m)	43ft 6in (13.25m)	43ft 6in (13.25m)
Wheel diameter:	3ft 6in (1.06m)	3ft 6in (1.06m)	3ft 6in (1.06m)
Min curve negotiable:	4 chains (80.46m)	4 chains (80.46m)	4 chains (80.46m)
Engine type:	GM 12N-710G3B-EC	GM 12N-710G3B-EC	GM 12N-710G3B-EC
Engine output:	3,300hp (2,462kW)	3,300hp (2,462kW)	3,300hp (2,462kW)
Power at rail:	3,000hp (2,238kW)	3,000hp (2,238kW)	3,000hp (2,238kW)
Tractive effort (Max):	92,000lb (409kN)	92,000lb (409kN)	92,000lb (409kN)
Tractive effort (Cont):	58,390lb (260kN)	58,390lb (260kN)	58,390lb (260kN)
Cylinder bore:	9^1/16in (0.23m)	9^1/16in (0.23m)	9^1/16in (0.23m)
Cylinder stroke:	11in (0.279m)	11in (0.279m)	11in (0.279m)
Design speed:	87.5mph (141km/h)	87.5mph (141km/h)	87.5mph (141km/h)
Maximum speed:	75mph (121km/h)	75mph (121km/h)	75mph (121km/h)
Brake type:	Air, Westinghouse PBL3	Air, Westinghouse PBL3	Air, Westinghouse PBL3
Brake force:	68 tonnes	68 tonnes	68 tonnes
Bogie type:	HTCR Radial	HTCR Radial	HTCR Radial
Route availability:	7	7	7
Heating type:	Not fitted	Not fitted	Not fitted
Multiple coupling type:	AAR	AAR	AAR
Traction alternator:	GM-EMD AR8	GM-EMD AR8	GM-EMD AR8
Companion alternator:	GM-EMD CA6	GM-EMD CA6	GM-EMD CA6
Traction motor type:	GM-EMD D43TR	GM-EMD D43TR	GM-EMD D43TR
No of traction motors:	6	6	6
Gear ratio:	81:20	81:20	81:20
Fuel tank capacity:	1,440 gal (6,550lit)	1,440 gal (6,550lit)	1,440 gal (6,550lit)
Lub oil capacity:	202 gal (920lit)	202 gal (920lit)	202 gal (920lit)
Sanding equipment:	Pneumatic	Pneumatic	Pneumatic
Special fittings:	EM2000 Q-Tron, GPS Combination coupler+ SSC	EM2000 Q-Tron, GPS 66411-430 - low emission	EM2000 Q-Tron, GPS
Sub-class variations:	Standard EWS locos	Standard DRS locos	Standard Freightliner locos
Note:	+ 66001/002 unable to be fitted with Combination couplers		66595-599 on order

Fact File

With American ownership of the new principal UK freight operator, it was not surprising that US traction to a UK profile was ordered by EWS. The same body structure used for the Class 59s was adopted, as this had operating authority in the UK, but an all-new interior using the 710-series power unit was incorporated.

The EWS order for 250 locomotives was soon followed by sizeable orders which are still being fulfilled for Freightliner, Direct Rail Services and GB Railfreight. Without doubt this design of locomotive has changed the face of UK rail freight.

Each operator has their own livery and few modifications have been made. All except the first two EWS locomotives are fitted with combination couplers, while a small batch has automatic uncouplers for banking duties.

The most significant change has been the installation of low-emissions technology by EMD, which changed the engine/cooler group layout, with an extra car-body external door on the 'A' side of the structure. This was tried on two Class 66/9s in 2004 and on all builds after mid 2006.

Specification changes to Group Standards have seen a number of different head, marker and tail light clusters fitted on different builds.

Several 'one-off' liveries are carried by most sub-classes.

66/6	66/7	66/9
66601-66625	66701-66727 (66728-32 on order)	66951-66952
General Motors	General Motors	General Motors
London, Canada &	London, Canada &	London, Canada
EMCC London, Canada	EMCC London, Canada	
JT-42-CWR	JT 42 CWR	JT-42-CWR
2000-2007	2001-2007	2004
Co-Co	Co-Co	Co-Co
126 tonnes	126 tonnes	126 tonnes
12ft 10in (3.91m)	12ft 10in (3.91m)	12ft 10in (3.91m)
70ft 0^{1}/$_{2}$in (21.40m)	70ft 0^{1}/$_{2}$in (21.40m)	70ft 0^{1}/$_{2}$in (21.40m)
8ft 8^{1}/$_{4}$in (2.65m)	8ft 8^{1}/$_{4}$in (2.65m)	8ft 8^{1}/$_{4}$in (2.65m)
56ft 9in (17.29m)	56ft 9in (17.29m)	56ft 9in (17.29m)
13ft 7in (4.15m)	13ft 7in (4.15m)	13ft 7in (4.15m)
43ft 6in (13.25m)	43ft 6in (13.25m)	43ft 6in (13.25m)
3ft 6in (1.06m)	3ft 6in (1.06m)	3ft 6in (1.06m)
4 chains (80.46m)	4 chains (80.46m)	4 chains (80.46m)
GM 12N-710G3B-EC	GM 12N-710G3B-EC	GM 12N-710G3B-T2
3,300hp (2,462kW)	3,300hp (2,462kW)	3,300hp (2,462kW)
3,000hp (2,238kW)	3,000hp (2,238kW)	3,000hp (2,238kW)
105,080lb (467kN)	92,000lb (409kN)	92,000lb (409kN)
66,630lb (296kN)	58,390lb (260kN)	58,390lb (260kN)
9^{1}/$_{16}$in (0.23m)	9^{1}/$_{16}$in (0.23m)	9^{1}/$_{16}$in (0.23m)
11in (0.279m)	11in (0.279m)	11in (0.279m)
87.5mph (141km/h)	87.5mph (141km/h)	87.5mph (141km/h)
65mph (105km/h)	75mph (121km/h)	75mph (121km/h)
Air, Westinghouse PBL3	Air, Westinghouse PBL3	Air, Westinghouse PBL3
68 tonnes	68 tonnes	68 tonnes
HTCR Radial	HTCR Radial	HTCR Radial
7	7	7
Not fitted	Not fitted	Not fitted
AAR	AAR	AAR
GM-EMD AR8	GM-EMD AR8	GM-EMD AR8
GM-EMD CA6	GM-EMD CA6	GM-EMD CA6
GM-EMD D43TR	GM-EMD D43TR	GM-EMD D43TR
6	6	6
83:18	81:20	81:20
1,440 gal (6,550lit)	66701-66717 – 1,440 gal (6,550lit)	1,220 gal (5,546lit)
	66718-66722 – 1,220 gal (5,546lit)	
	66723-66732 – 1,100 gal (5,000lit)	
202 gal (920lit)	202 gal (920lit)	202 gal (920lit)
Pneumatic	Pneumatic	Pneumatic
EM2000 Q-Tron, GPS	EM2000 Q-Tron, GPS	EM2000 Q-Tron, GPS
	66718-727 - low emission	

Freightliner locos with modified gearing

Standard GBRf locos

Development low-emission locos

Right: *The doyen of the Class 66 design, EWS Class 66/0 No 66001 is viewed from its No 2 end, showing the original marker, head and tail light style. On the left is Freightliner Class 66/5 No 66566 sporting a revised set of light groups incorporating one large high-powered headlight on each side and a single marker/tail light adjacent. Other differences include the tethering lugs on the buffer beam. No 66001 and 66002 have a different type of coupling pocket, which is unable to house the now standard EWS combination coupler. This view was taken at Burngullow, Cornwall.* **Kevin Wills**

Above (and inset right): *Standard Class 66/0 No 66052 viewed from its No 1 end showing the two-grille side. This locomotive is fitted with standard combination coupler and the retro-fitted 'wing mirrors' (detailed in the inset picture). This modification is only fitted to EWS locomotives. Both:* **Author**

Below Left & Right: *Front-end equipment positions. On the left is No 66043 showing original equipment; No 66951 on right shows revised equipment. A-Warning horns behind grille, B-radio aerial, C-high-level marker light, D-AAR jumper socket (cable kept in engine compartment), E-marker light, F-headlight, G-tail light, H-combined marker/tail light, I-combination coupler (stowed), J-coupling, K-main reservoir pipe (yellow), brake pipe (red). Both:* **Author**

Above & Below: *Class 66 bodyside equipment positions. A-No 1 end, B-No 2 end, C-Exhaust and silencer group, D-hinged inspection hatches for top of engine, E-cooling group air outlets, F-internal air filtration group, G-engine/ alternator group, H-cooling system air intakes, I-sand boxes, J-battery box, K-fuel tank, L-equipment rack. The No 1 cab of a Class 66 (and on a 59) is much larger than the No 2 cab, this is immediately identified by the larger space between the external cab door and the cab window group. No 66578 above is shown at Ipswich and No 66618 below at York. Both:* **Author**

Right: *The next operator to take delivery of Class 66s was Direct Rail Services, based in Carlisle and part of British Nuclear Fuels. By winter 2007 30 locomotives were in service powering flask and general freight services. Nos 66411-430 are fitted with the revised five-door design and have low-emissions equipment. Painted in house colours of blue and turquoise, No 66407 is seen from its No 1 end. One of the fleet, No 66411, is painted in Eddie Stobart Rail blue and white colours for a dedicated Daventry-Grangemouth flow for Tesco foods.* **Author**

Left: *GB Railfreight (GBRf) took delivery of its first Class 66s in 2001 for contract freight operations, mainly for the civil engineering functions. The company has quickly grown and is now part of FirstGroup, with a fleet of 27 locomotives and five on order. Three different 'standard' liveries and two body designs can be found. No 66703 of the original order is shown from its No 2 end at Willesden. This batch has the original light group clusters and is painted in mid-blue with orange GBRf logos.* **Author**

Left Middle: *Five additional locos, Nos 66723-66727, were delivered at the end of 2006, mainly for coal traffic in the North-East and Yorkshire. These have the revised front-end light clusters and sport FirstGroup dark blue livery offset by swirl branding. They are also of the five-door design fitted with reduced emissions equipment. No 66727 is seen from its No 1 end at Wembley.* **Author**

Below: *Five locomotives, Nos 66718-66722, were delivered in April 2006, to the five-door design with modified light clusters, and sporting a joint GBRf/Metronet livery of brighter blue. They are deployed on the massive Metronet London Underground surface-line modernisation project and are frequently used at nights and weekends on engineering trains between Wellingborough and the fringes of the LU surface network. No 66722 is illustrated.* **Author**

Right Top: *Freightliner Heavy Haul have applied a few advertising liveries to members of the Class 66 fleet, mainly in recognition of significant contracts with major customers, such as Shanks and Bardon Aggregates. Here the first joint Freightliner-customer-liveried '66' No 66522 displays Shanks livery of light and dark green. In the background is Class 66/6 No 66001.* **Kevin Wills**

Right Second: *Detail of the revised ventilation grilles found on the low-emissions Class 66s and the extra door. This is required as no through walkway exists between the two driving cabs on modified locomotives. The fifth door arrangement is seen on No 66951.* **Author**

Right Third: *The driving cab arrangement for the Class 66 is very much based on the Class 59 style, with some minor equipment repositioning and streamlining of the desk tops to improve cleanliness. The brake controls are operated by the driver's left hand, while power and direction controls are mounted on the EMD centre console. Above the driver's front screen is the on board computer system Q-tron, with repeaters for frontal illumination adjacent. When this view of No 66951 was taken, it retained CTRL construction radio equipment on the right side on the main desk.* **Author**

Right Bottom: *In addition to UK operations, a number of Class 66s can now be found at work in Mainland Europe, either EWS locomotives working for Euro Cargo Rail, or locomotives purchased/hired by mainstream European operators. Some 80 dedicated Euro 66s are now in Europe and 60 Euro Cargo Rail locomotives are now being delivered. This number is set to rise rapidly over the next few years. PB02, painted in Rail4Chem livery, is seen passing Tilburg in November 2006 with a container train from Rotterdam.* **Author**

■ **Several further orders for Class 66s are expected.**
   Five have been ordered by Fastline Freight for delivery in spring 2008, 10 by Freightliner for delivery by September 2008 and five by First/GBRf for delivery by February 2008.

TOPS number range:	67001-67030
Built by:	Alstom/General Motors, Valencia, Spain
GM model:	JT-42-HWHS
Years introduced:	1999-2000
Wheel arrangement:	Bo-Bo
Weight:	90 tonnes
Height:	12ft 9in (3.93m)
Length:	64ft 7in (19.71m)
Width:	8ft 9in (2.71m)
Wheelbase:	47ft 3in (14.43m)
Bogie wheelbase:	9ft 2in (2.80m)
Bogie pivot centres:	38ft 1in (11.63m)
Wheel diameter:	3ft 2in (965mm)
Min curve negotiable:	3.8 chains (75m)
Engine type:	GM 12N-710G3B-EC
Engine output:	2,980hp (2,223kW)
Maximum tractive effort:	31,750lb (141kN)
Continuous tractive effort:	20,200 (89.7kN) (with HEP active)
Cylinder bore:	$9^1/_{16}$in (0.23m)
Cylinder stroke:	11in (0.279m)
Maximum speed:	125mph (201km/h)
	67004/011 - 80mph (129km/h) as fitted cast iron brake blocks
Brake type:	Air, Westinghouse PBL3
Brake force:	78 tonnes (67004/011 - 68 tonnes)
Bogie type:	Alstom high speed
Route availability:	8
Heating type:	Electric - index 66 (in multiple each loco - 48)
Multiple coupling type:	AAR
Traction alternator:	GM-EMD AR9A
Companion alternator:	GM-EMD CA6HEX
Traction motor type:	GM-EMD D43FM
No of traction motors:	4
Gear ratio:	59:28
Fuel tank capacity:	1,201 gal (5,460lit)
Cooling water capacity:	212 gal (965lit)
Lub oil capacity:	202 gal (920lit)
Sanding equipment:	Pneumatic
Special fittings:	GPS (RETB-67004/007/008/009/011/030)
Operator:	EWS

Fact File

Designed and built as part of the EWS traction-modernisation project to provide the company with a 125mph capability, with specific intention to operate on Royal Mail postal and parcel trains. In the event, after just a few years the contract was lost and the locomotives have operated as part of the general EWS fleet, especially on passenger and 'Thunderbird' duties.

Ordered at the same time as the Class 66 freight locos, these 30 very expensive machines were assembled at the Alstom plant in Valencia, Spain and classified by General Motors as JT-42-HWHS.

Of the fleet of 30 all originally painted in EWS maroon and gold, two locomotives (67005/006) are now painted in Royal Train 'claret' and made available for Royal Train use when needed, while No 67029 is painted in silver VIP livery and used to power the EWS Management Train, formed of Mk3 stock and a DVT. To operate this train a revision to the jumpers has been made.

Some of the fleet are now deployed on Scottish sleeper services and ECML 'Thunderbird' work.

Below: *Class 67 equipment positions. A-No 2 end, B-No 1 end, C-exhaust and silencer module, D-hinged roof inspection doors, E-cooler group outlet, F-inertia air filter, G-power unit and alternator position, H-cooler group, I-air reservoirs, J-battery box, K-fuel tank, L-roof marker light with horns either side, M-TDM jumper, N-AAR multiple control socket (jumper cable kept in engine room), O-electric train supply socket, P-electric train supply jumper, Q-main reservoir pipe (yellow), brake pipe (red), R-light cluster (marker, tail, headlight), S-combination coupler.* **Author**

Right: *Viewed from its No 1 end, this semi-aerial view gives good detail of the roof section. The cooler-group roof grille is at the close end with the large exhaust and silencer module at the far end. When EWS operates charter passenger services, members of this fleet are usually deployed, as with a higher top speed of 125mph, pathing on the high speed railway is not a major problem. Also, their provision of ETS allows heating of stock. Although fitted with combination couplers, these are not usually used for coupling to passenger vehicles. No 67018 is seen on a passenger service at Torquay. Several members of the class now carry nameplates.* **Author**

Left: *Until introduction of the Class 67 fleet, the UK Royal Train, usually housed at Wolverton was powered by Class 47s, two being dedicated to the role and painted in Royal Claret livery. After introduction of Class 67s as the prime EWS traction, two locomotives became dedicated to Royal Train operation and have received minor modifications for this role. The most significant change is the livery, with both now painted in Royal Claret. Both were named by HM The Queen and carry the Royal insignia on the bodyside. When not required for Royal duties, usually around 20 times every year, they operate as part of the core Class 67 fleet. No 67005 is seen on a passenger working passing Dawlish.* **Author**

Right: *When introduced the Class 66s and 67s all carried etched maker's plates, giving details of construction, model and number and delivery date. Plate from 67003 illustrated.* **Author**

Right: *The driving desk on the Class 67 was of a totally new design to the UK, being based broadly on previous Alstom traction supplied to Mainland Europe. The driver sits just left of centre in the cab, with a very neat and well-styled wrap-around layout. His power controls, based on the traditional GM design with removable brass key, are desk-mounted and operated by the driver's right hand. Brake controls are located on the left side with desk displays on the angled panel in front. The computer system is also desk-mounted. The cab of No 67002 is illustrated before delivery to the UK.* **Author**

Class 73

Sub class:	73/1	73/2
TOPS number range:	73101-142	73201-235
1957 BR number range:	E6007-E6049	From Class 73/1 fleet
Southern Region class codes:	JB	JB
Built by:	English Electric, Vulcan Foundry	Modified by BR Stewarts Lane depot
Years introduced:	1965-67	1984-90
Wheel arrangement:	Bo-Bo	Bo-Bo
Weight:	77 tonnes	77 tonnes
Height:	12ft 5⁵⁄₁₆in (3.79m)	12ft 5⁵⁄₁₆in (3.79m)
Length - buffers retracted:	52ft 6in (16.00m)	52ft 6in (16.00m)
Length - buffers extended:	53ft 8in (16.96m) 73118/130 - 58ft 9in (17.95m)	53ft 8in (16.96m)
Width:	8ft 8in (2.64m)	8ft 8in (2.64m)
Wheelbase:	40ft 9in (12.42m)	40ft 9in (12.42m)
Bogie wheelbase:	8ft 9in (2.66m)	8ft 9in (2.66m)
Bogie pivot centres:	32ft 0in (11.27m)	32ft 0in (11.27m)
Wheel diameter:	3ft 4in (1.01m)	3ft 4in (1.01m)
Min curve negotiable:	4 chains (80.46m)	4 chains (80.46m)
Power supply:	660-850V dc third rail	660-850V dc third rail
Electric output (Nom):	1,600hp (1,193kW)	1,600hp (1,193kW)
Electric power at rail (Cont):	1,200hp (895kW)	1,200hp (895kW)
Electric power at rail (Max):	3,150hp (2,350kW)	3,150hp (2,350kW)
Engine type:	English Electric 4SRKT Mk2	English Electric 4SRKT Mk2
Engine output:	600hp (447kW)	600hp (447kW)
Diesel power at rail:	402hp (300kW)	402hp (300kW)
Electric tractive effort:	40,000lb (179kN)	40,000lb (179kN)
Diesel tractive effort:	36,000lb (160kN)	36,000lb (160kN)
Cylinder bore:	10in (0.25m)	10in (0.25m)
Cylinder stroke:	12in (0.30m)	12in (0.30m)
Maximum speed:	90mph (145km/h	90mph (145km/h)
Brake type:	Dual, with high level air pipes, some modified to air brake only	Dual, with high level air pipes. All modified to air brake only
Brake force:	31 tonnes	31 tonnes
Route availability:	6	6
Heating type:	Electric - index 66 (electric only)	Electric - index 66 (electric only)
Multiple coupling type:	Electric, 1951-1966 EMU jumpers Diesel - blue star	Electric, 1951-1966 EMU jumpers Diesel - blue star
Main generator type:	EE824-5D	EE824-5D
Aux generator type:	EE908-5C	EE908-5C
Traction motor type:	EE546-1B	EE546-1B
No of traction motors:	4	4
Gear ratio:	61:19	61:19
Fuel tank capacity:	310gal (1,409lit)	310gal (1,409lit)
Sanding equipment:	Pneumatic	Pneumatic
Special fittings:	Drop-head buck-eye, Loudaphone 73118/130 fitted with Scharfenberg couplings	Drop-head buck-eye, Loudaphone 73202 modified to multiple with Gatwick Express Class 460 stock
Present operators:	RT Rail, South West Trains, GBRF, Network Rail, private owners	Gatwick Express, GBRf, Network Rail, South West Trains
Sub class variations:	Production fleet, mounted on revised bogies with modified grilles	Locos originally dedicated to Gatwick Express operation

Fact File

These universal electro-diesel locomotives were the brainchild of the Southern, which wanted to exploit the most from its third rail electric supply, while having the ability to operate 'off juice'.

The original prototype Class 73/0 fleet has now been withdrawn and a handful of Class 73/1s and 73/2s remain operational. The fleet is best remembered in recent years for operating the Gatwick Express service between 1984 and 2006. One locomotive, No 73202, still remains with Gatwick Express for 'Thunderbird' duties.

On the privatised railway, operator GBRf has taken eight locomotives for freight service and the private sector has a number of machines available for working either on diesel or electric power.

Network Rail operate two locomotives for de-icing duties and Eurostar UK operated a pair for Eurostar tractor duties until November 2007, when the Eurostar operation transferred to Temple Mills, the pair transferring to private use.

The preservation sector has purchased a sizeable number of locomotives, many now operational.

Above: *The Southern operator's affiliation with the Class 73 dual-power fleet continued after privatisation, with South West Trains now operating a fleet of three for depot transfer and 'Thunderbird' duties. However, how long these will remain is in some doubt, as following withdrawal of Class 442s, the Class 73s are unable to directly couple to any of the remaining stock without the use of adaptor couplers. The three SWT locomotives, one Class 73/1 and two Class 73/2s are painted in full SWT blue livery and are maintained at either Bournemouth or Wimbledon depots. No 73235 above is viewed from the diesel or No 1 end, showing the 'B' side with two glazed windows and one grille panel. For operating in the multiple-unit area, the buck-eye couplers are in the raised position and buffers retracted.* **Author**

Below: *Following introduction of 'Juniper' Class 460 electric multiple-units on the Gatwick Express service, the fleet of Gatwick EDs was reduced to just one locomotive, No 73202, which is normally kept at Stewarts Lane for emergency rescue duties or hauling sets to maintenance depots if needed. It is painted in Gatwick Express 'InterCity' colours, is air brake fitted only and is fitted with an interlock light for operation with Juniper stock; this is side-mounted at the No 2 end (detail inset picture). The Class 73s still retain their dual position driving controls, allowing the locomotives to be driven from either side of the cab. Both:* **Author**

Above: *GB Railfreight currently operates a fleet of five Class 73/2s (73204-06/08/09), have use of 73/1 No 73136 and have two further locomotives in store (73203/07). These operate mainly in the South Thames electrified area and into non-electrified worksites on engineers' services, also powering 'spot-hire' freight services. With the exception of 73136 and 73208, which are painted in BR rail blue, the fleet is painted in GBRf blue, orange and yellow livery, with orange branding. The two blue-liveried locos, led by No 73208, are seen powering a passenger charter service near Virginia Water on 10 August 2006.* **Author**

Left Middle: *GB Railfreight standard livery of mid-blue offset by orange and yellow is seen on No 73205, viewed from its electrical end. The GBRf locos have all been modified for air-brake-only operation, but retain blue star compatibility with similarly-equipped diesel locomotives.* **Brian Garrett**

Left Bottom: *RT Rail are the owner/operators of No 73107, which is painted in two-tome grey livery and named* Spitfire. *The locomotive is main line certified and used for charter and spot hire use. It is seen working with two Hastings power cars at Ashford. When not in use it is usually kept at Hastings.* **Brian Stephenson**

Right Top & Right Middle: *At the time of the introduction of Eurostar operations, two Class 73/1s were transferred to the operator for use as 'Thunderbird' or 'Tractor' power. The pair were rebuilt by Crewe Works with a massive coupling adaptor plate on either end, incorporating a hinged Scharfenberg coupler, which if needed could be lowered to allow attachment to a Eurostar. To provide conventional draw gear in front of this arrangement, standard buffers and a coupling hook were also fitted. The nose end also sported a control jumper cable and socket, air pipes both high and low level and a headlight. When originally modified, it was said the coupling attachment could be 'easily removed and attached to any Class 73'; in reality, the equipment has remained on the dedicated locomotives, Nos 73118/130. Both are painted in double grey livery with Channel Tunnel roundels and until November 2007 were kept at North Pole International Depot. When the Channel Tunnel route first opened, the locomotives saw a lot of use hauling sets between London and Dollands Moor for testing, or powering training trips; however, today their use has drastically declined and they are more usually used as depot pilots. With the transfer of Eurostar UK maintenance facilities to Temple Mills, Stratford, in November 2007 the Class 73s were made redundant, as the dc operation of the Class 373 sets was removed. No 73130 is seen at North Pole Depot. Both locomotives have now been placed on long-term 'loan', one to RailSchool and the other to the Barry Railway.*
Both: **Author**

Right Bottom: *Some Class 73s which were withdrawn from mainstream operation and entered 'preservation' have now been returned to front-line use and are back at work on the National Network. One such example is Class 73/1 No 73133, modified with Group Standard light clusters and extra front window. It is owned by Cambrian Trains and is presently hired to Network Rail for use as a depot pilot at Taunton Fairwater Yard in connection with the HOBC and TRT West of England projects.*
The locomotive is painted in mid-blue with a grey roof and usually resides in one of the inner roads of Taunton Fairwater Yard. **Philip Izzard**

Sub class:	86/1, 86/2 & 86/9	86/5	86/6
TOPS number range:	86101, 86201-261, 86901-86902	86501	86602-86639
1957 BR number range:	E3101-E3200 series	E3180	E3101-E3200 series
Former class code:	AL6	AL6, Class 86	AL6, Class 86
Built by:	English Electric, Vulcan Foundry and BR Doncaster Rebuilt by BREL Crewe	Modified by Adtranz Crewe	Modified by BR Crewe
Years introduced:	1965-66	1965-66	1965-66
Years Modified:	86/1 - 1972, 86/2 - 1972-75, 86/9 - 2005	2000	2000
Wheel arrangement:	Bo-Bo	Bo-Bo	Bo-Bo
Weight:	85 tonnes	84 tonnes	84 tonnes
Height (pan down):	13ft 0⁹/₁₆in (3.97m)	13ft 0⁹/₁₆in (3.97m)	13ft 0⁹/₁₆in (3.97m)
Length:	58ft 6in (17.83m)	58ft 6in (17.83m)	58ft 6in (17.83m)
Width:	8ft 8¹/₄in (2.64m)	8ft 8¹/₄in (2.64m)	8ft 8¹/₄in (2.64m)
Wheelbase:	43ft 6in (13.25m)	43ft 6in (13.25m)	43ft 6in (13.25m)
Bogie wheelbase:	10ft 9in (3.27m)	10ft 9in (3.27m)	10ft 9in (3.27m)
Bogie pivot centres:	32ft 9in (9.98m)	32ft 9in (9.98m)	32ft 9in (9.98m)
Wheel diameter:	3ft 9¹/₄in (1.15m)	3ft 9¹/₄in (1.15m)	3ft 9¹/₄in (1.15m)
Min curve negotiable:	4 chains (80.46m)	4 chains (80.46m)	4 chains (80.46m)
Power supply:	25kV ac overhead	25kV ac overhead	25kV ac overhead
Traction output (max):	6,100hp (4,550kW)	5,900hp (4,400kW)	5,900hp (4,400kW)
Traction output (cont):	4,040hp (3,010kW)	3,600hp (2,680kW)	3,600hp (2,680kW)
Tractive effort:	46,500lb (207kN)	58,000lb (258kN)	58,000lb (258kN)
Maximum speed:	86/1 - 100mph (161km/h) 86/2 - 100mph (161km/h) 86/9 - 60mph (97km/h)	75mph (121km/h)	75mph (121km/h)
Brake type:	Dual, some air only	Air	Air
Brake force:	40 tonnes	40 tonnes	40 tonnes
Route availability:	6	6	6
Heating type:	Electric - index 66	Electric - isolated	Electric - isolated
Multiple coupling type:	Jumper system, then TDM	TDM	TDM
Control system:	HT tap changing	HT tap changing	HT tap changing
Traction motor type:	AEI G282BZ	AEI G282AZ	AEI G282AZ
No of traction motors:	4	4	4
Gear ratio:	22:65	18:70	22:65
Sanding equipment:	Pneumatic	Pneumatic	Pneumatic
Operator:	Network Rail, Private	Freightliner	Freightliner
Sub class variations:	Locomotives fitted with flexicoil suspension, SAB wheels and 282BZ traction motors	Trial conversion of Class 86/6 with lower gearing and improved sanding to provide better performance on Freightliner trains	Locos operated by Freightliner, vacuum brake equipment removed and restricted to 75mph

Note:
86/1 - Owned by the AC Locomotive Group.
86/2 - Presently out of service, 86/9s are mobile load banks and have traction equipment isolated at No 1 end.

Left: *Class 86/2, fitted with flexicoil suspension and nose end RCH jumpers for operating with RCH-fitted stock. This example, seen from its No 1 end, is painted in Anglia livery and sports a non-standard ventilation grille on the front end and the roof-mounted fire-fighting bottles fitted later. This view shows the equipment side, with nine grille panels providing ventilation to the electrical equipment. The other has a mix of windows and grille panels. Buffer-beam connections exist for air and vacuum braking, and electric train heating.* **Author**

Originally introduced for use on the West Coast Main Line in 1965-66 as the second generation of ac main-line power, this 100-strong fleet formed the backbone of services on the Euston main line for many years, working both passenger and freight services.

By the early 1970s, rebuilding with revised bogies to reduce track stress took place, which saw the introduction of several different sub-classes; 86/0 for original locomotives, 86/1 for development locos and 86/2 for flexicoil bogie fitted examples.

Newer WCML classes ousted most of the '86s' from front-line use with a batch transferring to the London-Norwich main line following electrification.

After privatisation the fleet was split between Virgin Trains, Anglia and the freight operators EWS and Freightliner.

Today, the passenger fleets are all out of service from the mainstream operators, but some privately owned examples are set to return to the main line. EWS no longer use the class, while Freightliner operate the Class 86/5 and 86/6 fleets on long distance liner services.

Network Rail operate two locomotives classified as 86/9 as mobile load banks.

A number of the stored locomotives might see further use with overseas administrations.

Above: *Class 86 equipment positions. A-No 1 end, B-No 2 end, C-pantograph, D-fire bottle, E-sandbox filler, F-flexicoil suspension, G-air compressor, H-battery charger, I-main rectifiers, J-transformer, K-control cubicle, L-traction motor blower. Class 86/6 No 86609 is seen from equipment side.* **Author**

Below: *One member of Class 86/5 exists, No 86501, which was re-equipped with revised gearing at Crewe as an experiment by Freightliner to improve adhesion. It is seen from its No 2 end walkway side at Ipswich.* **Author**

Below: *Two Class 86/2s Nos 86253 (86901) and 86210 (86902) were rebuilt at Barrow Hill as mobile load banks. The locomotives have revised internal equipment and operate with only one bogie taking power. When not required for line testing, they are used by Network Rail, often for overhead-wire ice scraping. No 86901 is viewed at Rugby, in NR yellow livery.* **John Wills**

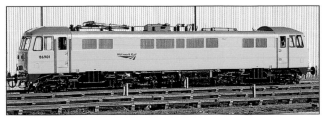

Locomotives

TOPS number range:	87001-87035
Number range:	BREL Crewe
Years introduced:	1973-1975
Wheel arrangement:	Bo-Bo
Weight:	83.3 tonnes
Height (pan down):	13ft 1¼in (3.99m)
Length:	58ft 6in (17.83m)
Width:	8ft 8¼in (2.64m)
Wheelbase:	43ft 6⅛in (13.25m)
Bogie wheelbase:	10ft 9⅛in (3.28m)
Bogie pivot centres:	32ft 9in (9.98m)
Wheel diameter:	3ft 9½in (1.16m)
Min curve negotiable:	4 chains (80.47m)
Power supply:	25kV ac overhead
Traction output (Max):	7,860hp (5,860kW)
Traction output (Con):	5,000hp (3,730kW)
Tractive effort:	58,000lb (258kN)
Maximum speed:	110mph (177km/h)
Brake type:	Air
Brake force:	40 tonnes
Route availability:	6
Heating type:	Electric - index 95
Multiple coupling type:	Originally multi-pin jumpers, modified to TDM
Control system:	HT tap changing
Traction motor type:	GEC G412AZ
No of traction motors:	4
Gear ratio:	32:73
Sanding equipment:	Pneumatic
Owner:	Porterbrook Leasing, private owners
Operator:	GBRf, private sector, BZK Bulgaria

Fact File

Built by BREL as the 'new' power for the West Coast 'Electric Scot' services, the Class 87s were the backbone of the Euston-Glasgow, Manchester and Liverpool routes until the introduction of Class 90s and eventually 'Pendolino' stock under privatisation.

The '87s' were always used by the passenger sector, except for trials locomotive No 87101 which was fitted on construction with advanced thyristor control equipment; this example eventually worked for the freight sector and withdrawn early.

Following withdrawal from Virgin Trains West Coast operations, the fleet owned by Porterbrook was stored, with several of the smaller operators, DRS and Cotswold testing the locomotives for short periods.

Export potential could be seen by the owners, with some of the Eastern European countries that used a similar power system being options for future use. In early 2007 two examples, Nos 87012/019 were exported to BZK in Bulgaria. The majority of the rest of the fleet is expected to follow in 2008.

Two others, Nos 87022 and 87028, are currently operating for GBRf on Mail Train flows, but the remainder are stored. Two more have so far been saved by the private sector in preservation and the pioneer of the fleet, No 87001, is now the property of the National Railway Museum, York.

Left: *Class 87 front end equipment. A-warning horns behind grille, B-TDM control jumper, C-marker and tail light group, D-headlight, E-electric train supply jumper receptacle, F-electric train supply jumper cable, G-coupling, H-air brake pipe (red), I-main reservoir pipe (yellow). When originally built the Class 87s had multiple control jumper cables mounted on the nose end, the position of which is identified by the blanking plates fitted today. Originally a smaller sealed beam headlight was fitted, being replaced in the 1980s by a Group Standard unit.* **Author**

Above: *Before the final demise of the Class 87 fleet from front line passenger services on the West Coast main line and their replacement by Pendolino stock, a number of 'one-off' and display liveries were applied. The owners of the fleet, Porterbrook Leasing, applied its mauve livery to No 87002, which then operated normal services in this non-standard colour. It is seen here passing Crewe with a northbound express on 29 July 2004.* **Author**

Below: *Operator GB Railfreight, part of FirstGroup, took over two Class 87s to power West Coast main line Royal Mail trains, following the awarding of the mail by rail contract by Royal Mail to GBRf. The trains are formed of Class 325 'Railnet' EMUs but are frequently piloted by Class 87s. Nos 87022/028 are painted in all-over blue livery, offset by orange cab surrounds and windows. Large numerals are applied. No 87028 is illustrated at Carlisle.* **Sam Felce**

TOPS number range:	90001-90050
Built by:	BREL Crewe
Years introduced:	1987-1990
Wheel arrangement:	Bo-Bo
Weight:	84.5 tonnes
Height (pan down):	13ft 0^1/$_4$in (3.96m)
Length:	61ft 6in (18.74m)
Width:	9ft 0in (2.74m)
Wheelbase:	43ft 6in (13.25m)
Bogie wheelbase:	10ft 9in (3.27m)
Bogie pivot centres:	32ft 9in (9.98m)
Wheel diameter:	3ft 9^1/$_2$in (1.16m)
Min curve negotiable:	4 chains (80.43m)
Power supply:	25kV ac overhead
Traction output (max):	7,860hp (5,860kW)
Traction output (con):	5,000hp (3,730kW)
Tractive effort:	58,000lb (258kN)
Maximum speed:	90001-90040 - 110mph (177km/h)
	90041-90050 - 75mph (121km/h)
Brake type:	Air
Brake force:	40 tonnes
Route availability:	7
Heating type:	90001-90040 - Electric - index 95
	90041-90050 - Electric - isolated
Multiple coupling type:	TDM
Control system:	Thyristor
Traction motor type:	GEC G412CY
No of traction motors:	4
Gear ratio:	32:73
Sanding equipment:	Pneumatic
Special fittings:	90001-90015 - Drop-head buck-eye couplings
Operator:	'one' Railway, EWS, Freightliner

Fact File

The 50 third generation main line ac electrics of Class 90 were intended for West Coast use, and when built in 1987-90 were used on both passenger and freight services. The first 15 were dedicated to InterCity operations and the balance to the freight, van and Royal Mail operations.

The Class 90/0s used on main West Coast passenger services were replaced by Pendolino stock and are now deployed on 'one' Anglia services between London and Norwich, while the remaining locomotives (now classified as 90/0) although at various times have operated as 90/1s and 90/2s) are now operated by EWS and Freightliner. 'one' Anglia locos now sport this operator's turquoise livery, while the EWS examples are in either EWS maroon, grey or First ScotRail colours for sleeper operation. The Freightliner locomotives are in green or grey with Freightliner branding. Many locomotives are named.

Below: *Class 90 equipment positions: A-No 1 end, B-No 2 end, C-equipment room (four grille side), D-battery box, E-air compressors, F-pantograph, G-light cluster (each side (head, tail and marker light), H-warning horns, I-electric train supply jumper, J-air brake pipes, main reservoir pipe (yellow), brake pipe (red), K-electric train supply jumper receptacle, L-pullman rubbing plate. M-sandbox filler port. The turquoise and grey livery adopted by operator 'one' Railway suits the body style of the Class 90 well, especially when in pristine condition. Viewed from its No 1 end on the two-grille side, No 90007 is illustrated. These passenger locomotives still retain buck-eye couplers and use TDM control to talk via train lines to remote driving van trailers (DVTs).* **Author**

Right Top: *Viewed from its No 2 end on the two-grille side, 'one' Railway No 90003 shows the original slightly darker blue applied to the first few repaints which also included the 'Anglia' trading name. The 'one' Railway-operated locomotives are based at Norwich Crown Point and power the Norwich-London Liverpool Street services. Buck-eye couplers and Pullman rubbing plates are retained, and thus retractable buffers are fitted.* **Author**

Right Second: *The largest batch of Class 90s - 25 locos - are operated by EWS; however in mid-2007 just 11 were fully operational, the rest being stored. They are allocated to Crewe International and power a mix of freight and charter passenger services, as well as providing power for the overnight Sleeper contract on behalf of First ScotRail. The EWS locomotives are in a mix of liveries including freight grey, EWS maroon and gold and EWS/First ScotRail for the dedicated passenger locomotives. All have lost their buck-eye couplers and Pullman rubbing plates (even those allocated to passenger services) and have thus been fitted with fixed buffers. No 90031 is illustrated from its No 2 end.* **Author**

Right Third: *By spring 2007 three EWS Class 90s Nos. 90019/021/024 were painted in a joint EWS/First ScotRail 'Barbie' livery, which surprisingly suits the body profile of this fleet. They should be dedicated to the four overnight services between Edinburgh/Glasgow and London (two each way), but rostering frequently finds them on other duties. Viewed from its No 2 end from the two grille side, No 90024 is seen at Euston.* **Nathan Williamson**

Right Bottom: *One of the main strengths of the Class 90 fleet from introduction was its true mixed traffic role, being able to operate both passenger and freight services. From introduction a batch was allocated to liner train use where services could be operated at up to 75mph. Today Freightliner operates a batch of 10 (Nos 90016/041-049) for powering long distance intermodal services, mainly linking Scotland and the North West with the Midlands, London and Essex. Locos are now being repainted in corporate green and yellow livery, as shown on No 90041. These have also had their buck-eye couplers and rubbing plates removed and conventional buffers installed.* **John Wills**

Class 91

Class:	91
TOPS number range:	91101-91132 (originally 91001-91031)
Built by:	BREL Crewe
Rebuilt:	Adtranz/Bombardier Doncaster
Years introduced:	1988-1991
Years refurbished to 91/1:	2000-2002
Wheel arrangement:	Bo-Bo
Weight:	84 tonnes
Height (pan down):	12ft 4in (3.75m)
Length:	63ft 8in (19.40m)
Width:	9ft 0in (2.74m)
Wheelbase:	45ft 4^1/$_2$in (13.85m)
Bogie wheelbase:	10ft 1^7/$_8$in (3.35m)
Bogie pivot centres:	34ft 5^1/$_2$in (10.50m)
Wheel diameter:	3ft 3^1/$_2$in (1.00m)
Min curve negotiable:	4 chains (80.49m)
Traction output (max):	6,300hp (4,700kW)
Traction output (con):	6,090hp (4,540kW)
Maximum design speed:	140mph (225km/h)
Maximum operating speed:	125mph (201km/h)
	110mph (177km/h) if slab end leading
Brake type:	Air
Brake force:	45 tonnes
Route availability:	7
Heating type:	Electric - index 95
Multiple coupling type:	TDM
Control system:	Thyristor
Traction motor type:	GEC G426AZ
No of traction motors:	4
Gear ratio:	1.74:1
Sanding equipment:	Pneumatic
Special fittings:	Drop-head buck-eye couplings
Operator:	National Express East Coast

Below: In normal operation the Class 91s usually work at the north end of trains on the ECML route, coupled to the standard class carriages. A like profiled driving van trailer (DVT) is marshalled at the London end, controlling the Class 91 via coded messages transmitted through TDM cables. Although designed for 140mph operation, route constraints, namely signalling and no automatic train protection means that a top speed of 125mph has to be observed. North of York at Shipton-by-Benningborough, No 91121 propels its train south. **Author**

Above: *The front-end equipment on a Class 91 is in the same places as the slab end detailed below, it is usual that the buck-eye coupling on the nose end is maintained in the lowered position and the buffer extended. Equipment locations within the main body section between the cabs from the leading end are: rheostatic brake unit and high voltage cubicle, thyristor cubicle, transformer bay and brake frame. No significant structural modifications have been carried out to this fleet since introduction. No 91129 is seen at Doncaster.* **Derek Porter**

Right Middle: *Class 91 cab layout. The illustration shows a refurbished layout, installed at the time of upgrading from Class 91/0 to 91/1. The power controller is on the driver's right side, together with the master switch (forward, off, reverse), AWS reset button and horn valve. On the left side is the brake controller. All other displays including AWS, driver's reminder appliance and TPWS are desk mounted on the front panel. The large blank space is for the eventual provision of ERTMS. The slab-end cab is of a slightly different layout.* **Author**

Right Bottom: *When the Class 91s were designed, one of the 'must have' features was the ability to drive from the inner or slab end; while this was not intended to power high speed trains on a regular basis, it was considered essential in case of on-line failure or light running, where the driver would need to operate the locomotive in the reverse direction. When driving from the inner or slab end, a top speed of 110mph has to be observed. Due to TDM jumper problems, Class 91s frequently have to run round trains at locations such as Newcastle, York or Doncaster and haul services southbound to London, avoiding the need of a pilot locomotive. Slab end equipment: A-TDM jumpers (behind doors), B-warning horn (behind grille), C-Group Standard light cluster (tail, marker and headlight), D-Pullman rubbing plate, E-buck-eye coupling, F-UIC control jumper, G-electric train supply jumper socket, H-air pipes, air brake pipe (red), main reservoir pipe (yellow), I-electric train supply jumper cable, J-sand filler port, K-water filler port. Illustrated is No 91107.* **Author**

Class 92

TOPS number range: 92001-92046
Built by: Brush Traction
Years introduced: 1993-95
Wheel arrangement: Co-Co
Power supply: AC overhead at 25kV or
DC third rail at 750V
Weight: 126 tonnes
Height (pan down): 13ft 0in (3.95m)
Length: 70ft 1in (21.34m)
Width: 8ft 8in (2.66m)
Wheelbase: 56ft 6in (17.22m)
Bogie wheelbase: 14ft 1in (4.29m)
Bogie pivot centres: 41ft 10¹/₂in (12.75m)
Wheel diameter: 3ft 9in (1.16m)
Min curve negotiable: 6 chains (120.7m)
Traction output (max): 6,700hp (5,000kW) - overhead power supply
5,360hp (4,000kW) - third rail power supply
Tractive effort: Normal - 81,000lb (360kN)
Boost - 90,000lb (400kN)
Maximum speed: 87mph (140km/h)
Brake type: Air, rheostatic and regenerative
Brake force: 63 tonnes
Route availability: 8
Heating type: Electric – ac supply – index 108,
dc supply - index 70
Multiple coupling type: TDM
Control system: Asynchronous 3-phase
Traction motor type: Brush
No of traction motors: 6
Special fittings: TVM430, CTO
Present operators: EWS, SNCF, Eurotunnel
Notes: Some locos stored

Fact File

Designed by the then BR Railfreight Distribution, with a major input from French operator SNCF and the Channel Tunnel authority, the 46-strong Class 92 fleet was built expressly for Cross-Channel services using the Channel Tunnel.

The design is basically two locomotives in one bodyshell, meaning that in all but the most serious failures a locomotive would be able to continue its journey through the Channel Tunnel.

They were ordered and funded by Railfreight Distribution (30), SNCF (9) and Eurostar UK (7). During the course of delivery from Brush Traction, the Eurostar overnight services were abandoned, rendering these locomotives redundant, and shortly after, the SNCF-owned examples were stored in the UK. The Railfreight Distribution locomotives were eventually transferred to EWS upon privatisation. To maintain as many in a serviceable condition as possible, a 'work around' was operated for some time, but today only the EWS locomotives remain operational.

Some hope exists that the SNCF locomotives might be reinstated for a French-owned UK freight service.

All are fitted for dual 25kV ac and 750V dc operation and fitted with TVM430 cab signalling.

In February 2007, five of the original Eurostar UK locomotives, Nos 92020/021/032/040/044 were sold to Eurotunnel.

Left: *The Class 92s have two identical bodysides and pantographs fitted at both ends, although only one is raised at a time. The majority still carry the 'as-built' Channel Tunnel triple-grey and blue livery offset by the Channel Tunnel segment logo and a cast BR double arrow logo below the driver's side window. All locomotives were named from delivery, originally these were applied in stick-on letters, but subsequent renamings have used cast plates. No 92019 is illustrated at Manchester Piccadilly.* **Author**

Right: *Class 92 front end: A-warning horns, B-high level marker light, C-Group Standard light cluster, side, head and tail light, D-electric train supply jumper socket, E-electric train supply jumper cable, F-main reservoir (yellow) and brake pipe (red), G-UIC jumper connection, H-UIC jumper receptacle, I-sandbox. Illustrated is the front end of the first complete locomotive, No 92002. Before it entered traffic, the two grey TVM430 boxes below the buffer were repainted from grey to black.* **Author**

Right Middle: *After the takeover of the Railfreight businesses by US-owned EWS, little attention was given to the Class 92 fleet in cosmetic terms. A couple were repainted by Toton in the new maroon and gold livery, but the majority retained their Railfreight grey colours and many kept the BR double-arrow logo. In 2005 a start was made on branding the fleet, using a large yellow sticker incorporating the EWS animal-head logo in maroon. Frankly, this looks hideous on the side of any locomotive. In many cases these stickers have partially or completely peeled off. No 92005 is viewed at Rugby.* **John Wills**

Below: *When originally constructed it was the wish of the UK operators to take the Class 92s deep into France, possibly to Lille or Paris on freight and Nightstar services; however, by the time deliveries came on stream, this plan had been abandoned and the '92s' are not permitted to operate further into France than Calais. Two, Nos 92001/031, are presently painted in EWS maroon and gold, retaining their Channel Tunnel logos and with cast nameplates located above the running numbers. No 92031 is illustrated at Rugby.* **John Wills**

Locomotives

Sub class:	9/0 & 9/1	9/7	9/8
Number range:	9/0 - 9001-9040, 9/1 - 9101-9113	9701-9707	9801-9840
Previous number range:	-	-	9001-9040
Former class code:	-	-	9/0
Built by:	Brush Traction, Loughborough	Brush Traction, Loughborough	Brush Traction, Loughborough
Years introduced:	1993-1999	2001	1993-1994
Years refurbished	-	-	2005-2008
Wheel arrangement:	Bo-Bo-Bo	Bo-Bo-Bo	Bo-Bo-Bo
Weight:	132 tonnes	132 tonnes	132 tonnes
Height (pan down):	13ft 9in (4.20m)	13ft 9in (4.20m)	13ft 9in (4.20m)
Length:	72ft 2in (22m)	72ft 2in (22m)	72ft 2in (22m)
Width:	9ft 9in (3.01m)	9ft 9in (3.01m)	9ft 9in (3.01m)
Wheelbase:	60ft 8in (18.51m)	60ft 8in (18.51m)	60ft 8in (18.51m)
Bogie wheelbase:	9ft 2in (2.8m)	9ft 2in (2.8m)	9ft 2in (2.8m)
Bogie pivot centres:	20ft 8in (6.33m)	20ft 8in (6.33m)	20ft 8in (6.33m)
Wheel diameter:	3ft $9^{1}/4$in (1.15m)	3ft $9^{1}/4$in (1.15m)	3ft $9^{1}/4$in (1.15m)
Power supply:	25kV ac overhead	25kV ac overhead	25kV ac overhead
Traction output (max):	7,725hp (5,760kW)	9,387hp (7,000kW)	9,387hp (7,000kW)
Tractive effort:	69,500lb (310kN)	90,000lb (400kN)	90,000lb (400kN)
Maximum speed:	87mph (140km/h)	87mph (140km/h)	87mph (140km/h)
Brake type:	Air	Air	Air
Brake force:	50 tonnes	50 tonnes	50 tonnes
Train supply:	Electric	Electric	Electric
Multiple coupling type:	Eurotunnel	Eurotunnel	Eurotunnel
Control system:	Asynchronous 3-phase	Asynchronous 3-phase	Asynchronous 3-phase
Traction motor type:	ABB 6PH	ABB 6PH	ABB 6PH
No of traction motors:	6	6	6
Operator:	Eurotunnel	Eurotunnel	Eurotunnel
Sub class variations:	9/0 - Original as built locos 9/1 - Dedicated freight locos	high-output freight locos	Refurbished 9/0 fleet fitted with higher output equipment

Fact File

Owned and operated by Eurotunnel for Channel Tunnel operations, these three classes of single-ended electric locomotives are locked within the Eurotunnel system due to their larger than UK loading gauge.

The original fleet of 38 Class 9/0 locomotives was introduced for the opening of the Channel Tunnel in 1994; the success of freight operations saw a follow-on order placed for 13 Class 9/1s, which were slightly modified from the original batch.

In 1999 a further batch of high-output freight shuttles were ordered, classified as 9/7.

All locomotives were built by Brush Traction, Loughborough with body shells produced by Qualter Hall Engineering of Barnsley. All are finished in Eurotunnel livery.

Due to the high levels of work undertaken by this captive fleet, refurbishment commenced in 2005 with all the original 9/0 locomotives being overhauled by Brush Traction and upgraded with 7,000kW traction equipment.

Left: *The Eurotunnel 'Shuttle' system is operated between Folkestone in the UK and Coquelles terminal in Calais, France. Massive 'loops' exist at each end and trains operate in one direction via a loop principle. All trains are operated with a locomotive at either end, with either a 'tourist' or 'freight' rake of stock between. Class 9/0 No 9024 is seen marshalled with a 'tourist' formation at the Coquelles terminal. Access to observe and photograph the Eurotunnel operation is very limited.*
Author

Right Top and Right Second:
Looking virtually identical to the original Class 9/0 fleet, the 13 members of Class 9/1 are dedicated to the operation of 'freight' shuttle services, transporting road trucks carried in skeleton frame wagons and one passenger coach (carrying the truck drivers). The original Class 9/0 locomotives were fitted with a cab at the inner or slab end, which was used for light locomotive or shunting operations. However, by the time the follow-on order was placed this facility was deemed as unnecessary and omitted. These two views show the cab and inner end of Class 9/1 No 9102 at the depot facility in Coquelles.
Both: **Author**

Right Third: *Stabling facilities exist at both the UK and French terminals of Eurotunnel, but the main servicing and locomotive repair facility is located at Coquelles, France, where special full train length maintenance sheds are provided for servicing complete trains without the need to remove the motive power. Specialist locomotive-repair facilities are also provided which look after all but the most major repairs to the locomotive fleet. The depot also looks after the diesel maintenance and emergency locomotives. Class 9/0 No 9025 is seen 'on shed' at Coquelles marshalled up with a full passenger rake of stock.* **Author**

Right Bottom: *The Class 9 'Shuttle' locomotives use the UK principle of cab configuration, with the driver sitting on the left side of the cab and operating the brake with his left hand and the power controller with his right. All other controls and indicators are provided on easy to see/reach screens and panels. The driver also controls the locomotive at the rear of the train via a fixed through-train link, and extra controls are provided for observation of the equipment at the rear of the train. The Train Manager on Eurotunnel services is also trained in driving, and if an emergency occurred during the cross-Channel journey, he would go to the rear of the train and operate the back locomotive separately from the front. The cab of locomotive No 9017 is shown.* **Author**

■ At the time of writing the refurbishment of the 90xx locomotives to 98xx classification was ongoing at Brush Traction. Renumbering consists of changing the second digit from a '0' to an '8'.

Class 121

Vehicle Type:	DMBS
Number range:	55020-55034
Set Numbers:	121020 & 121032 (operational sets)
TOPS Classification:	121
Introduced:	1960
Built by:	Pressed Steel
Vehicle length (over body):	64ft 6in (19.66m)
Height:	12ft 8^{1}/$_{2}$in (3.77m)
Width:	9ft 3in (2.81m)
Seating:	65S
Internal layout:	2+3
Gangway:	No
Toilets:	Not fitted
Weight:	38 tonnes
Brake type:	Vacuum
Power unit:	2 x Leyland of 150hp per vehicle
Horsepower (total):	300hp (224kW)
Transmission:	Mechanical
Max speed:	70mph (113km/h)
Coupling type:	Screw
Multiple restriction:	Blue square
Door type:	Slam
Special features:	Central Door Locking (passengers doors)
Body structure:	Steel
Owner/Operator:	Chiltern/Arriva Trains Wales
Certified for main line use:	55020 (Chiltern),
	55032 (Arriva Trains Wales)

Fact File

Built to the BR Derby high-density design for general branch-line use, these Pressed Steel railcars, which operated originally with unpowered single-ended driving trailers, were the equivalent of the original Great Western AEC single cars.

Sufficient power existed to haul one or two vehicles. A total of 15 powered, twin-ended cars were built in 1960.

Allocated to BR Western Region, the cars worked in the London, Bristol and Plymouth area.

After withdrawal the fleet became popular for departmental use, being of twin-cabbed design.

Recently two vehicles have been returned to main-line use, fitted with central door locking and upgraded to present running standards.

Left Top and Left Bottom: *Arriva Trains Wales operate 'Bubble' car No 55032 on its short-distance Cardiff Queen Street-Cardiff Bay line. The company did not want to use main resources for the route and purchased the single vehicle specially for the service. The coach was rebuilt heavily by LNWR Workshops in Crewe, with a new high-quality interior. To meet the latest rail safety standard, central door locking was required and a special system was developed that locked the doors at the base after closure. A standard 'doors released' orange light is thus provided at cant rail height towards the middle of the coach. Not all the external passenger doors of the original vehicle were required for its new role and the two middle doors on each side were sealed, providing four passenger doors on each side, plus the conductors double leaf door. The coach retains its original vacuum brakes and sports joint marker/tail lights and headlight on each end. The original route indicator has been plated over. The end exhaust stacks have been retained at the luggage van end, thus the two ends are of a slightly different style. Both ends are shown in the illustrations taken at Cardiff Queen Street. Both:* **Nathan Williamson**

Above & Below: *Chiltern Railways, based at Aylesbury, required a single vehicle to operate selected services on its Aylesbury-Princes Risborough route and obtained car No 55020. The vehicle was heavily rebuilt, with new-style seating, central door locking and repositioning of the original front mounted-exhaust stacks to clean up the cars' appearance. The car now sports combined marker/tail lights and a central headlight. The original vacuum brake has been retained. No 55020, or set No 121020, is allocated to Aylesbury and painted in Chiltern Railways mid-blue livery. The views above and below show both ends of the car at Princes Risborough. Both:* **John Wills**

Diesel Multiple-Units

Number range:	142001-142096
Introduced:	1985-1987
Built by:	Leyland bus body on BREL underframe, Assembled at BREL Derby
Formation:	DMS+DMSL
Vehicle numbers:	DMS - 55542-55591, 55701-55746
	DMSL - 55592-55641, 55747-55792
Vehicle length:	51ft 0^{1}/2in (15.55m)
Height:	12ft 8in (3.86m)
Width:	9ft 2^{1}/4in (2.80m)
Seating:	Total - 103-122S
	DMS - 53-62S (depending on layout)
	DMSL - 50-60S (depending on layout)
Internal layout:	2+3 or 2+2 (depending on operator)
Gangway:	Within set only
Toilets:	DMSL - 1
Weight:	Total - 49.5 tonnes
	DMS 24.5 tonnes
	DMSL - 25 tonnes
Brake type:	Air EP
Bogie type:	4-wheel chassis
Power unit:	1 x Cummins LTA10-R of 230hp per vehicle
Transmission:	Hydraulic
Transmission type:	Voith T211r
Horsepower (total):	460hp
Max speed:	75mph (121 km/h)
Coupling type:	Outer - BSI, Between cars - Bar
Multiple restriction:	Class 14x, 15x, 17x
Door type:	Twin leaf inward pivot
Body structure:	Aluminium alloy (bus body sections)
Owner:	Angel Trains
Operator:	Northern Railways, Arriva Trains Wales First Great Western
Notes:	Set No 142084 fitted with one Perkins 2006-TWH engine of 230hp per vehicle

Fact File

The largest fleet of 'Railbus' type vehicles, designed by the BRB as a low-cost replacement for branch line services, is the BREL/Leyland Class 142, introduced in several batches between 1985-87 for use on London Midland, Eastern and Western Regions.

The trains were not welcomed by staff or passengers, who thought their bus-style interior inappropriate for rail transport.

Today the sets owned by Angel Trains are operated by Northern, Arriva Trains Wales and FGW. Many refinements have been made to interiors, improving perception of the stock. In the medium term it is the desire of the owners to replace these units with more traditional vehicles.

Sets 142001-050 are officially 142/0 and 142051-096 are 142/1 but this is not reflected in numbering.

Below: *Painted in Regional livery, set No 142090, a unit from the second batch with small destination blind, is seen at Pontypridd working for Arriva Trains Wales.* **Author**

Right: *The Class 142 front end is very basic and an adaptation of a Leyland bus vehicle, built to strengthened principles to meet railway Group Standards. One major problem with the design has been with end-impact collisions, with the body shell parting company from the underframe. Main front end equipment items are as follows: A-route indicator; several different designs exist, with the first 50 units originally sporting a full width display, and the second batch of 46 sets having the smaller window display as shown. Some units now support dot-matrix displays. B lamp cluster (marker, head and tail lights), C-ventilation grilles (not all units have the small square grille), D-BSI coupling, incorporating electrical and air connection for multiple operation, E-warning horns. Set No 142070 is illustrated, painted in Regional Railways colours.* **Author**

Diesel Multiple-Units

Right: *The between vehicle connection of Class 142 (and 143 and 144) vehicles is by a 'bar' coupler. This has a metal face plate and a protruding pin, which interlocks into a like-facing plate on the other vehicle. These plates are then bolted together by four threaded bolts. Each vehicle has an exhaust stack on the non-driving side, which vents to atmosphere above vehicle height. The main equipment items at the inner end are: F-bar coupler, G-exhaust stack, H- between vehicle electrical jumper socket, I-air connection socket, J-battery box.* **Author**

Above: *Since their original delivery and application of British Railways Regional Railways livery and having bus seat interiors, the Class 142 fleet has come a long way, with several TOC liveries now applied showing how different colours can change the entire concept of a train. Based on a previous operator's deep blue and gold livery including a bodyside star, several of the Northern Rail '142s' can be found in this scheme, now with the Northern Rail logo applied on the bodyside. At the time of writing, Northern was in the process of a fleet shuffle, with a number of its 'Pacer' units mothballed and returned to the owning lease company. Set No 142034 is seen at Doncaster.* **Brian Morrison**

Left Middle & Left Bottom:
Operator Arriva Trains Wales, which uses members of the Class 142 fleet in the Cardiff suburban area, inherited a fleet painted in a mix of colours; several sported a 'Welsh Valleys' scheme of green, white and red which looked very smart, shown left middle on set No 142073 at Newport. The view left bottom shows the now corporate Arriva Trains Wales turquoise colour scheme now applied to all Cardiff sets. The offsetting of the main colour with an angled swirl at the cab ends and bodyside band and branding looks neat. Spring 2007 saw 15 of the fleet allocated to Cardiff Canton, all are internally refurbished with low-density 2+2 high-back seats.
John Wills/Brian Garrett

Above: *The MerseyTravel yellow, white and blue livery is applied to a number of Class 142s, mainly operating for Northern Rail and allocated to Newton Heath depot. These sets were previously used in the Liverpool funded area on suburban non-electrified services. As with other Northern Rail '142s', the fleet is scheduled for reduction and some sets will return to the lease owners. The livery is shown on set No 142020.*
John Wills

Right Middle: *Northern Rail, by far the largest operator of Class 152s, has two sets (as of Spring 2007), painted in former Northern Spirit turquoise-blue offset by a large green 'Northern' "N" on each coach; this livery is shown by No 142050 at Carlisle.*
Nathan Williamson

Right Bottom: *When originally introduced, the Class 142s had basic 2+3 bus seats in airline and longitudinal style, as one would have found in a Leyland bus of the period. Huge criticism was levelled at the rail industry at the time and slowly, following privatisation, new operators sought to replace the interiors with comfortable rail-standard seats. A number of different designs can be found in both the 3+2 and 2+2 style, supplied by different manufacturers. Here a Northern Class 142 shows the 2+2 high-back seat with hinged middle armrests and separate headrest, covered in a mid-grey moquette.*
Brian Morrison

Traction Recognition

Class 143 'Pacer'

Number range:	143601-143625
Introduced:	1985-1986
Built by:	Walter Alexander body mounted on Andrew Barclay underframe from Leeds, assembled in Kilmarnock
Formation:	DMS+DMSL
Vehicle numbers:	DMS - 55642-55666
	DMSL - 55667-55691
Vehicle length:	51ft 0^1/$_2$in (15.55m)
Height:	12ft 2^3/$_4$in (3.73m)
Width:	8ft 10^1/$_2$in (2.70m)
Seating:	Total - 104S
	DMS - 54S
	DMSL - 50S
Internal layout:	2+2
Gangway:	Within set only
Toilets:	DMSL - 1
Weight:	Total - 49.5 tonnes
	DMS - 24.5 tonnes
	DMSL - 25 tonnes
Brake type:	Air EP
Bogie type:	4-wheel chassis
Power unit:	1 x Cummins LTA10-R of 230hp per vehicle
Transmission:	Hydraulic
Transmission type:	Voith T211r
Horsepower (total):	460hp (343kW)
Max speed:	75mph (121 km/h)
Coupling type:	Outer - BSI
	Between cars - Bar
Multiple restriction:	Class 14x, 15x
Door type:	Twin leaf inward pivot
Body structure:	Aluminium alloy (bus body sections)
Owner:	Porterbrook, Rail Assets Investments, Bridgend Council, Cardiff City Council
Operator:	Arriva Trains Wales, First Great Western

Fact File

Built concurrently with the Class 142 fleet, these 'Pacer' sets were assembled at the Kilmarnock plant of Andrew Barclay, with coach bodies from Walter Alexander using frames built by Hunslet in Leeds. These sets were originally allocated to the North East, based at Heaton. However after a short period the sets were transferred south and allocated to Cardiff in South Wales.

When originally built the sets were numbered in the 1430xx series, this later changes to the 1433xx series and subsequently to the 1436xx batch.

Most sets are owned by Porterbrook Leasing, two are owned by Rail Assets Investments Ltd and three by South Wales Councils.

Today the interiors are refurbished and have 2+2 'Chapman' seats. The livery varies between FGW 'Bristol Blue' and Arriva Trains Wales 'Valley' colours. Front end equipment is the same style as the Class 142.

Few modifications exist in the class, which is allocated to Cardiff Canton and Exeter.

Below: *Displaying Arriva Trains Wales 'Valley Lines' livery, set No 143605 arrives at Pontypridd station with its DMSL coach leading. This vehicle is identifiable by the frosted glass window at the inner end. The roof-mounted square just to the rear of the driving cab is the National Radio Network pick-up aerial.* **Author**

Above: *In early 2007, First Great Western operated eight Class 143s, all painted in 'Bristol Blue' advertising livery. Officially allocated on paper to Exeter, in reality they receive maintenance at Bristol St Philips Marsh. In the near future these sets are to emerge in First Great Western Local Lines colours. Set No 143611 is seen at Newport.* **Author**

Right Middle: *The original 2+3 seating, as used in the North East and when first allocated to the Cardiff area has now all been replaced by good quality 2+2 'Chapman' seats, covered in a mix of green and maroon moquette. The mainly airline seating has fold-down tables, with luggage racks provided above the seats.* **Author**

Right Bottom: *Class 143 driving cab layout. The 'Pacer' breeds saw the introduction of a new driving-desk layout, based broadly on previous multiple-unit styles, with the power controller operated by the driver's right hand and the electronic brake controller his left hand. The later-fitted National Radio Network telephone is on the right side, with a fan above.* **Author**

Class 144 'Pacer'

Number range:	144001-144023
Introduced:	1986-1987
Built by:	Walter Alexander body on BREL underframe assembled at BREL Derby Litchurch Lane
Formation:	144001-144013 - DMS+DMSL
	144014-144023 - DMS+MS+DMSL
Vehicle numbers:	DMS - 55801-55823
	MS - 55850-55859
	DMS - 55824-55846
Vehicle length:	50ft 2in (15.25m)
Height:	12ft 2³/₄in (3.73m)
Width:	8ft 10¹/₂in (2.70m)
Seating:	144001-144013 - Total - 87S
	144014-144023 - Total - 145S
	DMS - 45S
	MS - 58S
	DMSL - 42S
Internal layout:	2+2
Gangway:	Within set only
Toilets:	DMSL - 1
Weight:	Total - 72 tonnes
	DMS - 24 tonnes
	MS - 23.5 tonnes
	DMSL - 24.5 tonnes
Brake type:	Air EP
Bogie type:	4-wheel chassis
Power unit:	1 x Cummins LTA10-R of 230hp per vehicle
Transmission:	Hydraulic
Transmission type:	Voith T211r
Horsepower (total):	144001-144013 - 460hp (343kW)
	144014-144023 - 690hp (515kW)
Max speed:	75mph (121 km/h)
Coupling type:	Outer - BSI
	Between cars - Bar
Multiple restriction:	Class 14x, 15x, 17x
Door type:	Twin leaf inward pivot
Body structure:	Aluminium alloy (bus body sections)
Owner:	Porterbrook (MSs owned by West Yorks PTE)
Operator:	Northern Railways
Note:	As built fitted with Leyland TL11 engine of 200hp (149kW) per vehicle, with mechanical transmission

Fact File

The 23 members of Class 144 form the final 'Pacer' breed, using Walter Alexander bus body sections mounted on a BREL-produced underframe. Assembly of the trains was undertaken at Derby.

The first 13 sets are two-car, with the remaining 10 having an intermediate MS, funded by West Yorkshire PTE to strengthen services.

Originally seating was in the 2+3 bus style, but refurbishment has seen a more pleasing 2+2 interior layout using Richmond seating.

All sets are painted in West Yorkshire PTE Metro red and silver grey. Units are allocated to Leeds Neville Hill and operate on West Yorkshire local services.

Below: *Painted in West Yorkshire PTE Metro colours, set No 144013 is seen from its DMS vehicle at Colton Junction, York. The semi-circle livery is opposite on each side of each vehicle. Front-end equipment and the driving cab is the same as on Class 143 units.*
Author

Diesel Multiple-Units

Above: *The final 10 units of the Class 144 build, delivered as two-car sets, were strengthened to three-car length by the addition of an MS vehicle in 1987, funded by West Yorkshire PTE to overcome overcrowding. All sets are allocated to Leeds Neville Hill depot and have the same body profile as the Class 143. Set No 144014 is viewed just north of York.* **Sam Felce**

Below: *Detail of Class 144 intermediate Motor Standard (MS) vehicle. Each vehicle has a twin-leaf inward-opening pivot door at each corner, feeding a cross-vehicle vestibule. Seating is in the 2+2 style for 58 passengers. MS No 55851 is illustrated at Doncaster.* **Richard Tuplin**

Class 150 'Sprinter'

	Sub class:	150/0	150/1 (2-car)	150/1 (3-car)	150/2
Number range:		150001-150002	150101-150150	150003-150022	150201-150285
Introduced:		1984	1985-86	Orig - 1985-86 As 3-car - 1995	1986-87
Built by:		BREL York	BREL York	BREL York	BREL York
Formation:		DMSL+MS+DMS	DMSL+DMS	DMSL+DMS(L)+DM	DMSL+DMS
Vehicle numbers:		DMSL - 55200-55201 MS - 55400-55401 DMS - 55300-55301	DMSL - 52101-52150 DMS - 57101-57150 -	DMSL - 52103-52119 DMS(L) - 522xx, 572xx DMS - 52110-57119	DMSL - 52201-52285 DMS - 57201-57285 -
Vehicle lengths:		DMSL - 65ft 9³/₄in (23.62m) DMS - 65ft 9³/₄in (23.62m) MS - 66ft 2¹/₂in (20.18m)	DMSL - 65ft 9³/₄in (23.62m) DMS - 65ft 9³/₄in (23.62m)	DMSL - 65ft 9³/₄in (23.62m) DMS - 65ft 9³/₄in (23.62m)	DMSL - 65ft 9³/₄in (23.62m) DMS - 65ft 9³/₄in (23.62m)
Height:		12ft 4¹/₂in (3.77m)	12ft 4¹/₂in (3.77m)	12ft 4¹/₂in (3.77m)	12ft 4¹/₂in (3.77m)
Width:		9ft 3¹/₈in (2.82m)	9ft 3¹/₈in (2.82m)	9ft 3¹/₈in (2.82m)	9ft 3¹/₈in (2.82m)
Seating:		Total - 240S DMSL - 72S MS - 92S DMS - 76S	Total - 124-141S DMSL - 59-71S DMS - 65-70S -	Total - 224S DMSL - 76S DMS(L) - 76S DMS - 72S	Total - 130-149S DMSL - 62-73S DMS - 68-76S -
Internal layout:		2+3	2+3	2+3	2+3 or 2+2
Gangway:		Within set	Within set	Within set	Throughout
Toilets:		DMSL - 1	DMSL - 1	DMSL - 1	DMSL - 1
Weight:		Total - 105.8 tonnes DMSL - 35.8 tonnes MS - 34.4 tonnes DMS - 35.6 tonnes	Total - 76.4 tonnes DMSL - 38.3 tonnes DMS - 38.1 tonnes -	Total - 109-110.8 tonnes DMSL - 36.5 tonnes DMS(L) - 34.9/ 35.8 tonnes DMS - 38.5 tonnes	Total - 74 tonnes DMSL - 37.5 tonnes DMS - 36.5 tonnes -
Brake type:		Air EP	Air EP	Air EP	Air EP
Bogie type:		Powered - BX8P Trailer - BX8T	Powered - BP38 Trailer - BT38	Powered - BP38 Trailer - BT38	Powered - BP38 Trailer - BT38
Power unit:		1 x NT855R4 of 285hp per vehicle	1 x NT855R5 of 285hp per vehicle	1 x NT855R5 of 285hp per vehicle	1 x NT855R5 of 285hp per vehicle
Transmission:		Hydraulic	Hydraulic	Hydraulic	Hydraulic
Transmission type:		Voith T211r	Voith T211r	Voith T211r	Voith T211r
Horsepower:		855hp (638kW)	570hp (425kW)	855hp (638kW)	570hp (425kW)
Max speed:		75mph (121km/h)	75mph (121km/h)	75mph (121km/h)	75mph (121km/h)
Coupling type:		Outer - BSI Between cars - Bar	BSI	BSI	BSI
Multiple restriction:		Class 14x, 15x, 170	Class 14x, 15x, 170	Class 14x, 15x, 170	Class 14x, 15x, 170
Door type:		Bi-parting sliding (cab door slam)	Bi-parting sliding (cab door slam)	Bi-parting sliding (cab door slam, slide on 150/2 car)	Bi-parting sliding (cab door slide)
Body structure:		Steel	Steel	Steel	Steel
Owner:		Angel Trains	Angel Trains	London Midland	Northern, London Midland
Operator:		London Midland	London Midland, TfL, FGW		FGW, ATW
Notes:		Prototype sets			

Diesel Multiple-Units

Fact File

By the early 1980s the BRB had to act to procure new-generation suburban and mid-distance DMU stock, as the 1950s-built first-generation units were quickly becoming life expired.

Prototypes from two builders, BREL and Metro-Cammell were ordered and tested on the main line. The BREL train was classified as 150 and the Met-Cam product as 151.

The BREL product was selected as the squadron replacement and two designs of 150 were ordered from BREL York. The Class 150/1s were two-car sets without end gangways, while the later 150/2s were gangway fitted throughout.

Although basic in design, these sets revolutionised rail travel and over the years much refurbishment has been carried out, resulting in a substantial number now sporting 2+2 seating. Many sets working for London Midland in the Birmingham area retain 2+3 seating to increase passenger loadings.

Some reformations have taken place; a number of 150/1 sets reformed with a 150/2 car marshalled between, providing three-car units for busy London Midland routes.

Class 150s can be found operating throughout England and Wales.

Above: *After trials throughout the UK, the two prototype three-car Class 150/0 sets settled down to work in the Midlands, firstly in the Derby area and then the Birmingham commuter region, now operating under the London Midland banner. The two sets are immediately recognisable from modified three-car sets by having a genuine motor second (without driving cab) marshalled between the two driving cars. From their original prototype status the sets have been 'standardised' with the remainder of the fleet. No 150001 is illustrated.* **John Wills**

Right Middle: *The production two-car 150/1 sets are recognisable in having no end corridor connection and a slam cab door rather than a sliding door on the later 150/2 builds. Viewed from its DMS vehicle, set No 150125 stands at Doncaster painted in Central Trains/Centro livery. All units have obstacle deflector plates on the front.* **Derek Porter**

Right Bottom: *In early 2007, 18 three-car Class 150/1 sets were in traffic, allocated to Tyseley. Each '150/1' set has been split and either a DMS or DMLS from a 150/2 inserted in the centre, thus permitting a through gangway throughout the three car set. Set No 150010, formed with the DMS of set No 150226 and the driving cars of set No 150110, shows the new Network West Midlands livery of sky blue, green and white, styled in the Central Trains theme at the cab ends.* **John Whitehouse**

 *(Diesel Multiple-Units)*

Above: *It is quite surprising what a different coat of paint does for a unit. Here we see a Silverlink (now TfL) Class 150/1, viewed from its DMS vehicle at Bletchley. These sets have been refurbished, but retain 3+2 seating as they are basically used on suburban high-usage routes. The eight TfL sets, allocated to Willesden, are all named and operate non-electrified services around London as well as the Bedford-Bletchley route. Set No 150128 is illustrated.* **Author**

Left Middle & Bottom: *The Class 150/2 is the most numerous sub-class of the '150' breed, with 85 two-car sets originally being built. In original condition the sets had 3+2 seating, one toilet in the DMSL vehicle and cramped vestibule areas. Refurbishment by most operators has seen good-quality 2+2 seating installed and a more pleasing environment offered. Some sets working in high-density areas still retain 3+2 seats. The set illustrated middle is an Arriva Trains Wales set in Cardiff Valleys red/green pictogram livery viewed from its DMS vehicle. The bottom view is a bit of a made-up livery. This set formerly operated for Anglia and was then transferred to Central Trains where white swirl ends were added to the turquoise livery; this set is viewed from the DMSL end. The main external difference between the 150/1 and 150/2 apart from the end gangway door on the 150/2 is the fitting of a sliding cab door in place of the previous slam type.* **Author/John Wills**

Above: *Love it or hate it, the Wessex Trains maroon pictogram-livery applied to the Class 150/2 fleet operating in the West Country was distinctive and quite attractive. In addition to the livery, the majority of sets were named following a major local initiative by Exeter-based management. Sets were all refurbished with 2+2 low density seating, and fold-down seats provided accommodation for bikes and prams. Set No 150243 is illustrated. Main equipment areas are: A-DMS vehicle, B-DMSL vehicle, C-fuel tank, D-battery box, E-power unit, F-silencer group.* **Author**

Below: *In early 2007 First Great Western started to roll out Class 150/2s sporting the new Local Lines livery for the Wessex, Bristol, Devon and Cornish areas. This is based on the FirstGroup blue, with the previous 'dynamic lines' replaced by dozens of route-associated names. Passenger doors are finished in bright pink. With yellow-painted obstacle deflector plate, set No 150244 is illustrated from the DMS vehicle at Exeter.* **Author**

Left: *Class 150 front end equipment. Items are the same on all sub-classes, except a gangway is fitted to Class 150/2s which incorporates a route indicator in a section above the driver's and assistant's window. A-National Radio Network aerial, B-destination indicator (above cab front windows on 150/2s, C-BSI coupling incorporating physical, air and electrical connections, D-obstacle deflector plate. E-light cluster (tail, head and marker lights). Set No 150124 illustrated in Central Trains Centro-livery.* **Author**

Below: *The Northern Rail franchise operates a fleet of 39 Class 150 units, a mix of Class 150/1s and 150/2s. Gradually, as overhauls fall due, sets are emerging in the blue and purple house colours, as shown here on set No 150277 at Doncaster. This livery variant calls for yellow light-cluster surrounds and grey passenger/staff access doors.* **Brian Morrison**

Above: *The early members of Class 150/0 and 150/1 had squared-off vestibule walls separating passenger saloons from the seating area, whereas the 150/2 sets have angled glass dividers. This view shows a 150/1 operating for Silverlink with squared dividers and orange grab poles.*
Brian Morrison

Right Middle: *The modern design of rolling stock, with seats fitted on floor tracks, makes it easy to alter the configuration of coaches from high-density (3+2) to low-density (2+2) seating. Originally the 150s were constructed with 3+2 seating, but as passenger aspirations of travel developed market research found that the 2+2 mode was preferred and indeed on some routes the centre seat of three would remain empty while passengers stood. The view above shows a London Midland-operated 150/2, with 3+2 seats and a narrow centre aisle. The seating is a mix of airline and facing groups; no tables are provided.* **Author**

Right Bottom: *The sets operated by Arriva Trains Wales and First Great Western use Chapman high-back seating finished in either pink and grey (FGW) or green and red (Arriva). In common with all Class 150s, emergency tools and equipment is housed adjacent to one door vestibule. Some of the Cardiff-allocated 150/2s operated by Arriva are now having Primarius seating installed.* **Author**

Class 153 'Super Sprinter'

Number range:	153301-153385
Introduced:	As 153 - 1991-1992
	Originally as Class 155 2-car sets - 1987-1988
Rebuilt by:	Hunslet-Barclay, Kilmarnock
Original build:	Leyland Bus, Workington
Formation:	DMSL
Vehicle numbers:	52301-52335, 57351-57385
Vehicle length:	76ft 5 in (23.29m)
Height:	12ft 3³/₈in (3.75m)
Width:	8ft 10in (2.70m)
Seating:	69 - 72S depending on operator
Internal layout:	2+2
Gangway:	Throughout
Toilets:	1
Weight:	41.2 tonnes
Brake type:	Air EP
Bogie type:	Powered - BREL P3-10
	Trailer - BREL BT38
Power unit:	1 x Cummins NT855R5
Transmission:	Hydraulic
Transmission type:	Voith T211r
Horsepower (total):	285hp (213kW)
Max speed:	75mph (121 km/h)
Coupling type:	BSI
Multiple restriction:	Class 14x, 15x, 17x series
Door type:	Single leaf sliding plug
Body structure:	Steel
Owner:	Angel Trains, Porterbrook
Operator:	Northern, FGW, ATW, 'One', EMT, LM
Notes:	Rebuilt from 35 Class 155 twin sets

Fact File

The 70 single-car Class 153s were rebuilt from 35 two-car Class 155 sets for secondary and branch line use, where on grounds of economy two-car trains could not be justified.

The rebuilding work was undertaken at Hunslet-Barclay and included the fitting of a very small cab in the original vestibule end of the '155', and building a new cab end.

The vehicles usually referred to as 'bubble' cars are operated by five TOCs on branch line work. Interiors are refurbished in the 2+2 style with a bicycle and luaggage space and a toilet at one end.

A number of different promotional liveries is applied.

Right & Below: *Class 153 equipment positions: A-No 2 end National Radio Network aerial, B-light cluster group (marker, head, tail light), C-folding front communicating door, D-BSI coupling, incorporating physical, air and electrical connections, E-emergency jumper cable socket, F-warning horn (emergency air plug to rear), G-obstacle deflector plate, H-No 1 end (original), I-No 2 end (new), J-local door controls, K-passenger door open button, L-air intake, (cooler filler port on opposite side), M-toilet water filler port, N-National Radio Network aerial, O-fuel tank, P-auxiliary heater, Q-power unit, R-silencer system and exhaust. The front end shown is the 'new' end added during the conversion from two-car units to single vehicles, equipment positions were selected to fit items in the very cramped space available. The side elevation below shows No 153368 with its original end to the left. Both:* **Author**

Right: *London Midland and East Midlands Trains each operate a fleet of 10 Class 153s. Set No 153384 arrives at Peterborough on a Lincoln service and sports a recent modification, the fitting of revised light clusters incorporating a joint marker/tail light using LED technology. The former position of the squared off marker light is now blanked off. To conform with stock requirements the gauge envelope has to be displayed on the vehicle end 'C3'; this is usually applied on the end between vehicles.* **Author**

Left: *The ex Wessex and Arriva Trains Wales '153s' were painted in promotional liveries in recent years. Several were given this black and gold scheme 'Scenic Lines Devon and Cornwall' livery, sponsored by the Devon and Cornwall Rail Partnership. Viewed from its No 1 end, set No 153377 is seen at Bristol. All the now FGW-operated sets have Chapman seats, but many are due for internal refurbishment.* **Author**

Right: *Under the Wessex banner, now Arriva Trains Wales, Class 153s were painted in an orange promotional livery for the Heart of Wales line, offset by yellow passenger doors. The livery, applied at Cardiff Canton, incorporated a pictogram and branding. Set No 153353 is seen from its No 2 (small) end at Exeter.* **Author**

Left: *When converted to single cars one of the biggest problems was to incorporate a new driving cab in the original vestibule end. The available space only allowed a very small cab to be assembled and its design reflects the lack of space. Before introduction the train drivers' union expressed some concerns about how their more portly members would be able to access the cab and operate the controls. With power controller on the right, brake controller on the left and all other equipment squeezed on the fascia panel, the small cab of 153301 is shown.* **Author**

Class 155 'Super Sprinter'

Number range:	155341-155347
Introduced:	1988
Built by:	Leyland Bus, Workington
Formation:	DMSL+DMS
Vehicle numbers:	DMSL - 52341-52347
	DMS - 57341-57347
Vehicle length:	76ft 5 in (23.29m)
Height:	12ft 3³/₈in (3.75m)
Width:	8ft 10in (2.70m)
Seating:	Total - 156S
	DMSL - 76S
	DMS - 80S
Internal layout:	2+2
Gangway:	Throughout
Toilets:	DMSL - 1
Weight::	Total - 77.7 tonnes
	DMSL - 39.4 tonnes
	DMS - 38.6 tonnes
Brake type:	Air EP
Bogie type:	Powered - BREL P3-10
	Trailer - BREL BT38
Power unit:	1 x Cummins NT855R5 per vehicle
Transmission:	Hydraulic
Transmission type:	Voith T211r
Horsepower (total):	570hp (425kW)
Max speed:	75mph (121 km/h)
Coupling type:	BSI
Multiple restriction:	Class 14x, 15x, 17x series
Door type:	Single leaf sliding plug
Body structure:	Aluminium alloy
Owner:	West Yorkshire PTE, managed by Porterbrook
Operator:	Northern

Fact File

These seven Class 155s are all that is left of the original order for 42 Class 155s, the other 35 sets having been rebuilt into single-car Class 153s.

Built by Leyland Bus and using bus technology and original fittings, these sets are owned by West Yorkshire PTE and are now refurbished with 2+2 facing and uni-directional seats; one toilet is provided per set. The fleet is maintained at Leeds Neville Hill depot and can usually be found operating in and around the Leeds area.

Main equipment positions are the same as the Class 153s detailed in the previous section.

Below: *The seven West Yorkshire PTE Class 155 sets are operated by Northern and have recently undergone refurbishment, being adorned in a new pictogram livery based on the Northern blue and mauve colours and advertising places of interest in the operating area. Set No 155345 is illustrated.* **Richard Tuplin**

Above: *Class 155/3 was built in 1988 following the main Regional Railways (Provincial) order, specifically for West Yorkshire area use. Allocated to Leeds Neville Hill, the sets now operated by Northern are principally used on the Leeds - Manchester route. Front end equipment is the same as on Class 153 (which were rebuilds from Class 155s). Set No 155345 is illustrated. Note the yellow snowplough/obstacle deflector plate, a common feature to this class.* **Richard Tuplin**

Right Middle: *The refurbishment of the Class 155 fleet in 2006 has seen a joint Northern and West Yorkshire Metro livery applied using high-quality graphics of features of the Leeds - Manchester route. As these are applied in vinyl, any damage can be quickly repaired.* **Richard Tuplin**

Right Bottom: *The interior of the Class 155/3 is set out in low-density 2+2, with a predominance of airline seats with fold-down tables. A small number of group seats around tables is provided. Each coach seats 76. Since their introduction, more comfortable high-back seats with hinged armrests have been installed. One toilet per train is provided and luggage racks are located above seats. As no air conditioning is installed, opening hopper windows are fitted throughout.* **Richard Tuplin**

Class 156 'Super Sprinter'

Number range:	156401-156514
Introduced:	1987-1989
Built by:	Metro-Cammell, Birmingham
Formation:	DMSL+DMS
Vehicle numbers:	DMSL - 52401-52514
	DMS - 57401-57514
Vehicle length:	7ft 6in (23.03m)
Height:	12ft 6in (3.81m)
Width:	8ft 11in (2.73m)
Seating:	Total - 140-152S
	DMSL - 68-74S
	DMS - 72-78S
Internal layout:	2+2
Gangway:	Throughout
Toilets:	DMSL - 1
Weight:	Total - 76.5 tonnes
	DMSL - 38.6 tonnes
	DMS - 37.9 tonnes
Brake type:	Air EP
Bogie type:	Powered - BREL P3-10
	Trailer - BREL BT38
Power unit:	1 x Cummins NT855R5 of 285hp per vehicle
Transmission:	Hydraulic
Transmission type:	Voith T211r
Horsepower (total):	570hp (425kW)
Max speed:	75mph (121 km/h)
Coupling type:	BSI
Multiple restriction:	Class 14x, 15x, 17x series
Door type:	Single leaf sliding
Body structure:	Steel
Owner:	Porterbrook, Angel Trains
Operator:	East Midlands Trains, 'one' Railway, Northern, ScotRail

Fact File

The largest batch of 'Super Sprinter' units was ordered by the BRB Provincial Sector from Metro-Cammell and delivered between 1987-89.

Although destined for outer suburban use, the sets have a top speed of 75mph. Seating is in the 2+2 style with a mix of airline and group seats; today, configurations depend on the operator. External equipment follows the design of the Class 153 and 155.

In 2007, four national operators use the fleet with the majority operating in northern areas.

Few major modifications have been made since this fleet, which is one of the most reliable in the UK, was delivered.

Below: Nine Class 156s are allocated to Norwich Crown Point and operated by 'one' Railway on Norwich/Ipswich area local services. The fleet is in 'one' turquoise and grey livery with strip cab sides and yellow ends. 'one' set, No 156416, is named Saint Edmund, *illustrated at Ipswich.* **Author**

Right: *Derby-based East Midlands Trains operates a fleet of 11 Class 156s for longer-distance regional services. All are painted in two-tone green livery with blue and red angled cab sides. This batch has Chapman-style seats set out in airline and group configuration. Set No 156406 is illustrated from the DMSL vehicle.* **John Wills**

Right Second: *A sizeable fleet of Class 156s works in Scotland, where batches operate for Strathclyde Passenger Transport and FirstGroup. All sets sport the same passenger configuration and are allocated to Corkerhill Depot. Set No 156500, painted in Strathclyde carmine and cream livery, is approaching Ayr.* **Author**

Right Third: *With Scottish rail services now operated by FirstGroup, the company's corporate livery style has been applied as vehicles pass through depot for classified overhaul. The 'swirl' or 'Barbie' livery is seen on set No 156446 at Glasgow Central. The swirl of the livery cuts through the single windows directly behind the cab end vestibules which are not adjacent to seating positions.* **John Wills**

Right Bottom: *The Northern franchise operates a sizeable fleet of Class 156s; these are painted in either the Northern turquoise, white and mauve or pictogram liveries. Set No 156484, illustrated at Leeds, was unveiled in May 2007 sporting a Settle & Carlisle promotion livery, with a colour scheme based on the Northern mauve and white but incorporating some high-quality graphics of the picturesque route. This set is one of a small number dedicated to S&C line duties (but does operate on other duties) and has S&C route maps laminated into the tables.* **Brian Morrison**

Sub class:	158/0	158/9
Number range:	158701-158890	158901-158910
Introduced:	1989-1992	1991
Built by:	BREL Derby	BREL Derby
Formation:	158701-158890-	DMSL(A)+DMSL(B)
	DMSL(A) + DMCL or DMSL + MS + DMCL	
Vehicle numbers:	DMSL(A) 57701 - 57890	DMSL(A) - 52901-52910
	DMSL(B) or DMCL -52701 - 52890	DMSL(B) - 57901-57910
	* MSL 58701-58717	
Vehicle length:	76ft 1³/₄in (23.21m)	76ft 1³/₄in (23.21m)
Height:	12ft 6in (3.81m)	12ft 6in (3.81m)
Width:	9ft 3¹/₄in (2.82m)	9ft 3¹/₄in (2.82m)
Seating:	158701-158890 - Total - 9-32F / 96-121S	Total - 142S
	DMSL - 64-68S	DMSL(A) - 70S
	DMCL - 9-32F / 32-53S	DMSL(B) - 72S
	Three-car sets - Total - 32F/170S	
	DMSL - 68S	
	MSL - 70S	
	DMCL - 32F/32S	
Internal layout:	2+2S 2+1F	2+2
Gangway:	Throughout	Throughout
Toilets:	DMSL, DMCL, MSL - 1	DMSL - 1
Weight:	Total - 77 tonnes or 115.5 tonnes	Total - 77 tonnes
	DMSL - 38.5 tonnes	DMSL(A) - 38.5 tonnes
	DMCL - 38.5 tonnes	DMSL(B) - 38.5 tonnes
	MSL - 38.5 tonnes	
Brake type:	Air EP	Air EP
Bogie type:	Powered - BREL P4	Powered - BREL P4
	Trailer - BREL T4	Trailer - BREL T4
Power unit:	158701-158814 1 x NT855R of 350hp per vehicle	1 x NT855R of 350hp per vehicle
	158815-158862 1 x Perkins 2006-TWH	
	of 350hp per vehicle	
	158863-158872 1 x NT855R of 400hp per vehicle	
	158880-158890 1 x NT855R of 350hp per vehicle	
Transmission:	Hydraulic	Hydraulic
Transmission type:	Voith T211r	Voith T211r
Horsepower (total):	158701-158862/158880-158890 - 700hp (522kW)	700hp (522kW)
	158863-158872 2-car sets 800hp (597kW)	
	3-car sets 1,200hp (895kW)	
Max speed:	90mph	90mph
Coupling type:	BSI	BSI
Multiple restriction:	Class 14x, 15x, 170	Class 14x, 15x, 170
Door type:	Bi-parting sliding plug	Bi-parting sliding plug
Special features:	RETB ready	
Body structure:	Aluminium	Aluminium
Owner:	Porterbrook, Angel Trains	Midland Montague
Operator:	FSR, FGW, Northern, EMT, SWT, ATW	West Yorkshire PTE
Notes:	* Originally sets 158798-158814 formed	
	DMSL(A)+DMCL or DMSL(B)	

Fact File

In the late 1980s the BRB's Provincial Sector was in need of main line-capable stock to operate long-distance 'local' services. A new design of multiple unit was put forward and a sizeable fleet ordered from the then BREL Works at Derby, using aluminium body technology and including a quality passenger interior, carpets throughout and air conditioning. Classified as '158', the first 'Express' vehicles emerged in 1989.

With various follow-on orders and derivatives, a fleet of over 200 two- and three-car sets was built.

The Class 158s soon became commonplace in all areas of the UK, operating short-distance domestic services as well as long-distance cross-country trains.

Today a large number of different interiors can be found, as operators tailor trains to their local needs. Some sets sport first class in differing qualities.

All seating in standard class is 2+2 and in first there is a mix of 2+2 and 2+1. A diverse variety of external liveries is carried with several 'one-off' colour schemes.

Few modifications have been carried out externally since construction.

The Class 159s were originally built as '158s' and then upgraded before entry into service.

A number of Class 158s are now refurbished.

Above: *The entire fleet of Class 158 vehicles was fabricated and fitted out at BREL Derby Litchurch Lane, providing a constant throughput of work at the site for around three years. All 158s for the Provincial Sector order were finished in a new 'Express' livery of grey offset by mid- and light-blue body stripes. Sets ordered for West Yorkshire PTE were finished in their maroon livery and the vehicles allocated for Class 159 modification were finished in NSE colours. Three brand new Class 158s for use in Scotland carrying the 'Express' branding stand side by side at Derby Litchurch Lane.* **Author**

Right: *Class 158 (and 159) front end equipment layout. A-air conditioning intake, B-destination and route indicator, C-Group Standard light cluster, marker, tail and headlight, D-front communicating door (different designs are to be found), E-BSI coupling incorporating physical, electrical and pneumatic connections, F-radio aerial, G-emergency air connection (behind flap), H-warning horns adjacent and set back from coupling.* **Author**

Above: *Class 158 equipment positions. A-obstacle deflector or snowplough, B-BSI coupling (incorporating physical, air and electrical connections), C-light cluster group, behind plastic screen, consisting of head, marker and tail lights, D-destination and route indicators, E-National Radio Network aerial pick-up, F-air conditioning modules (revised style fitted to only a handful of Class 158s and all 159s), G-fuel tank, H-battery box, I-auxiliary heater, J-power unit (mounted centrally under train), K silencer and exhaust system, L-door release valve, M-coolant indicator, N-door release light. The set illustrated is branded in an advertising livery applied by Wessex. Equipment positions are the same for all members of Class 158 and 159, although some small local variants might be found, especially in air conditioning equipment. This unit is ex-Scottish Region and has a snowplough rather than an obstacle deflector plate. Two staff-operated hopper windows are provided on each side of each coach, these are officially for emergency use if the air conditioning has failed.* **Author**

Below: *A huge number of different liveries can be found within the Class 158 fleet; in recent times a number of sets have been transferred around the network following delivery of new stock to some localities, giving a general improvement to passenger stock in most areas; for example a number of ex-First Trans Pennine Express Class 158s have moved south to First Great Western and South West Trains taking these distinctive maroon and blue sets which used to operate the Manchester-Newcastle route to the south and west of the UK. In most cases re-branding will be carried out quickly. With these sets working for FGW, first-class seating has been made available on local services for the first time in many years. Set No 158769 is illustrated.* **Author**

Left: *The Alphaline trading title was used by both Wessex and Wales & West franchises for its longer distance services and a number of units sport the stylised 'A' symbol on their bodyside. This is shown on Wessex (now FGW) set No 158870. This set sports standard obstacle deflector plates. Interiors on these sets were upgraded using Chapman seating.* **Author**

Right: *With Arriva Trains now operating the all-Wales franchise, the company's house colour of bright turquoise is being applied to sets during overhaul. To meet with the Disability Discrimination Act, contrasting colour doors have to be fitted. These sets incorporate Chapman seats and, since the closure of Cardiff Canton depot are now maintained at Machynlleth. Set No 158837 is illustrated.* **Author**

Left: *The Northern franchise operates a sizeable number of Class 158 two-car sets. A diverse selection of liveries can be found, including this former mid-blue North West Trains livery carried by set No 158752, seen at Doncaster. This unit has an inspection cover missing from the obstacle deflector plate below the driver's front window. It is quite amazing how a different livery can change the entire appearance of identical units.* **John Wills**

Right: *East Midlands Trains operates Class 158s on a number of longer-distance routes; they still sport Central Trains house colours of two-tone green, offset by green passenger doors. In 2005-07 several of the then Central Trains sets became surplus to requirements in the Midlands and were hired to other operators to assist with unit shortages. Here East Midlands Trains set No 158796 stands at Exeter on hire to First Great Western.* **Author**

Above: *A sizeable batch of two-car Class 158s is operated by First ScotRail on outer suburban and main line services. These are predominantly the early numeric sets and incorporate first and standard class seating, with a push-through door between the classes. Originally painted in 'Express' colours, then original ScotRail, the sets are now being rebranded in the First house colours as shown on set No 158741, which sports a snowplough rather than a standard deflector plate.* **Author**

Left Middle: *South West Trains currently operates a fleet of 11 Class 158s (158880-890); these are fully refurbished as per the operator's Class 159s and are used on 'short haul' services as well as to strengthen the Waterloo-Exeter-Paignton/Plymouth services. Set No 158886 is seen at Cockwood Harbour, forming a Penzance-London service.* **Author**

Left Bottom: *First Great Western commenced the major refurbishment of its Class 158 fleet in autumn 2007, with the upgrade contract awarded to Wabtec Doncaster. The work has seen a slightly revised passenger seating area, improved lighting and upholstery, better cycle stowage, and a technical upgrade. Externally the sets are finished in a version of FGW 'dynamic lines' blue using names of beauty spots, pubs, clubs and schools in place of lines. Set No 158761 is illustrated.* **Brian Morrison**

Above: *At the end of the general Class 158 built, a follow-on order for 10 Class 158/9 sets was placed, funded by West Yorkshire PTE. These sets are of the standard design, but with seating for 142 standard-class passengers in the 2+2 style. Only one toilet is provided per set. The units, now all painted in Northern livery, are allocated to Leeds Neville Hill and usually operate services within the PTE boundary.* **John Wills**

Right Middle: *A considerable number of different seating styles and moquettes have been seen within the Class 158 formations. All the original seats have now been replaced with improved-quality chairs, many with hinged armrests to improve access. Better tables are now fitted, and decorated dado and end panels are common. This group seating around a table shows Chapman seating as fitted to most FGW sets, sporting a maroon and grey moquette.* **Author**

Right Bottom: *One of the most significant Class 158 refurbishments in terms of customer perception was to the two sets taken over by South West Trains in 2005 for Bristol-London services. These sets were gutted and re-fitted at Fratton depot with Class 159 style interiors. This included a first-class section behind the driving cab in one vehicle. Upgrading was also carried out to the vestibule areas, toilets and ceilings. The first-class area is shown; note the luggage stack at the far end and the PIS display above the end door.* **Author**

	159/0	159/1
Sub Class:	159/0	159/1
Number range:	159001-159022	159101-159109
Former number range:	-	158800-158814 range
Introduced:	1992-1993	As 158 - Originally 1991.
		As 159 - 2006 (Rebuilt from Class 158)
Built by:	BREL Derby,	Rebuilt: Wabtec Doncaster
	fitted out by Rosyth Dockyard	
Formation:	DMCL+MSL+DMSL	DMCL+MSL+DMSL
Vehicle numbers:	DMCL - 52873-52894	DMCL - 52800-52814 range
	MSL - 58718-58739	MSL - 58701-58717 range
	DMSL - 57873-57894	DMSL - 57800-57814 range
Vehicle length:	76ft 1³/₄in (23.21m)	76ft 1³/₄in (23.21m)
Height:	12ft 6in (3.81m)	12ft 6in (3.81m)
Width:	9ft 3¹/₄in (2.82m)	9ft 3¹/₄in (2.82m)
Seating:	Total - 24F/172S	Total - 24F/170S
	DMCL - 24F/28S	DMCL - 24F/28S
	MSL - 72S	MSL - 70S
	DMSL - 72S	DMSL - 72S
Internal layout:	2+1F/2+2S	2+1F/2+2S
Gangway:	Throughout	Throughout
Toilets:	DMCL, DMSL, MSL - 1	DMCL, DMSL, MSL - 1
Weight:	Total - 114.3 tonnes	Total - 114.3 tonnes
	DMCL - 38.5 tonnes	DMCL - 38.5 tonnes
	MSL - 38 tonnes	MSL - 38 tonnes
	DMSL - 37.8 tonnes	DMSL - 37.8 tonnes
Brake type:	Air EP	Air EP
Bogie type:	Powered - BREL P4-4	Powered - BREL P4-4
	Trailer - BREL T4-4	Trailer - BREL T4-4
Power unit:	1 x Cummins NTA855R per vehicle	1 x Cummins NTA855R per vehicle
Transmission:	Hydraulic	Hydraulic
Transmission type:	Voith T211r	Voith T211r
Horsepower (total):	1,200hp (895kW)	1,200hp (895kW)
Max speed:	90mph (121km/h)	90mph (121km/h)
Coupling type:	BSI	BSI
Multiple restriction:	14x, 15x, 170 series	14x, 15x, 170 series
Door type:	Bi-parting swing plug	Bi-parting swing plug
Body structure:	Aluminium	Aluminium
Owner:	Porterbrook	Porterbrook
Operator:	South West Trains	South West Trains

Below: *Viewed from its DMS end (always at the country end of formations), set No 159018 passes Surbiton, bound for Exeter St Davids via Yeovil. Exterior detail follows the Class 158 style, no major structural changes having been made by South West Trains. All 159/0s and 159/1s are to be fitted with CCTV and passenger information displays in 2007-2008.* **Author**

Fact File

Built as Class 158s and upgraded before entry into service, the original 22 Class 159s were the Rolls-Royce of the 'Express' build.

Replacing loco-hauled services on the Waterloo-West of England route, these sets have proved to be most popular. Seating is in 2+2 for standard and 2+1 for first.

The sets are allocated to Salisbury and are always maintained to a high standard.

In 2006-07 an additional nine 3-car Class 158s were converted to '159' standards by Wabtec to supplement SWT services and replace Class 170s on local services.

All units are painted in SWT 'white' express livery and operate as far west as Penzance, Plymouth and Paignton.

Above: *Viewed from its DMCL or first class vehicle, identified by a '1' to the rear of the cab door but no yellow 'first' strip, No 159021 is seen at Exeter. All the 159/0 sets now have revised air conditioning, identifiable by the larger air louvre above the passenger doors.* **Author**

Right: *The intermediate MS vehicles seat 72 standard passengers in the 2+2 mode; 1 toilet is provided. Unlike Class 158s, each 159/0 vehicle has four crew-operated opening hopper windows on each side of each vehicle. With the air conditioning usually working well on this fleet the windows are kept closed.* **Author**

Above: *The first of the 'new' Class 159/1 fleet started to enter service from the end of 2006. A number of detail changes exist on this sub-class, in terms of livery, branding and internal decor. Here a Class 159/0 is seen on the left and a Class 159/1 on the right. Branding, paint style and door colours are all different, thus providing an immediate recognition factor for this group of units.* **Author**

Above: *The 'new' breed of Class 159/1s were upgraded to '159' status by Wabtec Doncaster. The vehicles were completely gutted and new interiors fitted, including toilets, luggage stacks and a new design of seating in both standard and first class. Some of the vehicles sport slightly different bodywork detail, as shown here on set No 159102 with a window in the centre front door and a snowplough in place of an obstacle deflector. Modern high-intensity headlights have also been fitted. No 159102 is seen at Doncaster.*
Derek Porter

Left Middle: *Standard-class interior of 159/1, showing the quality 2+2 seats covered in SWT red moquette, a good number of group seats around tables are provided for family travel and good luggage space is given. Upgraded ceiling lighting is installed and a push-through door installed between the standard and first class seating areas. Anti-slide dividers have also been fitted along the above seat luggage racks.* **Author**

Left Bottom: *First Class seating on Class 159/1. This can only be described as some of the most comfortable ever fitted to a DMU. The seats installed are former Class 170 modules made redundant from Anglia sets. First seating is provided in the 2+1 style, with each seat having a good-size table. The first-class section has curtains and down lights fitted to the underside of the luggage rack. It is a shame that such a quality rebuild did not include power supply sockets for laptop computers, a feature becoming standard with most operators.* **Author**

Right: *Detail of middle MSL vehicle from Class 159/1. These have been upgraded from Class 158 First TransPennine Express status to SWT and now reflect the interior of the Class 159/0 vehicles.* **Author**

Right: *Class 159 cab layout. Equipment positions also apply to Class 158 stock. A-door release light, B-Automatic warning system sunflower indicator and buzzer, C-driver's reminder appliance (DRA), D-cab ventilator, E-one shot sander button, F-cab fan, G-headlight, marker light and tail light switch with display below, H-main reservoir and brake cylinder pressure gauge, I-speedometer, J-couple button, K-uncouple button (below cover), L-signal button, M-transmission fault unit, N-transmission fault train, P-wheel slip protection (WSP) fault, Q-engine stop button, R-engine start button, S-fault lamp test button, T-safety systems isolated indicator, U-brake controller, V-windscreen wiper control, W-warning horn valve, X-automatic warning system (AWS) reset button, Y-power controller, Z-master key switch. The cab illustrated is from Class 159/1 No 159102.* **Author**

Sub class:	165/0	165/1
Number range:	165001-165039	165101-165137
Introduced:	1990-1992	1992-1993
Built by:	BREL/ABB York	BREL/ABB York
Formation:	165001-165028 -DMSL+DMS	165101-165117 - DMCL+MS+DMS
	165029-165039 -DMSL+MS+DMS	165118-165137 - DMCL+DMS
Vehicle numbers:	165001-165028	165101-165117
	DMSL - 58801-58822, 58873-58878	DMCL - 58953-58969
	DMS - 58834-58855, 58867-58872	MS - 55415-55431
	165029-165039	DMS - 58916-58932
	DMSL - 58823-58833	165118-165137
	MS - 55404-55414	DMCL - 58879-58898
	DMS - 58856-58866	DMS - 58933-58952
Vehicle length:	DMSL - 75ft 2^1/$_2$in (22.91m)	DMCL - 75ft 2^1/$_2$in (22.91m)
	MS - 74ft 6^1/$_2$in (22.72m)	MS - 74ft 6^1/$_2$in (22.72m)
	DMS - 75ft 2^1/$_2$in (22.91m)	DMS - 75ft 2^1/$_2$in (22.91m)
Height:	12ft 5^1/$_4$in (3.79m)	12ft 5^1/$_4$in (3.79m)
Width:	9ft 2^1/$_2$in (2.81m)	9ft 2^1/$_2$in (2.81m)
Seating:	165001-165028 - Total - 183S	165101-165117 - Total - 16F/270S
	DMSL - 89S	DMCL - 16F/66S
	DMS - 94S	MS - 106S
	165029-165039 - Total - 289S	DMS - 98S
	DMSL - 89S	165118-165137 - Total - 16F/170S
	MS - 106S	DMCL - 16F/72S
	DMS - 94S	DMS - 98S
Internal layout:	2+2/2+3S	2+2F/2+3S
Gangway:	Within set	Within set
Toilets:	DMSL - 1	DMCL - 1
Weight:	165001-165028 - Total - 79.5 tonnes	165101-165117 - Total - 112 tonnes
	DMSL - 40.1 tonnes	DMCL - 38 tonnes
	DMS - 39.4 tonnes	MS - 37 tonnes
	165029-165039 - Total - 116.5 tonnes	DMS - 37 tonnes
	DMSL - 40.1 tonnes	165118-165137 - Total - 75 tonnes
	MS - 37 tonnes	DMCL - 38 tonnes
	DMS - 39.4 tonnes	DMS - 37 tonnes
Brake type:	Air EP	Air EP
Bogie type:	Powered - BREL P3-17	Powered - BREL P3-17
	Trailer - BREL T3-17	Trailer - BREL T3-17
Power unit:	1 x Perkins 2006TWH per vehicle	1 x Perkins 2006TWH per vehicle
Transmission:	Hydraulic	Hydraulic
Transmission type:	Voith T211r	Voith T211r
Horsepower (total):	165001-165028 - 700hp (522kW)	165101-165117 - 1,050hp (783kW)
	165029-165039 - 1,050hp (783kW)	165118-165137 - 700hp (522kW)
Max speed:	75mph (121 km/h)	75mph (121 km/h)
Coupling type:	BSI	BSI
Multiple restriction:	Class 165, 166 and 168 only	Class 165, 166 and 168 only
Door type:	Bi-parting swing plug	Bi-parting swing plug
Special features:	Chiltern ATP/trip-cocks , air conditioning	
Body structure:	Welded aluminium	Welded aluminium
Owner:	Angel Trains	Angel Trains
Operator:	Chiltern	First Great Western

Fact File

Designed and introduced in the period of Network SouthEast operation to modernise the Chiltern Lines from Marylebone and the Paddington suburban network, these two- and three-car trains brought new levels of comfort to these lines.

Upon privatisation Chiltern Railways acquired all the Class 165/0 sets in both two- and three-car form, while Thames, the operator of the Paddington routes took all the 165/1s.

Chiltern later embarked on a major refurbishment exercise in which new interiors were provided, which eliminated first-class travel and increased the number of passengers per vehicle. To permit operation over the London Underground-equipped line between Harrow-on-the-Hill and Amersham, 'trip-cock' apparatus is fitted. The livery of the 165/0 sets is Chiltern white and blue.

The Thames sets have been facelifted and are now operated as part of the First Great Western franchise. These units still retain first and standard class accommodation and in 2007 were being re-branded in First 'dynamic lines' livery.

Above: *Refurbishment of the Chiltern Railways-operated Class 165/0 fleet saw a major revision to the original build. On the front, the most noticeable change was the fitting of new flush-mounted light clusters, incorporating a headlight and joint marker/tail light on each side; windows were changed to solid glass with no opening hoppers as air conditioning was installed and new roof-mounted air conditioning vents were fitted. Internally the sets were reconfigured for standard class only. Set No 165033 is seen at Marylebone.* **Author**

Right Middle: *Trial refurbishment was carried out before the squadron contract was placed and this saw set No 165013 partially upgraded; it is seen showing off the new front end and livery. Note the 'trip-cock' on the leading bogie. On these sets the different door colour required by the Disability Discrimination Act has been carefully worked to blend in with the train.* **Author**

Right Bottom: *Three-car Class 165/0 No 165031 is seen from a slightly elevated position at Quainton, showing the different roof detail following the provision of air conditioning. Today the Chiltern and FGW sets are quite different from exterior appearance.* **Author**

Above: *Class 165 (Chiltern) intermediate vehicle, showing the revised roof layout installed during refurbishment and the fitting of air conditioning equipment. To meet the Disability Discrimination Act the passenger doors have been carefully colour blended, with the inner end door of the DMS having a yellow cant rail band to indicate disabled accommodation. The rubber-covered button on the near corner post of the vehicle is a local door close/lock switch.* **Author**

Below: *Refurbished interior of Chiltern Railways Class 165/0, showing the high-back seats now installed, complete with hinged armrests. Seats are set out in airline and group styles and a small table is fitted above the dado panel by group seats. Orange hand grips are provided. This view shows a DMSL, with the small toilet compartment on the left side by the passenger operated bi-parting vestibule doors. Above-seat luggage racks are provided. As these sets are predominantly used on short-haul services, floors are covered in lino rather than carpets.* **Author**

Right Top and Second: *The Class 165/1 sets are operated by First Great Western on the Thames Valley services. Two- and three-car formations exist and these have yet to be fully refurbished, although sets were 'facelifted' in recent years. One driving car of each train has first class accommodation for 16 in the 2+2 style. All sets are now repainted in First Group 'dynamic lines' livery with pink passenger doors. The upper two illustrations show the two- and three-car versions; as these sets do not have air conditioning, opening hopper windows are provided and the roof lines are plain. The upper view shows the interim FGW white, blue and green livery while the second view shows the 'dynamic lines' colours on set No 165101.* **Author / John Wills**

Right Third: *Class 165/1 intermediate MS coach. These vehicles have accommodation for 106 in the 2+2 style. Passenger access is by two pairs of bi-parting swing plug doors, operated locally by passengers as required. An orange 'door unlock' light is provided at cant rail height on all vehicles.* **Author**

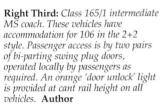

Right Bottom: *In 2005, when London was seeking the 2012 Olympic Games, a number of trains used by various London operators were branded in a Transport for London joint advertising livery. Great Western Link applied the colours in vinyl form to two-car Class 165/1 No 165136, seen here at Reading forming a local service to Basingstoke. This unit has a camera mounted in the non-driving side front window. A number of TOCs are now fitting this equipment to record lineside incidents which can be used in any subsequent court or legal action.* **Author**

Number range:	166201-166221
Introduced:	1992-1993
Built by:	BREL/ABB York
Formation:	DMCL(A)+MS+DMCL(B)
Vehicle numbers:	DMCL(A) - 58101-58121
	MS - 58601-58621
	DMCL(B) - 58122-58142
Vehicle length:	DMCL - 75ft 2^1/$_2$in (22.91m)
	MS - 74ft 6^1/$_2$in (22.72m)
Height:	12ft 5^1/$_4$in (3.79m)
Width:	9ft 2^1/$_2$in (2.81m)
Seating:	Total - 32F/243S
	DMCL(A) - 16F/75S
	MS - 96S
	DMCL(B) - 16F/72S
Internal layout:	2+2/2+3S, 2+1F
Gangway:	Within set
Toilets:	DMCL - 1
Weight:	Total - 117.2 tonnes
	DMCL(A) - 39.6 tonnes
	MS - 38 tonnes
	DMCL(B) - 39.6 tonnes
Brake type:	Air EP
Bogie type:	Powered - BREL P3-17
	Trailer - BREL T3-17
Power unit:	1 x Perkins 2006TWH of 350hp per vehicle
Transmission:	Hydraulic
Transmission type:	Voith T211r
Horsepower (total):	1,050hp (783kW)
Max speed:	90mph (145km/h)
Coupling type:	BSI
Multiple restriction:	Class 165, 166 and 168 only
Door type:	Bi-parting swing plug
Special features:	Air conditioning
Body structure:	Welded aluminium
Owner:	Angel Trains
Operator:	First Great Western

Fact File

Introduced as the long-distance or main-line version of the Class 165, the 'Network Express Turbo' sets were designed for use on the 'Express' network between Paddington-Oxford and Newbury, taking over from locomotive-hauled services.

These sets were air-conditioned from new and therefore have only emergency hopper windows. First class seating is provided in each driving car behind the cab position. Seating is a mix of 2+2 and 2+3. Luggage stacks are provided.

All Class 166s by early 2007 were branded in the First Great Western 'dynamic lines' livery, replacing the grey and blue 'Thames' colours, offset by a green 'S' logo over the door positions.

Below: *Displaying the latest First Great Western 'Dynamic Lines' livery with bright pink passenger doors, Class 166 No 166215 stops at Reading while forming an Oxford-Paddington service. The first class area is identified by a yellow cant rail strip and a silver '1' on the bodyside.* **Author**

Right: *Class 166 intermediate MS vehicle, providing seating for 96 mainly in the 3+2 style. This view shows the exhaust stack from the underfloor engine going up the end of the carbody and venting at roof height. In the vehicle roof are ventilation grilles for the air conditioning. On the end of the vehicle, about halfway up, is a key-operated switch, which when activated closes the passenger doors on that vehicle.* **Author**

Left: *If this and the view above are compared it will be seen that the same basic body structure was used for all Class 166 vehicles, but with the cab end replacing one coach end section on DMCL vehicles. Underframe equipment from the far end consists of a fuel tank, battery box, electrical equipment, power unit and exhaust/silencer system.* **Author**

Right: *Class 166 cab end equipment, also applicable to Class 165 stock. A-route indicator display, dot matrix type controlled by driver, B-Group Standard light cluster (marker, head and tail light), C-BSI coupling, incorporating physical, air and electrical connections, D-emergency air connection. On this unit, No 166206 at Reading, part of the underside front valance had been broken off by an impact collision. These sets with a glass-fibre front panel are very prone to this type of damage.* **Author**

Class 168 'Clubman'

Sub class:	168/0	168/1	168/2
Design:	Networker outline	Turbostar outline	Turbostar outline
Number range:	168001-168005	168106-168113	168214 - 168219
Introduced:	1997-1998	2000-2002	2003-2006
Built by:	Adtranz Derby	Adtranz/Bombardier Derby	Bombardier Derby
Formation:	DMSL(A)+MSL+MS+DMSL(B)	168106 - 168107	168214, 168218-168219
		DMSL(A)+MSL+MS+DMSL(B)	DMSL(A)+MS+DMSL(B)
		168108 - 168113	168215 - 168217
		DMSL(A)+MS+DMSL(B)	DMSL(A)+MSL+MS+DMSL(B)
Vehicle numbers:	DMSL(A) - 58151-58155	DMSL(A) - 58156-58163	DMSL(A) - 58164 - 58169
	MSL - 58651-58655	MSL - 58756-58757	MSL 58365-58367
	MS - 58451-58455	MS - 58456-58463	MS - 58464-58469
	DMSL(B) - 58251-58255	DMSL(B) - 58256-58263	DMSL(B) - 58264 - 58269
Vehicle length:	77ft 6in (23.62m)	77ft 6in (23.62m)	77ft 6in (23.62m)
Height:	12ft 4^{1}/$_{2}$in (3.77m)	12ft 4^{1}/$_{2}$in (3.77m)	12ft 4^{1}/$_{2}$in (3.77m)
Width:	8ft 10in (2.69m)	8ft 10in (2.69m)	8ft 10in (2.69m)
Seating:	Total - 278S	168106 - 168107 - Total - 277S	168214/218/219 - Total 204S
	DMSL(A) - 60S	168108 - 168113 - Total - 204S	168215 - 168217 - Total 277S
	MSL - 73S	DMSL(A) - 59S	DMSL(A) - 59S
	MS - 77S	MSL - 73	MSL - 73S
	DMSL(B) - 68S	MS - 76S	MS - 76S
		DMSL(B) - 76S	DMSL(B) - 69S
Internal layout:	2+2	2+2	2+2
Gangway:	Within set	Within set	Within set
Toilets:	DMSL, MSL - 1	DMSL, MSL - 1	DMSL, MSL - 1
Weight:	168.8 tonnes	168106-107 - 175.1 tonnes	168214/218/219 - 134.9 tonnes
	DMSL(A) - 43.7 tonnes	168108-113 - 132.2 tonnes	168215-168217 - 178.2 tonnes
	MSL - 41 tonnes	DMSL(A) - 45.2 tonnes	DMSL(A) - 45.4 tonnes
	MS - 40.5tonnes	MSL - 42.9 tonnes	MSL - 43.3 tonnes
	DMSL(B) - 43.6 tonnes	MS - 41.8 tonnes	MS - 44 tonnes
		DMSL(B) - 45.2 tonnes	DMSL(B) - 45.5 tonnes
Brake type:	Air EP	Air EP	Air EP
Bogie type:	Powered -P3-23	Powered - P3-23	Powered - P3-23
	Trailer - T3-23	Trailer - T3-23	Trailer - T3-23
Power unit:	1 x MTU 6R183TD13H per car	1 x MTU 6R183TD13H per car	1 x MTU 6R183TD13H per car
Transmission:	Hydraulic	Hydraulic	Hydraulic
Transmission type:	Voith T211r	Voith T211r	Voith T211r
Horsepower (total):	1,688hp (1,259kW)	168106 -107 - 1,688hp (1,259kW)	168214/18/19 - 1,266hp (944kW)
		168108 -113 - 1,266hp (944kW)	168215-217 - 1,688hp (1,259kW)
Max speed:	100mph (160 km/h)	100mph (160 km/h)	100mph (160 km/h)
Coupling type:	Outer - BSI	Outer - BSI	Outer - BSI
	Inner - Bar	Inner - Bar	Inner - Bar
Multiple restriction:	Class 165, 166, 168	Class 165, 166, 168	Class 165, 166, 168
Door type:	Bi-parting swing plug	Bi-parting swing plug	Bi-parting swing plug
Special features:	Fitted with Chiltern ATP	Fitted with Chiltern ATP	Fitted with Chiltern ATP
	and trip-cocks	and trip-cocks	and trip-cocks
Body structure:	Welded aluminium,	Welded aluminium,	Welded aluminium,
	bolt on steel ends	bolt on steel ends	bolt on steel ends
Owner:	Porterbrook	Porterbrook, HSBC	Porterbrook
Operator:	Chiltern Railways	Chiltern Railways	Chiltern Railways

Diesel Multiple-Units

Fact File

The first of the 'new generation diesel units to be ordered were these Class 168 'Clubman' sets for Chiltern line routes from Marylebone to Birmingham. The design was the forerunner of the massive Class 170 'Turbostar' fleet which is now in use throughout the UK network.

The first five 'Clubman' sets, laid out for one class accommodation, 'Club', are built to a different body profile and front end design to the remainder of the fleet. These were originally three-car sets which were later augmented to four car status.

As passenger growth took off on the Chiltern route, especially the London-Birmingham corridor extra 'Clubman' vehicles were ordered, but by this time Adtranz had standardised on the more pleasing front end of the 170 design, therefore all subsequent orders are basically Class 170s.

Interiors of all vehicles are set out in the 2+2 low density mode, with above-seat luggage stacks, toilets provided in both driving cars and one MS vehicle in four-car sets.

Units are equipped with 'trip-cock' equipment to allow operation over the London Underground controlled line between Harrow-on-the-Hill and Amersham.

Livery is Chiltern Railways blue and white.

Above: *Four-car Class 168/0 showing the original body style, painted in the new Chiltern Railways white and blue livery. The 168/0s operate as a mixed fleet with the 168/1 and 168/2 four-car sets on longer-distance and peak-hour services. During the off-peak periods these units can frequently be found stabled at either Aylesbury or Wembley depots. All sets are fitted with 'trip-cock' apparatus, seen mounted on the leading bogie.* **John Wills**

Right: *Class 168/0 front end layout. In many respects the revised 'Turbostar' body styling was much more pleasing to the eye. A-roof level marker light, B-electronic route indicator display, C-Group Standard light cluster, incorporating marker, head and tail lights. D-BSI coupling. Set No 168001 is displayed when new.* **Author**

Above: *By the time the second batch of Class 168s was ordered, Adtranz had established the 'Turbostar' production line at Derby and these units were built under this design, looking a little more pleasing to the eye. The first of the build, No 168106, is seen at Marylebone. The main equipment positions follow the same basic layout, except that the head, marker and tail lights are no longer in a box assembly.* **Author**

Left Middle: *Clearly showing the design differences between the 'Turbostar' and 'Networker Turbo' breeds, set No 168111, a three-car set is pictured under the roof at Marylebone station. Even though these units have a lot of white on the bodywork, high-quality maintenance at both Wembley and Aylesbury ensures these sets are always in pristine condition.* **Author**

Left Bottom: *Class 168 'Clubman' interior, showing the 2+2 seating in a mix of airline and group. The group seats have tables, and on the first five units dividing screens are positioned through the vehicle to break up the tube appearance. Above-seat luggage racks are provided, plus fold-down tables on airline-type seats. Carpets are fitted throughout.* **Author**

Above: *Two views showing the bi-parting sliding plug doors as fitted to the Class 168 design. The 'door open' button is on the left door with an 'out of use' light above. The yellow band at the top of the door indicates disabled and cycle access/storage. The open view shows the wide vestibule, suitable for two persons to pass in the door opening, thus speeding up loading and unloading at busy times.*
Both: **John Wills**

Right Second: *The expansion of the Chiltern Railways sets was carefully managed with extra middle vehicles ordered as required and then inserted into either two- or three-car sets to provide a fleet today of 10 four-car and nine three-car sets. A brand new fully finished middle vehicle, MSL No 58456 is illustrated in the works yard at Derby. Note the exhaust stack on the vehicle end, the glazed dividing doors and the bar coupler.* **Author**

Right Third: *The 'trip-cock' device attached to the side of the leading bogies (looking like a third-rail power-collection shoe) is required for use over the London Underground section between Harrow-on-the-Hill and Amersham. Signals on this section have 'trips' and with the signal at danger the trip is raised, if this is struck by the trip-cock on the train the brake pipe is vented and the brakes applied. The 165s/0s and 168s are the only DMUs so fitted.* **Author**

Right Bottom: *By the time the Class 168/2 sets were ordered from Bombardier from 2003, the 'Turbostar' design had again been slightly amended with larger headlights and a combined marker/tail light, as demonstrated here on set No 168218 alongside a Class 168/1 unit. A slight revision was also made to the roof-mounted marker light. All other equipment and interior fittings were the same.* **Author**

Class 170 'Turbostar'

	170/1	170/2	170/3	170/3
Sub class:	170/1	170/2	170/3	170/3
Number range:	170101-170117	170201-170208 and 170270-170273	170399	170393-170398
Introduced:	1998-1999 (2001 MC)	170201-170208 - 1999 170270-170273 - 2002	20001	2002-2003
Built by:	Adtranz Derby	170201-170208 - Adtranz Derby 170270-170208 - Bombardier Derby	Adtranz Derby	Adtranz Derby/ Bombardier Derby
Formation:	170101-170110/117 DMCL(A)+MC+DMCL(B) 170111-170116 DMCL(A)+DMCL(B)	170201-170208 DMCL+MS+DMSL 170270-170273 DMSL+DMCL	DMCL(A)+DMCL(B)	170393-170396 DMCL+MSLRB+DMSL 170397-170398 DMCL+MC+DMCL
Vehicle Nos.:	170101-170110/117 DMS(A) - 50101-110/117 MC - 55101-55110 DMS(B) - 79101-110/117 170111-170116 DMC(A) - 50111-50116 DMC(B) - 79111-79116	170201-170208 DMCL - 50201-50208 MS - 56201-56208 DMSL - 79201-79208 170270-170273 DMSL - 50270-50273 DMCL - 79270-79273	DMCL(A) - 50399 DMCL(B) - 79399	170393-170396 DMCL - 50393-50398 MSLRB-56393-56398 DMSL - 79393-79398 170397-170398 DMCL(A) - 50397-50398 MC - 56397-56398 DMCL(B) - 79397-79398
Vehicle length:	77ft 6in (23.62m)	77ft 6in (23.62m)	77ft 6in (23.62m)	77ft 6in (23.62m)
Height:	12ft 4^1/$_2$in (3.77m)	12ft 4^1/$_2$in (3.77m))	12ft 4^1/$_2$in (3.77m)	12ft 4^1/$_2$in (3.77m)
Width:	8ft 10in (2.69m)	8ft 10in (2.69m)	8ft 10in (2.69m)	8ft 10in (2.69m)
Seating:	170101-170110 Total 24F/118S 170111-170117 Total - 24F/97S 170101-170110/117 DMCL(A) - 12F/45S MC 21F/22S DMCL(B) - 12F/52S 170111-170116 DMCL(A) - 12F/45S DMCL(B) - 12F/52S	170201-170208 Total - 29F/127S 170270-170273 Total - 9F/110S 170201-170208 DMCL - 29F/3S MS - 58S DMSL - 66S 170270-170273 DMCL(B) - 9F/53S DMSL - 57S	Total - 18F/96S DMCL(A) - 9F/43S DMCL(B) - 9F/53S	170393-170396 Total - 29F/136S 170397-170398 Total - 40F/132S 170393-170396 DMCL - 29F/5S MSLRB - 60S DMSL - 71S 170397-170398 DMCL(A) -9F/43S MC - 22F/36S DMCL(B) - 9F/53S
Internal layout:	2+2F, 2+2S	2+1F, 2+2S	2+1F, 2+2S	2+1F/2+2
Gangway:	Within set	Within set	Within set	Within set
Toilets:	DMCL -1	One per vehicle	One per vehicle	One per vehicle
Weight:	170101-170110/117 Total - 132.8 tonnes 170111-170116 Total - 89.8 tonnes DMCL(A) - 44.8 tonnes MC - 43.0 tonnes DMCL(B) - 44.8 tonnes	170201-170208 Total - 133.7 tonnes 170270-170273 Total - 91.4 tonnes DMC L- 45 tonnes MS - 45.3 tonnes DMSL(B) – 43.4 tonnes	Total - 91.6 tonne DMCL(A) - 45.8 tonnes DMCL(B) - 45.8 tonnes	170393-170396 Total - 137.5 tonnes 170397-170398 Total - 134.2 tonnes DMCL - 45.4-46.5 tonnes MSL - 43-44.7 tonnes DMSL - 46.3 tonnes
Brake type:	Air	Air	Air	Air
Bogie type:	One P3-23c and one T3-23c per car	One P3-23c and one T3-23c per car	One P3-23c and one T3-23c per car	One P3-23c and one T3-23c per car

Diesel Multiple-Units

170/3	170/4	170/5	170/6
170301-170308	170401-170434	170501-170523	170630-170639
	170450-170478		
2000-2001	1999-2005	1999-2000	2000
170301-170308	Adtranz Derby/	Adtranz Derby	Adtranz Derby
Adtranz Derby	Bombardier Derby		
DMCL(A)+DMCL(B)	170401-170434	DMSL(A)+DMSL(B)	DMSL(A)+MS+DMSL(B)
	DMCL(A)+MS+DMCL(B)		
	170450-170461		
	DMSL(A)+MS+DMSL(B)		
	170470-170478		
	DMSL(A)+MS+DMSL(B)		
170301 - 170308	170401-170424	DMSL(A) - 50501-50523	DMSL(A) - 50630-50639
DMCL(A) - 50301-50308	DMCL(A) - 50401-50434	DMSL(B) - 79501-79523	MS - 56630-56639
DMCL(B) - 79301-79308	MS - 56401-56434		DMSL(B) - 79630-79639
	DMCL(B) - 79401-79434		
	170450-170478		
	DMSL(A) - 50450-50478		
	MS - 56450-56478		
	DMSL(B) - 79450-79478		
77ft 6in (23.62m)	77ft 6in (23.62m)	77ft 6in (23.62m)	77ft 6in (23.62m)
12ft 4^1/$_2$in (3.77m)	12ft 4^1/$_2$in (3.77m)	12ft 4^1/$_2$in (3.77m)	12ft 4^1/$_2$in (3.77m)
8ft 10in (2.69m)	8ft 10in (2.69m)	8ft 10in (2.69m)	8ft 10in (2.69m)
Total - 18F/96S	170401-170434	Total - 122S	Total - 196S
DMCL(A) - 9F/43S	18F/172S	DMSL(A) - 55S	DMSL(A) - 55S
DMCL(B) - 9F/53S	170450-170461	DMSL(B) - 67S	MS - 74S
	Total - 198S		DMSL(B) - 67S
	170470-170478		
	Total - 210S		
	170401-170434		
	DMC(A) -9F/43S		
	MS - 76S		
	DMC(B) - 9F/53S		
	170450-170461		
	DMSL(A) - 55S		
	MS - 76S		
	DMSL(B) - 67S		
	170470-170478		
	DMS(A) - 56S		
	MS - 76S		
	DMSL(B) - 67S		
2+1F, 2+2S	2+1F, 2+2S	2+2S	2+2S
Within set	Within set	Within set	Within set
One per vehicle	One per vehicle	One per vehicle	One per vehicle
Total - 92.4 tonnes	Total - 133.2 tonnes	Total - 91.7 tonnes	Total - 134.1 tonnes
DMCL(A) - 45.8 tonnes	DMCL(A) - 45.8 tonnes	DMSL(A) - 45.8 tonnes	DMSL(A) - 45.9 tonnes
DMCL(B) - 46.6 tonnes	MS - 41.4 tonnes	DMSL(B) - 45.8 tonnes	MS - 42.3 tonnes
	DMS(B) – 45.8 tonnes		DMSL(B) - 45.8 tonnes
Air	Air	Air	Air
One P3-23c and	One P3-23c and	One P3-23c and	One P3-23c and
one T3-23c per car	one T3-23c per car	one T3-23c per car	one T3-23c per car

Diesel Multiple-Units

Sub class:	170/1	170/2	170/3	170/3
Power unit:	1 x MTU 6R 183TD of 422hp per car	1 x MTU 6R 183TD of 422hp per car	1 x MTU 6R 183TD of 422hp per car	1 x MTU 6R 183TD of 422hp per car
Transmission:	Hydraulic Voith T211r to ZF final drive	Hydraulic Voith T211r to ZF final drive	Hydraulic Voith T211r to ZF final drive	Hydraulic Voith T211r to ZF final drive
Horsepower:	3-car - 1,266hp (944kW) 2-car - 844hp (629kW)	3-car - 1,266hp (944kW) 2-car - 844hp (629kW)	2-car - 844hp (629kW)	3-car - 1,266hp (944kW)
Max speed:	100mph	100mph	100mph	100mph
Coupling type:	BSI	BSI	BSI	BSI
Multiple working:	Class 15x	Class 15x	Class 15x	Class 15x
Door type:	Bi-parting slide plug	Bi-parting slide plug	Bi-parting slide plug	Bi-parting slide plug
Special features:	Air conditioned Some - RETB	Air conditioned RETB	Air conditioned Some - RETB	Air conditioned Some - RETB
Body structure:	Welded aluminium	Welded aluminium	Welded aluminium	Welded aluminium
Owner:	Porterbrook	Porterbrook	Porterbrook	Porterbrook
Operator:	Arriva Cross Country (AXC)	One Anglia	FTPE	First ScotRail/ Arriva Cross Country

Fact File

The most popular of the 'new generation' of MUs is the Adtranz/Bombardier 'Turbostar', of which 140 sets are in operation. The aluminium-built vehicles, assembled in Derby are principally owned by Porterbrook with a handful funded by HSBC. The sets come in two- or three-car formations and by nature of their design can have virtually any interior configuration.

All exteriors are of the same basic design, with some minor revision on later sets in the design of the main light clusters.

Sets are fully air conditioned and are relatively low-noise considering each vehicle has a 422hp underfloor engine. The top speed is 100mph and the sets can be seen throughout the UK rail network. In 2007 the product was still offered by Bombardier.

Above: *Class 170/1 two-car set now operated by Arriva Cross Country, previously used by Midland Main Line. These units still sport turquoise/green livery now off-set by Cross Country branding. This represents the first production run of the 'Turbostar' product range.* **Author**

Left: *Two batches of Class 170/2 exist, both operating for 'one' Railway. This view illustrates the two-car fleet, used for Norwich-area provincial services including East Anglia to London trains. Set No 170270 passing Stratford shows the early 'one' Railway livery, using a slightly darker blue bodywork, offset by turquoise doors.* **Author**

170/3	170/4	170/5	170/6
1 x MTU 6R 183TD	1 x MTU 6R 183TD	1 x MTU 6R 183TD	1 x MTU 6R 183TD
of 422hp per car	of 422hp per car	of 422hp per car	of 422hp per car
Hydraulic	Hydraulic	Hydraulic	Hydraulic
Voith T211r to	Voith T211r to	Voith T211r to	Voith T211r to
ZF final drive	ZF final drive	ZF final drive	ZF final drive
2-car - 844hp (629kW)	3-car - 1,266hp (944kW)	2-car - 844hp (629kW)	3-car - 1,266hp (944kW)
100mph	100mph	100mph	100mph
BSI	BSI	BSI	BSI
Class 15x	Class 15x	Class 15x	Class 15x
Bi-parting slide plug	Bi-parting slide plug	Bi-parting slide plug	Bi-parting slide plug
Air conditioned	Air conditioned	Air conditioned	Air conditioned
	Some - RETB	Some - RETB	Some - RETB
Welded aluminium	Welded aluminium	Welded aluminium	Welded aluminium
Porterbrook	Porterbrook, HSBC	Porterbrook	Porterbrook
First Transpennine	First ScotRail	London Midland /	London Midland /
		Arriva Cross Country	Arriva Cross Country

Right: *The first eight of the Class 170/2s are three-car sets; these were introduced for East Anglia-Woking and London-Norwich services. Over the years considerable modification has been made to these sets to increase passenger loadings. The middle car seats 58 standard class passengers, houses a buffet bar (some sets) and a guard's office.* **Author**

Below: *Showing the slightly lighter standard 'one' Railway livery, set No 170201 is seen at Colchester forming a King's Cross-Peterborough service. Front-end equipment is the same as on Class 168. This unit unusually sports the 'one' logo on the front valance.* **Author**

Diesel Multiple-Units

Left: *In early 2007, following a shuffle of stock after introduction of Class 185 units, a number of Class 158s was made available to South West Trains and their Class 170s moved to First TransPennine Express and Southern. The FTPE sets are allocated to Crofton and have been rebranded in full FTPE 'Barbie' livery which surprisingly suits the body lines of the 'Turbostar'. Set No 170301 is illustrated.*
Richard Tuplin

Right: *Scotland is the largest user of Class 170s, with a sizeable fleet operated by both First ScotRail and Strathclyde Passenger Transport. The latter fleet, Nos 170470-478, are painted in carmine and cream livery. and do not have first class accommodation, being mainly used on the outer suburban network around Glasgow. Set No 170470 is illustrated at Croy on 8 September 2005. Sets Nos 170472-478 also sport a turquoise body strip.*
John Wills

Left: *The main First ScotRail-operated fleet of Class 170s, Nos 170401-170461, were all originally painted in ScotRail white and green livery; however, following franchise changes the new FirstGroup colours are now being applied. Sets all have first and standard class accommodation and are allocated to Haymarket depot. The units are used on longer distance services between Edinburgh/Glasgow and Aberdeen/Inverness as well as on the main Edinburgh-Glasgow artery. Set No 170401 is seen at Haymarket on 17 October 2005.*
Bill Wilson

Right: *Members of Class 170/5 and 170/6 are operated by London Midland Trains and Arriva Cross Country on medium-long distance services. The 170/5 fleet are two-car units and the 170/6s are three-car sets. All units are set out for standard class only occupation and are allocated to Tyseley depot. Sets sport Central Trains green and blue livery, offset by yellow passenger doors and London Midland or Arriva Cross Country branding. Set No 170510 is illustrated at Wolverhampton.*
Author

Above: *During the course of the 'Turbostar' build, Porterbrook produced a small number of 'spot hire' units which could be made available to any TOC. Numbered 170397-399, the trains are painted in white with mauve doors and sport the operator's decals, such as here on 170397 showing Central Trains branding. The interior layout is set out for composite travel, but frequently the first class is declassified.* **Author**

Right Middle: *Class 170 interior. A large number of different interior designs can be found within the 170 fleet, this shows the original 'one' Railway standard class 2+2 seating in a mix of airline and group styles. All 170 vehicles have passenger information systems, are carpeted throughout and have complementary colour grab poles to suit the seating and company branding.* **Author**

Right Bottom: *A new design of driving cab was devised for the 'Turbostar' product range. Incorporating for the first time on a DMU a joint power and brake controller operated by the driver's left hand, the desk also incorporated as fixed features such devices as driver's reminder appliance and TPWS. Wiring in each '170' is provided for Radio Electric Token Block (RETB) equipment, but the interface boxes are only carried on selected sets. On the driver's right side is the NRN radio and horn valve. Door controls are provided on both sides.* **Author**

Traction Recognition

Class 171 'Turbostar'

	171/7	171/8
Sub class:	171/7	171/8
Number range:	171721 - 171730	171801 - 171806
Introduced:	2003-2005	2004
Built by:	Bombardier Derby	Bombardier Derby
Formation:	DMCL+DMSL	DMCL(A)+MS+MS+DMCL(B)
Vehicle numbers:	DMCL - 50721 - 50729,	DMCL(A) - 50801 - 50806
	50392	MS - 54801 - 54806
	DMSL - 79721 - 79729	MS - 56801 - 56806
	79392	DMCL(B) - 79801 - 79806
Vehicle length:	77ft 6in (23.62m)	77ft 6in (23.62m)
Height:	12ft 4¹/₂in (3.77m)	12ft 4¹/₂in (3.77m)
Width:	8ft 10in (2.69m)	8ft 10in (2.69m)
Seating:	Total 9F/107S	Total - 18F/241S
	(171730= 9F/111S)	DMCL(A) 9F/43S
	DMCL 9F/43S	MS 74S
	(171730=9F/47S)	MS 74S
	DMSL 64S	DMCL(B) 9F/50S
Internal layout:	2+1F, 2+2S	2+1F, 2+2S
Gangway:	Within set	Within set
Toilets:	DMCL, DMSL - 1	DMCL - 1
Weight:	Total - 95.4 tonnes	Total - 180.4 tonnes
	DMCL - 47.6 tonnes	DMCL(A) - 46.5 tonnes
	DMSL - 47.8 tonnes	MS - 43.7 tonnes
		MS - 43.7 tonnes
		DMCL(B) - 46.5 tonnes
Brake type:	Air	Air
Bogie type:	One P3-23c and one	One P3-23c and one
	T3-23c per car	T3-23c per car
Power unit:	1 x MTU 6R 183TD of	1 x MTU 6R 183TD of
	422hp per car	422hp per car
Transmission:	Hydraulic	Hydraulic
Transmission type:	Voith T211r to	Voith T211r to
	ZF final drive	ZF final drive
Horsepower:	Total - 844hp (629kW)	Total 1,688hp (1,259kW)
Max speed:	100mph (161 km/h)	100mph (161km/h)
Coupling type:	Dellner 12	Dellner 12
Multiple restriction:	Class 171	Class 171
Door type:	Bi-parting slide plug	Bi-parting slide plug
Special features:	Air conditioned	Air conditioned
Body structure:	Aluminium	Aluminium
Owner:	Porterbrook	Porterbrook
Operator:	Southern	Southern

Fact File

When operator South Central (later Southern) re-equipped its diesel multiple-unit fleet for non-electrified lines, it chose the Bombardier 'Turbostar' range. They opted for Class 170s, but soon after delivery of the original two-car sets to Selhurst depot, decided to change the couplers from BSI to Dellner 12s, in keeping with their 'Electrostar' EMU fleet and to give assistance if needed. The refitting changed the classification to 171.

Two sub-classes exist; two-car sets and four-car sets. Two-car units are usually used on the non-electrified Ashford-Hastings route, while a mix of two- and four-car sets are to be found on the London Bridge-Oxted-Uckfield route.

Units are finished in Southern green and white livery, and have good quality interiors in the 2+2 low-density style.

Below: Identical to the Class 170s in structural design, except for the fitting of Dellner couplers, two-car set No 171721 (the first of the build) is viewed from its Driving Motor Composite Lavatory (DMCL) vehicle at Brighton. All Class 171s are based at Selhurst where special maintenance facilities have been constructed. All sets are painted in Southern green and white livery and have the two-light style lamp cluster. **Brian Morrison**

Above: *The two and four-car Southern-operated 'Turbostar' sets of Class 171 were built alongside the Class 170s at the Bombardier plant in Derby. The sets were built over a protracted period to suit the operator's fleet deployment, with the two-car units delivered first. All sets are maintained at Selhurst depot, which was modified for its new role. In full Southern livery, set No 171802 is seen passing Norwood Junction on 7 January 2005.* **Chris Wilson**

Right Middle: *The intermediate Motor Standard (MS) cars of the four-car sets are in the open style having 2+2 seating, accommodating 74; the only difference from the driving cars is the omission of the cab end and access doors. Car No 54802 is illustrated from set No 171802.* **James Stearn**

Right Bottom: *Interiors of the Southern sets are finished in turquoise and use the low-density 2+2 style, a mix of group seats around tables and airline seats are provided. In the area directly behind the driving cab in one car on two-car sets and both driving cars on four-car sets, is a first class area. An automated passenger information system is fitted throughout.* **Nathan Williamson**

	175/0	175/1
Sub class:	175/0	175/1
Number range:	175001-175011	175101-175116
Introduced:	1999-2000	1999-2001
Built by:	Alstom, Birmingham	Alstom, Birmingham
Formation:	DMSL(A)+DMSL(B)	DMSL(A)+MSL+DMSL(B)
Vehicle numbers:	DMSL(A) - 50701-50711	DMSL(A) - 50751-50766
	DMSL(B) - 79701-79711	MSL - 56751-56766
		DMSL(B) - 79751-79766
Vehicle length:	75ft 7in (23.06m)	DMSL(A), DMSL(B) - 75ft 7in (23.71m)
		MSL - 75ft 5in (23.03m)
Height:	12ft 4in (3.75m)	12ft 4in (3.75m)
Width:	9ft 2in (2.80m)	9ft 2in (2.80m)
Seating:	Total - 118S	Total - 186S
	DMSL(A) - 54S	DMSL(A) - 54S
	DMSL(B) - 64S	MSL - 68S
		DMSL(B) - 64S
Internal layout:	2+2	2+2
Gangway:	Within set	Within set
Toilets:	DMSL(A), DMSL(B) - 1	DMSL(A), MSL, DMSL(B) - 1
Weight:	Total - 101.4 tonnes	Total - 148.9 tonnes
	DMSL(A) - 50.7 tonnes	DMSL(A) - 50.7 tonnes
	DMSL(B) - 50.7 tonnes	MSL - 47.5 tonnes
		DMSL(B) - 50.7 tonnes
Brake type:	Air	Air
Bogie type:	Alstom FBO-LTB, MBSI, TB, MBI	Alstom FBO-LTB, MBSI, TB, MBI
Power unit:	One Cummins N14 of	One Cummins N14 of
	450hp (335kW) per car	450hp (335kW) per car
Transmission:	Hydraulic	Hydraulic
Transmission type:	Voith T211rzze to ZF final drive	Voith T211rzze to ZF final drive
Horsepower (total):	900hp (671kW)	1,350hp (1,007kW)
Max speed:	100mph (161km/h)	100mph (161km/h)
Coupling type:	Scharfenberg	Scharfenberg
Multiple restriction:	Within type and Class 180	Within type and Class 180
Door type:	Single leaf swing plug	Single leaf swing plug
Special features:	Air conditioned	Air conditioned
Body structure:	Steel	Steel
Owner:	Angel Trains	Angel Trains
Operator:	Arriva Trains Wales	Arriva Trains Wales

Below: *A three-car Class 175/1, painted in the original FirstGroup 'Barbie' livery is seen working over the North Wales Coast route, a stronghold of this class. The two driving vehicles, while the same in structure, are laid out with different interior designs.* **Author**

Fact File

When longer-distance new-generation DMUs were sought in the late 1990s, Alstom put forward its 'Coradia 1000' product range, which was taken by FirstGroup for its then North Western and Great Western franchises. The North Western sets are now operated by Arriva Trains Wales.

The type comes in both two- and three-car formations, all with 2+2 seating in a mix of airline and group layouts.

The fleet is allocated to purpose-built accommodation at Chester and can be found forming the main line services of Arriva Trains Wales.

Originally sets were painted in FirstGroup 'Barbie' livery, but this is now being replaced by ART turquoise.

Above: *Class 175 front end equipment: A-high level marker light, B-horns behind grilles, C-marker/tail light, D-headlight, E-Scharfenberg coupling incorporating physical, air and electrical connections, F-electrical shore supply socket, G-emergency brake pipe connection, H-emergency main reservoir pipe connection.* **Author**

Above Right: *Two-car version of the Class 175/0. No external changes have taken place since construction, apart from livery. Set No 175008 is illustrated from its DMS(A) vehicle. Roof detail consists of an NRN radio aerial, air-conditioning module and fresh air ventilators.* **Author**

Right Middle: *Following franchise changes in 2005, and the formation of an 'all Wales' franchise operated by Arriva Trains Wales, the Class 175s became the operating property of this company, although for the first year a number of sets were sub-leased to another TOC. The Arriva Trains Wales turquoise and cream livery has been applied to a small number of sets. Set No 175110 is illustrated at Cardiff. This livery is quite unusual with the colours on the middle vehicle fading to white in the centre, giving a pleasing impression when the entire train is seen.* **Nathan Williamson**

Right Bottom: *Interior of Class 175 unit, showing the pleasant interior styling, good lighting and seats set out in a mix of airline and group styles. Fold-down tables are provided with above-seat luggage racks.* **Author**

Class 180 'Adelante'

Number range:	180101-180114
Introduced:	2000-2002
Built by:	Alstom, Birmingham
Formation:	DMSL(A)+MFL+MSL+RMSL+DMSL(B)
Vehicle numbers:	DMSL(A) - 50901-50914
	MFL - 54901-54914
	MSL - 55901-55914
	MSLRB - 56901-56914
	DMSL(B) - 59901-59914
Train length:	116.5m
Vehicle length:	DMSL(A), DMSL(B) - 75ft 7in (23.71m)
	MFL, MSL, RMSL - 75ft 5in (23.03m)
Height:	12ft 4in (3.75m)
Width:	9ft 2in (2.80m)
Seating:	Total - 42F/226S
	DMSL(A) - 46S
	MFL - 42F
	MSL - 68S
	MSLRB - 56S
	DMSL(B) - 56S
Internal layout:	2+1F, 2+2S
Gangway:	Within set
Toilets:	DMSL(A), MFL, MSL, MSLRB, DMSL(B) - 1
Weight:	Total - 252.5 tonnes
	DMSL(A) - 51.7 tonnes
	MFL - 49.6 tonnes
	MSL - 49.5 tonnes
	MSLRB - 50.3 tonnes
	DMSL(B) - 51.4 tonnes
Brake type:	Air
Bogie type:	Alstom MB2
Power unit:	One Cummins QSK19 of 750hp (560kW) per car
Transmission:	Hydraulic
Transmission type:	Voith T312br to ZF final drive
Horsepower (total):	3,750hp (2,796kW)
Max speed:	125mph (201km/h)
Coupling type:	Outer - Scharfenberg, Inner - Bar
Multiple restriction:	Within type and Class 175
Door type:	Single leaf swing plug
Body structure:	Steel
Special features:	FGW ATP, Air conditioned
Owner:	Angel Trains
Operator:	First Great Western (due off lease 12/07-03/08)

Diesel Multiple-Units

Fact File

The second main line breed of 'Coradia 1000' products by Alstom are the First Great Western five-car 125mph 'Adelante' sets used on all FGW routes except west of Plymouth and Cardiff.

Unlike the Class 175s, these sets are streamlined and look very impressive.

Passenger accommodation is of a high standard with a mix of 2+2 in airline and group layouts in standard class and 2+1 in airline and groups in first class. A small buffet is provided in one MS vehicle which reduces seating by 12, while a small serving bay is provided at one end of the first class vehicle to deal with FGW's first class 'at seat' service.

These sets have end Scharfenberg couplings which are housed behind a hinged front panel; when two sets are required to attach, the driver opens the doors and the coupling is made available; all connections are automatically made and operated from the cab.

As FGW do not have locomotives fitted with compatible couplings, if the need arises to attach a locomotive, a special adaptor coupler and air pipes are required.

With FGW concentrating on IC125 stock, the Class 180s were scheduled to be returned to Angel Trains from December 2007.

Left: *Class 180 intermediate coach; an MSLRB is shown. Each vehicle has one single-leaf sliding plug door at each end of each side, these feed a full-width vestibule, with access to the seating saloons by passenger-controlled sliding doors. In keeping with many modern designs, seats do not line up with all windows and in both first and standard class some seats are lined by a window divider. Underframe equipment is housed in air smoothed boxes. All vehicles are fully air-conditioned and no opening hopper windows are provided.* **Author**

Above: *Making an impressive sight pulling through Dawlish, set No 180102 forms a Paddington-Plymouth service. The '180s' tend to only operate as far as Exeter in the West Country with just one service each day to/from Plymouth. The cab ends of the '180s', while pleasing to the eye, have experienced a number of problems with panels falling off and the coupling covers becoming broken and removed. By 2007, very few sets still had all horn covers, coupling door and light cluster covers. A special arrangement exists with these sets for the emergency egress of the driver in case of accident, with the cab side window being removable and the driver being able to escape by rope ladder!* **Author**

Right Middle: *First-class seating area, showing both airline and group seating. Good quality tables are provided around group seats, but only fold down flaps are provided for airline seats, which are restrictive for business travellers. 'Pullman' style table lamps are provided but no power sockets for computers. All armrests are hinged to ease access.* **Author**

Right Bottom: *Emergency end coupling arrangement. If a '180' needs attachment to a locomotive, an emergency coupling adaptor on the Class 180 has to be attached to the Scharfenberg, which has a special draw hook. Special air pipes are then used to provide a main reservoir and brake pipe feed to the Class 180. No train supply of electrical connection is made.* **Author**

Class 185 'Desiro'

Number range:	185101-185151
Introduced:	2005-2007
Built by:	Siemens Transportation, Germany
Formation:	DMCL+MSL+DMS
Vehicle numbers:	DMCL - 51101 - 51151
	MSL - 53101 - 53151
	DMS - 54101 - 54151
Train length:	Total: 233ft 10in (71.28m)
Vehicle length:	DMCL, DMS - (77ft 11in) (23.76m)
	MSL – 77ft 10in (23.750m)
Height:	12ft 4in (3.75m)
Width:	9ft 3in (2.84m)
Seating:	Total - 15F/154S + 12 tip-up
	DMCL 15F/18S
	MSL 72S
	DMS 64S
Internal layout:	2+2S, 2+1F
Gangway:	Within set
Toilets:	MSL - 1, DMCL - 1
Weight:	Total - 163.4 tonnes
	DMCL - 55.6 tonnes
	MSL - 52.8 tonnes
	DMS - 55 tonnes
Brake type:	Air
Bogie type:	Siemens
Power unit:	One Cummins OSK19 of 750hp (560kW) per car
Transmission:	Hydraulic
Transmission type:	Voith Turbopack T312 and SK-485 final drive
Horsepower (total):	2,250hp (1,680KW)
Max speed:	100mph (161km/h)
Coupling type:	Dellner 12
Multiple restriction:	Within Class only
Door type:	Bi-parting sliding plug
Body structure:	Aluminium
Special features:	Air conditioned, power points, CCTV
Owner:	HSBC
Operator:	First TransPennine

Fact File

The first Siemens Transportation diesel-powered 'Desiro' stock for the UK is this fleet of 51 three-car '185s' introduced for First TransPennine Express services.

The high-quality sets were constructed and tested in Germany and shipped to the UK via the Channel Tunnel. The sets are allocated to a Siemens-operated depot at Ardwick, Manchester.

The '185' is a low-density train with 2+2 standard and 2+1 first class seating, trains are fully air conditioned, have passenger information displays and are very quiet even though each vehicle has a 750hp underslung power unit. Units are in FirstGroup's 'dynamic lines' livery.

Speculation exists that either additional vehicles or extra units might be ordered as passenger growth on the TransPennine routes will soon require longer trains.

Below: *The Class 185s are the backbone of First TransPennine Express services. Set No 185131 is viewed from the DMS vehicle at Doncaster. All sets are painted in FirstGroups 'Dynamic Lines' livery.* **Derek Porter**

Above: *Side detail of Driving Motor Standard vehicle. The full-width driving cab is provided with a single-leaf sliding plug door (finished in train livery), while passenger entrance/exit is by a pair of bi-parting sliding plug doors (finished in pink to meet Disability Discrimination Act regulations). Underframe equipment consists of a Cummins QSK19 750hp power unit, transmission unit, fuel tank and control equipment boxes. On the roof, air conditioning modules are located over the driver's compartment and centrally over the passenger saloon area. A centrally located cant-rail height 'door release' light is provided, as are emergency (green) door release valves just above sole bar height.*
Derek Porter

Right Middle: *The intermediate vehicle of the Class 185 is classified as Motor Standard Lavatory (MSL) and as illustrated is seen from the toilet end. Two pairs of passenger doors are provided and underframe and bodyside equipment is the same as on driving cars. The middle passenger window includes an electronic destination indicator, with text of a sensible size that can be seen and read by passengers on platforms.* **Derek Porter**

Right Bottom: *The Class 185 front end style is unique amongst UK trains, but based on the Siemens electric 'Desiro' product. Main equipment locations are: A-cab air conditioning module, B-roof level marker light, C-destination/route indicator, D-Group Standard light cluster units, including a joint marker/tail light unit and a headlight, E-Dellner 12 coupling, including physical, electric and pneumatic connections, F-warning horns, G-anti-climber plates (if during a collision two vehicles come into contact, the 'teeth' on the anti-climber engage and restrict upward movement and thus overriding of the vehicles. The coupling also has 'controlled' deformation to reduce impact).*
Derek Porter

Number range:	201001 (1001)
Introduced:	1957
Built by:	BR Eastleigh
Formation:	DMBS, TSL, TSL, TSRB, TSL, DMBS
	unit formed of a mixture of Class 201,
	202, 411 and 422 vehicles
Vehicle numbers:	DMBS - 60000 (201), 60116 (202), 60118(202)
	TSL - 60501 (201), 60529 (202), 70262 (411)
	TSRB - 69337 (422)
Vehicle length:	DMBS (201) 58ft 0in (17.67m) , DMBS (202) 64ft 6in (19.65m)
	TSL (201) - 58ft 0in (17.67m), TSL (202) 64ft 6in (19.65m)
	TSL (411) 64ft 9in (19.75m), TSRB – 64ft 9in (19.75m)
Height:	12ft 6in (3.82m)
Width:	Class 201-202 - 9ft (2.74m),9ft 3in (2.84m)
	Class 411, 422 9ft 3in (2.81m)
Seating:	DMBS (201) - 22S, DMBS (202) - 31S
	TSL (201) - 72S . TSL (202) - 60S
	TSL (411) - 64S. TSRB (422) - 40S
Internal layout:	2+2S
Gangway:	Within set
Toilets:	TSL - 1
Weight:	DMBS (201) - 55 tonnes, DMBS (202) - 56 tonnes
	TSL (201)- 29.5 tonnes, TSL (202) 53.5 tonnes
	TSL (411) 31.5 tonnes, TSRB (422) - 35 tonnes
Brake type:	Air/EP
Bogie type:	BR (SR) Mk4 and Commonwealth
Power unit:	DMBS - One English Electric 6K of 600hp (450kW) per car
Transmission:	Hydraulic
Main generator:	English Electric EE824
Traction motors:	DMBS - 2
Traction motor type:	EE 507
Horsepower (train):	1,200hp (895kW)
Max speed:	75mph (121km/h)
Coupling type:	drophead buckeye
Multiple restriction:	Not permitted
Door type:	Slam
Body structure:	Steel
Owner:	Privately owned
Operator:	Hastings Diesels

Diesel Multiple-Units

Below: *Technically the spare DMBS No S60116 (originally S60016) from a Class 202, the vehicle now named* Mountfield *stops at Exeter while working a charter in 2005. The 6L driving cars had four seating bays at the inner end, while the 6S vehicles only had three. This car also has a brass whistle mounted on the front end, in addition to its Group Standard air horns.* **Author**

Fact File

Introduced in 1957 for the dieselisation of the London-Hastings line, a number of Southern Region DEMU vehicles have been saved by Hastings Diesels and now augmented with other stock, including former EMU vehicles and returned to main line status.

Usually referred to as set No 1001, the set is formed of a mixture of vehicles from various Class 201, 202, 411 and 422 units. The set is made available for main line charter train use and is painted in Southern Region multiple unit green livery. When not in use the set is kept at St Leonards Depot, Hastings. Two of the three preserved DMBS vehicles can operate with one or more intermediate vehicles.

Above: *Class 202 DMBS equipment positions: A-warning horns, B-waist height main reservoir (yellow) and brake (red) pipes (joint isolating handle), C-multiple unit control jumper, D-multiple unit control jumper receptacle, E-headlight, F-drophead buck-eye coupling, G-emergency cab door, H-cab door, I-engine air intake, J-engine room door, K-cooler group with fan on roof, L-guard's van, M-battery box, N-fuel tank, O-removable roof section over engine. Car No S60118 (the original S60018) from a 6L Class 202 unit.*
John Wills

Right Middle: *The pioneer 'Hastings' power car No S60000 from 6S (Class 201) set 1001. If this and the illustration above are compared this vehicle is noticeably shorter being on a short underframe and having one less seating compartment. Restoration of this 'Hastings' set is exemplary, with the vehicle returned to as near original condition as possible while maintaining modern Group Standards, with such items as headlights.* **Author**

Right Bottom: *One of the advantages of SR DEMU preservation is that the power cars can operate with intermediate vehicles of former SR 4xx series electric multiple-units with some modifications. To expand the size of the Hastings set, two ex EMU vehicles are currently in stock, a Class 422 (4BIG) buffet and this TSL from a Class 411 No 70262. The coach retains its modern hopper windows but has been restored to 1950s multiple-unit green with yellow numbers.* **Author**

Class 220 'Voyager'

Diesel Multiple-Units

Number range:	220001-220034
Introduced:	2000-2001
Built by:	Bombardier Transportation*
Formation:	DMSL+MSRMB+MSL+DMFL
Vehicle numbers:	DMSL - 60301-60334 - DC2010A
Design codes:	MSRMB - 60701-60734 - DD2010A
	MSL - 60201-60234 - DD2020A
	DMFL - 60401-60434 - DC1010A
Vehicle length:	77ft 6in (23.67m)
Height:	12ft 4in (3.75m)
Width:	8ft 11in (2.73m)
Seating:	Total - 26F/160S
	DMSL - 42S
	MSRMB - 58S
	MSL - 60S
	DMFL - 26F
Internal layout:	2+1F, 2+2S
Gangway:	Within set
Toilets:	DMSL, MSL, DMFL - 1
Weight:	Total - 185.6 Tonnes
	DMSL - 48 tonnes
	RMS - 45 tonnes
	MSL - 44.5 tonnes
	DMFL - 48.1 tonns
Brake type:	Air, EP rheostatic
Bogie type:	Bombardier B5005
Power unit:	1 x Cummins of 560kW (750hp) per car
Transmission:	Electric
Transmission package:	Onix
Traction motor type:	8 x Alstom Onix 800 per train
Horsepower:	3,000hp (2,237kW)
Max speed:	125mph (201km/h)
Operating range:	1,350 miles (2,173km)
Route availability:	2
Coupling type:	Outer: Dellner 12, Inner: Bar
Multiple restriction:	Class 220, 221 and Class 57/3
Door type:	Single leaf swing plug
Body construction:	Steel
Special fittings:	Air conditioning, Non tilt
Owner:	Halifax/Bank of Scotland
Operator:	Arriva Cross Country)

* Body shells assembled in Belgium, fitted out at Bombardier plants in Wakefield, UK and Brugge, Belgium.

Fact File

After privatisation in the mid-1990s and Virgin Group's takeover of two of the most important franchises, CrossCountry and West Coast, new train orders followed.

For CrossCountry a diesel train was needed, as the majority of services operated for all or part of their journey away from power supplies. A number of options were studied and eventually a significant number of four- and five-car DMUs were ordered from Bombardier.

To facilitate tilting on selected routes two distinct fleets of trains, which became known as 'Voyager', were ordered; 34 sets with conventional running gear and 44 sets with full body tilt. The Class 220s, which come in four-car formations, are the non-tilt variety.

The sets are high-powered with 3,000hp available for just four cars, using underfloor mounted power units.

Passenger accommodation is limited, with a single four-car train seating just 160 standard and 24 first class passengers, compared to around 400 in an HST they replaced.

One driving car in each set is for first class, identified by a yellow cant-rail band. All sets were named. These sets were transferred to Arriva Cross Country from November 2007.

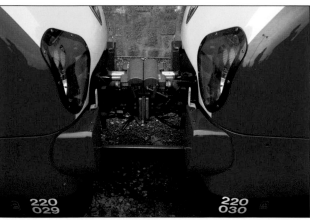

Left: *Voyager sets are fitted with fully automatic Dellner 12 couplers, which when together perform the physical as well as air and electrical connections. Units of Class 220 and 221 are permitted to multiple together, and Class 57/3 'Thunderbird' locomotives fitted with drop-head Dellner couplers are authorised to attach. Sets 220029 and 220030 are seen coupled. The physical connection is the lower section, with the pneumatic and electrical connections above; as sets are 'pushed' together a roll-open cover reveals the connections which push together. Coupling and un-coupling is controlled by push buttons in the driver's cab.* **Author**

Above: *Recognition of the standard Class 220 'Voyager' sets from a Class 221 'Super Voyager' can be achieved by noting the bogies, which on a 220 are frameless. Following the franchise changes in November 2007 when Arriva took over the Cross Country operation, one set, No 220017 was totally rebranded in a new maroon and silver livery offset by pink passenger doors. Other sets have received Cross Country XC branding. Set No 220017 is seen at Bristol Parkway.*
Chris Perkins

Right Middle: *In first class the seating on Class 220s and 221s (which is identical) is very comfortable, with individual seats each with a table. Power points are provided for laptop computers and 'Pullman' style lights are adjacent to the windows. Luggage accommodation is limited with small overhead racks and end of vehicle stacks.* **Author**

Right Bottom: *The cab layouts of the Class 220 and 221 are slightly different to take into account the tilting features of the '221'. The layout conforms to the latest standard with a joint power and brake controller on the left side, and door control buttons (the drivers on Voyagers operate the doors at all times) are on both sides, while other controls and indicators are easily visible.*
The large space in the centre of the desk will (hopefully) be taken one day by ERTMS. The screen on the left side is the onboard computer system. **Author**

Class 221 'Super Voyager'

	221 (5-car)	221 (4-car)
Class:	221 (5-car)	221 (4-car)
Number range:	221101-221140	221141-221144
Introduced:	2001-2002	2002
Built by:	Bombardier Transportation*	Bombardier Transportation*
Formation:	DMSL+MSRMB+MSL(A)+MSL(B)+DMFL	DMSL+MSRMB+MSL+DMFL
Vehicle numbers:	DMSL - 60351-60390 - DF2010A	DMSL - 60391-60394 - DF2010A
Design codes:	MSRMB - 60751-60790 - DG2010A	MSRMB - 60791-60794 - DG2010A
	MSL(A) - 60951-60990 - DG2020A	MSL - 60991-60994 - DG2020G
	MSL(B) - 60851-60890 - DG2020B	DMFL - 60491-60494 - DF1010A
	DMFL - 60451-60490 - DF1010A	-
Vehicle length:	77ft 6in (23.67m)	77ft 6in (23.67m)
Height:	12ft 4in (3.75m)	12ft 4in (3.75m)
Width:	8ft 11in (2.73m)	8ft 11in (2.73m)
Seating:	Total - 26F/220S	Total - 26F/160S
	DMSL - 42S	DMSL - 42S
	MSRMB - 58S	MSRMB - 58S
	MSL(A) - 60S	MSL - 60S
	MSL(B) - 60S	DMFL - 26F
	DMFL - 26F	
Internal layout:	2+1F, 2+2S	2+1F, 2+2S
Gangway:	Within set	Within set
Toilets:	DMSL, MSL, DMFL - 1	DMSL, MSL, DMFL - 1
Weight:	Total - 281.9 tonnes	Total - 227 tonnes
	DMSL - 56.6 tonnes	DMSL - 56.6 tonnes
	MSRMB - 53.1 tonnes	MSRMB - 53.1 tonnes
	MSL(A) - 56.6 tonnes	MSL - 56.6 tonnes
	MSL(B) - 53.1 tonnes	DMFL - 56.6 tonnes
	DMFL - 56.6 tonnes	-
Brake type:	Air, EP rheostatic	Air, EP rheostatic
Bogie type:	Bombardier HVT	Bombardier HVT
Power unit:	1 x Cummins of 560kW (750hp)	1 x Cummins of 560kW (750hp)
	at 1800rpm per car	at 1800rpm per car
Transmission:	Electric	Electric
Transmission package:	Onix	Onix
Traction motor type:	10 x Alstom Onix 800 per train	8 x Alstom Onix 800 per train
Horsepower:	3,750hp (2,796kW)	3,000hp (2,237kW)
Max speed:	125mph (201km/h)	125mph (201km/h)
Operating range:	1,200 miles (1,931km)	1,200 miles (1,931km)
Route availability:	4	4
Coupling type:	Outer: Dellner 12, Inner: Bar	Outer: Dellner 12, Inner: Bar
Multiple restriction:	Class 220/221 only	Class 220/221 only
Door type:	Single leaf swing plug	Single leaf swing plug
Body construction:	Steel	Steel
Special fittings:	Air conditioning, tilt fitted	Air conditioning, tilt fitted
Owner:	Halifax/Bank of Scotland	Halifax/Bank of Scotland
Operator:	Arriva Cross Country	Arriva Cross Country

* Body shells assembled in Belgium, fitted out at Bombardier plants in Wakefield UK and Brugge, Belgium.

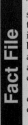

Diesel Multiple-Units

Fact File

To enable higher speeds to be accomplished in selected areas on the West Coast Main Line and on the Didcot-Birmingham line, a tilt system was introduced by Virgin Trains, where trackside beacons supplied 'authority' for tilting trains to activate its tilt system on selected sections of route and travel around 10 per cent faster without discomfort to passengers and in total safety.

These 'tilt' sets were considerably modified from conventional 'Voyager' units and incorporate different bogies and control equipment.

After testing in France, the system was activated in the UK and today both Class 221 'Super

Voyagers' and Class 390 'Pendolino' stock use the tilt system.

The 'Super Voyager' stock comes in both five- and four-car formations. The five-car sets were designed for general use, while the four-car sets were originally destined for use on the Euston-Holyhead route.

The Class 221s are basically the same train as the '220' interiors are identical. Following the November 2007 franchise changes, Sets 221101-113/142-144 are operated by Virgin Trains and sets 22114-141 are operated by Arriva Cross Country.

Above: *When first introduced passengers had difficulty in locating the first or club class accommodation, as no exterior branding was provided. After a short time, the traditional yellow cant rail band was applied to first-class coaches and to assist staff in seeing which way around trains were operating a yellow cover was attached to the electrical drum cover of the coupling at the first class end, as seen here on set No 221105, showing the exterior configuration of a five-car 'Super Voyager' set.* **Author**

Right Second: *All Virgin Voyager doors are hatched with 'zebra' stripes and each vehicle has one section of windowless construction by the toilet area. On the middle vehicle of five-car sets and the 609xx vehicle of four-car sets the cast nameplates are carried. The plate* Amy Johnson *on No 221120 is illustrated.* **Author**

Right third: *Standard class interior as applicable to both Class 220 and 221 stock. Seats are set out in a mix of airline and groups and tables are provided at group seats. Seats are covered in a mix of red and blue moquette. All seats have hinged armrests to assist in reaching inner seats. Mid-length luggage stacks are provided as well as above-seat racks for light small items.* **Author**

Right Bottom: *The front end equipment of the Voyager and Super Voyager stock consists of a cant rail height marker light, two light groups either side of the bodywork above buffing height consisting of marker, head and tail lights. In the centre is the Dellner 12 coupling incorporating physical, pneumatic and electrical connections. The jumper socket on the right is for a shore supply. A dot matrix destination display is fitted at the base of the front window.* **Author**

Diesel Multiple-Units

	222/1 'Pioneer'	222/4 'Meridian' (4-car)	222/4 'Meridian' (5-car)
Sub class:	222/1 'Pioneer'	222/4 'Meridian' (4-car)	222/4 'Meridian' (5-car)
Number range:	222101 - 222104	222008 - 010/018-222023	222011 - 222017
Introduced:	2005	2004-2005	Built 2004-05, Modified 2006
Built by:	Bombardier Transportation Brugge	Bombardier Transportation Brugge	Bombardier Transportation Brugge
Formation:	DMRFO+MSO+MSRMB+DMSO	DMRFO+MCO+ MSRMB+DMSO	DMRFO+MCO+ MSRMB+MSO+DMSO
Vehicle numbers:	DMRFO - 60271 - 60274 MSO - 60571 - 60574 MSRMB - 60681 - 60684 DMSO - 60191 - 60194	DMRFO - 60248 - 60263 MCO - 60918 - 60933 MSRMB - 60628 - 60643 DMSO - 60168 - 60183	DMRFO - 60251 - 60257 MCO - 60921- 60927 MSRMB - 60631 - 60637 MSO - 60531 - 60537 DMSO - 60171 - 60177
Vehicle length:	Driving - 78ft 2in (23.85m) Int - 75ft 4in (23.00m)	Driving - 78ft 2in (23.85m) Int - 78ft 2in (23.85m)	Driving - 78ft 2in (23.85m) Int - 78ft 2in (23.85m)
Height:	12ft 4in (3.75m)	12ft 4in (3.75m)	12ft 4in (3.75m)
Width:	8ft 11in (2.73m)	8ft 11in (2.73m)	8ft 11in (2.73m)
Seating:	Total - 22F/170S DMRFO - 22F MSO - 68S MSRMB - 62S DMSO - 40S	Total - 50F/124S DMRFO - 22F MCO - 28F/22S MSRMB - 62S DMSO - 40S	Total - 50F/192S DMRFO - 22F MCO - 28F/22S MSRMB - 62S MSO - 68S DMSO - 40S
Internal layout:	2+1F, 2+2S	2+1F, 2+2S	2+1F, 2+2S
Gangway:	Within set	Within set	Within set
Toilets:	3-per unit	3-per unit	4-per unit
Weight:	Total - 202 tonnes DMRFO - 52.8 tonnes MSO - 48.6 tonnes MSRMB - 49.6 tonnes DMSO - 51 tonnes	Total - 202 tonnes DMRFO - 52.8 tonnes MCO - 48.6 tonnes MSRMB - 49.6 tonnes DMSO - 51 tonnes	Total - 250.6 tonnes DMRFO - 52.8 tonnes MCO - 48.6 tonnes MSRMB - 49.6 tonnes MSO - 48.6 tonnes DMSO - 51 tonnes
Brake type:	Air, EP regenerative	Air, EP regenerative	Air, EP regenerative
Bogie type:	Bombardier B5005	Bombardier B5005	Bombardier B5005
Power unit:	1 x Cummins QSK9R of 560kW (750hp) per car	1 x Cummins QSK9R of 560kW (750hp) per car	1 x Cummins QSK9R of 560kW (750hp) per car
Transmission:	Electric 8 x Alstom Onix 800 per train	Electric 8 x Alstom Onix 800 per train	Electric 10 x Alstom Onix 800 per train
Horsepower:	3,000hp (2,237kW)	3,000hp (2,237kW)	3,750hp (2,796kW)
Max speed:	125mph (201km/h)	125mph (201km/h)	125mph (201km/h)
Operating range:	1,350 miles (2,173km)	1,350 miles (2,173km)	1,350 miles (2,173km)
Route availability:	2	2	2
Coupling type:	Dellner 12	Dellner 12	Dellner 12
Multiple restriction:	Class 222/1 only	Class 222/4 or 222/9 only	Class 222/4 or 222/9 only
Door type:	Single leaf swing plug	Single leaf swing plug	Single leaf swing plug
Body construction:	Steel	Steel	Steel
Owner:	HSBC	HSBC	HSBC
Operator:	Hull Trains	East Midlands Trains	East Midlands Trains

Left: *Soon after Hull Trains introduced the 'Pioneer' fleet it was agreed to name each set after a pioneer of Hull. The names, in stick-on style, are applied to both driving cars. The 'plates' also carry the Hull Trains and FirstGroup logo and the 'Pioneer' legend.* **John Wills**

222/9 'Meridian' (8-car)
222001 - 222007
2004-2005
Bombardier Transportation, Brugge
DMRFO+MFO+MFO+
MSRMB+MSO+MSO+
MSO+DMSO
DMRFO - 60241 - 60147
MFO - 60441 - 60447
MFO - 60341 - 60347
MSRMB - 60621 - 60627
MSO - 60561 - 60567
MSO - 60551 - 60557
MSO - 60541 - 60547
DMSO - 60161 - 60167
Driving - 78ft 2in (23.85m)
Int - 78ft 2in (23.85m)
12ft 4in (3.75m)
8ft 11in (2.73m)
Total - 106F/304S
DMRFO - 22F
MFO - 42F
MFO - 42F
MSRMB - 62S
MSO - 68S
MSO - 68S
MSO - 68S
DMSO - 38S
2+1F, 2+2S
Within set
8 per unit
Total - 395.6 tonnes
DMRFO - 52.8 tonnes
MFO - 48.2 tonnes
MFO - 48.2 tonnes
MSRMB - 49.6 tonnes
MSO - 48.6 tonnes
MSO - 48.6 tonnes
MSO - 48.6 tonnes
DMSO - 51.0 tonnes
Air, EP regenerative
Bombardier B5005
1 x Cummins QSK9R of
560kW (750hp) per car
Electric 16 x Alstom Onix
800 per train
6,000hp (4,474kW)
125mph (201km/h)
1,350 miles (2,173km)
4
Dellner 12
Class 222/4 or 222/9 only
Single leaf swing plug
Steel
HSBC
East Midlands Trains

Right: *The five-car Class 222s emerged in autumn 2006 when one MSO from each nine-car set was inserted behind the DMSO vehicle of a four-car set, increasing seating by 69 per train. Set No 222013 is seen at St Pancras.* **Author**

When Midland Mainline and Hull Trains ordered new stock, Bombardier's 'Voyager' style product was ordered. This time a more luxurious product with improved seating was built, solely at the Brugge plant.

Hull Trains operates four 4-car sets and MML three batches (seven 8-car, seven 5-car and eight 4-car sets). The body structure of these sets differs slightly from the Virgin product.

All trains are maintained by Bombardier under contract at either Crofton or Central Rivers. Hull Trains sets are finished in green and grey livery, while the MML sets are finished in blue and white.

On the MML, originally seven 9-car sets were built, but these were reformed to give one MSO to an equal number of sets during peak periods.

Under the 2007 franchise changes, MML's routes were transferred to East Midlands Trains, a part of Stagecoach Rail. From early November, sets then started to appear in the new company colours based on the South West Trains style. The first set to be repainted was No 222017.

Above & Below: *The East Midlands Trains '222s' have different style driving cars at either end of the train, reflecting the internal layout. Above is the DMSO with five saloon windows, whereas the DMRFO has only four window positions; the window directly behind the front passenger door is missing and the space inside is taken by the first class catering area. The equipment positions are the same as on Class 220/221 stock, and a yellow cover to the BSI coupler is provided to indicate the first class end of the train. The actual nose end structure on the Class 222 breed is much improved to that of the Class 220 and 221 being more streamlined and having an under-coupling valance. Both:* **Author**

Left: *With both the East Midlands Trains and Hull Trains sets being of the non-tilt type, the smaller lightweight bogies are used. Intermediate MSO No 60541 from eight-car set 222001 is illustrated. These vehicles have seven large and one small windows on this side, while electronic route, next stop and destination indicators are provided, seen here between the near passenger door and first window. Passenger doors are operated locally, but automatically close after a pre-determined time.* **Author**

Left Middle: *First class interior, showing the high quality high-back seats, each seat has a table, with the airline-style seats also having a fixed table rather than a fold-down table. Curtains are provided and diffused lighting giving a very pleasing travelling atmosphere. An MFO from set No 220001 is illustrated.* **Author**

Below: *The East Midlands Trains 'Meridian' sets are allocated on paper to Central Rivers depot, Burton-on-Trent, operated by Bombardier Transportation, but in practice the sets are stabled at Derby. The Class 222s share operations on all the EMT main line routes with HST stock, the five-car sets tend to be used on the stopping services and the eight-car formations on the principal fast services. Full at-seat catering in first class is possible from the kitchens on the 222s. Four-car set No 222022 is seen at Derby forming a stopping service to London.* **Author**

Above: *The four Class 222 'Pioneer' units, operated by Hull Trains on its dedicated Hull-King's Cross service are high-quality sets, derived from the MML fleet in external design. First Class seating is provided on one driving car, with the other three cars set out for standard class travel. The middle of the three vehicles includes a buffet. The sets are finished in mid-green and silver livery with yellow ends. First class is identified by a yellow cant rail band and yellow plate on the coupling head. All sets are allocated to Bombardier's Crofton depot near Wakefield. All sets are named after local personalities from the Hull area. Set No 222104 is illustrated at Doncaster.* **John Wills**

Right Middle: *The 'Pioneer' first class interior layout is in the 2+1 style, with each seat having a good size table. The interior ambience is improved by the provision of curtains and a sympathetic choice of seat and floor colouring. A full 'at-seat' service is offered to first class travellers.* **Brian Morrison**

Right Bottom: *Standard class accommodation on the 'Pioneer' fleet is provided in the 2+2 style, with a mix of airline and group seating. Comfort is improved by good lighting, luggage racks and hinged armrests to all seats, assisting passengers gaining access to window seats. Power sockets are provided throughout for telephone and laptop computer charging.* **Brian Morrison**

Departmental DMUs

Departmental DMU stock

Number	Former number	Type	Use	Set No.
975042	55019	DMB	Sandite unit	960015
977391	51433	DM	Ultrasonic test train power	901001
977392	53167	DM	Ultrasonic test train power	901001
977693	53222	DM	Iris 2 test unit	901002
977694	53338	DM	Iris 2 test unit	901002
977723	55021	DMB	Sandite/service unit	960021
977858	55024	DMB	Sandite/service unit	960010
977859	55025	DMB	Sandite/service unit	960011
977860	55028	DMB	Sandite/service unit	960012
977866	55030	DMB	Sandite/service unit	960013
977870	60660	TS	Sandite/de-icing unit	930301
977873	55022	DMB	Sandite/service unit	960014
977939	60145	DMB	Sandite/de-icing unit	930301
977940	60149	DMB	Sandite/de-icing unit	930301
977968	55029	DMB	Driver training unit	-
977975	55027	DMB	Severn Tunnel emergency unit	960302
977976	55031	DMB	Severn Tunnel emergency unit	960303
977987	51371	DMB	Water spray unit	960301
977988	51413	DMB	Water spray unit	960301
977992	51375	IMV	Water spray unit	960301
999660	-	DM	Track assessment unit	950001
999661	-	DM	Track assessment unit	950001
999700	-	DM	Track assessment/recording	-
999701	-	DM	Track assessment/recording	-
999800	-	DM	Track assessment/recording	-
999801	-	DM	Track assessment/recording	-

Fact File

Over the years a number of obsolete operational passenger DMU vehicles have been taken into departmental or service stock and operated for various non-passenger functions, such as the former BR Research or Network Rail.

The two principal uses for departmental DMU stock are for Network Rail track assessment trains and sandite/service units.

Vehicles carry a six-digit vehicle number and many carry six-digit, class-prefixed unit numbers. The majority of vehicles are from first-generation DMMU vehicles, however in more recent times purpose-built stock has started to emerge. This started in 1987 when a two class Class 150 style unit was purpose built as a track recording unit and more recently four vehicles (two 2-car units) have been supplied by Plasser & Theurer of Austria.

Left: *The former Class 121 and 122 'Bubble' cars feature strongly in the departmental listings, as these twin-cabbed cars are ideally suited to specialist roles. Track assessment and recording, including photography of the network has been carried out in recent years using these vehicles under the Network Rail and Carillion Rail banner. These vehicles are well suited for driver route or refresher training and some have stepped seats in the former passenger saloon for this role. No 977968 operated by Carillion Rail is seen from its non-brake-van end at Dawlish during a driver's route training run on the Exeter-Plymouth line. This vehicle sports marker/tail lights and a headlight. Note the middle window is fitted with a windscreen wiper.* **Author**

Left Bottom: *Two ex-Class 121s, Nos 977975/976 are heavily modified as Severn Tunnel Emergency Rescue vehicles. Painted in NR yellow and kept close to the tunnel, the cars have illuminated drop-down sides and can effect a 'train to train' passenger transfer if a train was disabled within the tunnel. With windows boarded against vandalism, the cars are seen at Severn Tunnel Junction.* **Nathan Williamson**

Above: *A very popular 'Bubble' car is No 960012, rebuilt by Crewe from DMB No 55028. It is now based at Salisbury on South West Trains and used for drivers' and conductors' route training. Its interior has been modified to a classroom with stepped seating allowing a good view of the road ahead for up to 12 trainees. The vehicle is finished in full SWT blue livery and is named* John Cameron *(after a director of the company and owner of A4 No 60009). It is shown from its exhaust (brake) end at Salisbury.* **Author**

Right Middle: *Unit No 901002 is formed of Driving Motor cars 977693 and 977694, which are ex Class 101 rebuilds. The set, painted in Network Rail yellow and based at the RTC Derby is known as Iris II and used for radio strength reception tests. The set retains vacuum brakes, sports extra nose end jumpers and can be found operating anywhere in the UK. The set is scheduled for early withdrawal.* **Author**

Right Bottom: *Set No 901001 is a heavily rebuilt ex-Class 101 pair of driving cars now fitted with air brakes and internally fitted out as staff mess and riding accommodation. The two vehicles form the Ultrasonic Test Unit, the actual test car of which is No 999602, a rebuilt ex REP emu vehicle (and illustrated in the departmental emu section). The unit with Group Standard marker light clusters is seen in Railtrack livery, today it carries standard Network Rail yellow.* **Author**

Inset Left: *Detail of 'bolt-on' equipment carried on the front of car No 977391 to illuminate and film the track. With this attached the set cannot be coupled to any other vehicle.* **Nathan Williamson**

Left Top: *The sole surviving departmental vehicle modified from a Gloucester Class 122 DMBS is No 975042 (960015) which was rebuilt from car No 55019. It is now painted in Network Rail yellow livery and modified for sandite laying. In keeping with the majority of retained 'heritage' DMMU vehicles it is usually kept at Aylesbury. The vehicle is seen from its brake or exhaust end in this view. Note the 'trip cock' beam on the leading bogie allowing operation over the LUL-controlled lines in the Chiltern area.*
Brian Morrison

Left Second: *Rebuilt from Pressed Steel-built Class 121 DMBS No 55022, departmental No 977873 or set No 960014 is also allocated to Aylesbury and available for Sandite and rail cleaning use. This unit is painted in 1970s BR blue-grey livery, has a sealed-up route indicator, standard headlight, dual marker/tail lights and a radio aerial on the roof. Some minor body changes were made in the centre of the vehicle to accommodate a ventilation grille.*
Nathan Williamson

Left Third and Left Bottom: *Only one three-car departmental DMMU is in use, operated by Chiltern Railways and Network Rail as set No 960301. Formed of three former Class 117 driving vehicles, the set is used as a 'Water-Jetting Unit' for rail head cleaning. It is allocated to Aylesbury. This is a very interesting unit, as the middle vehicle, No 977992 is actually rebuilt driving vehicle No 51375, with the cab end removed and a standard corridor end added, thus making it an intermediate coach, fitted with power equipment. The set is painted in BR lined green livery and has had a number of structural modifications made. The view third left shows the set stabled at Aylesbury, while the view below shows the former driving end on the now intermediate coach 977992. A new roller shutter door has been installed at the near end to load commodities.*
Brian Morrison and Nathan Williamson

Above: *Two special bodyshells were built alongside the Class 150/1 production run at BREL York in the late 1980s and transferred to the RTC Derby where the pair were fitted out as a state-of-the art Track Assessment Train. One vehicle, the nearest in the view above, retains virtually standard window positions, while the other coach is to a special design incorporating instrumentation equipment, both hinged and sliding doors are provided on this vehicle. The set is now painted in Network Rail yellow and allocated to the RTC Derby. During the course of the year the set traverses most lines in the UK. Some revisions to the window positions were made to the instrumentation vehicle in late 2005 when an extra window was installed to the left of the two equipment doors.* **Author**

Below: *Allocated classification 960 are two twin-car sets formed 999700-01 and 999800-01; these are the very latest in track assessment technology. 999700-01 is a Plasser & Theurer UFM160-1 and 999800-01 is a Plasser & Theurer EM-SAT 100/RT. Both are based at the RTC Derby and look very continental in their outward appearance. Set No 999700-01 is seen at Ipswich.* **Author**

Sub class:	313/0	313/1
Number range:	313018-313064	313101-313134
Former number range:	-	313001-313034
Introduced:	1976-1977	As 313/1 - 1997-2002
Built/rebuilt by:	BREL York	As 313/1 - Adtranz/Bombardier Ilford
Formation:	DMSO+PTSO+BDMSO	DMSO+PTSO+BDMSO
Vehicle numbers:	DMSO - 62546-62592	DMSO - 62529-62562
	PTSO - 71230-71276	PTSO - 71213-71246
	BDMSO - 62610-62656	BDMSO - 62593-62626
Set length:	199ft 6in (60.83m)	199ft 6in (60.83m)
Vehicle length:	DMSO/BDMSO - 64ft 11^{1}/2in (19.80m)	DMSO/BDMSO - 64ft 11^{1}/2in (19.80m)
	PTSO - 65ft 4^{1}/4in (19.92m)	PTSO - 65ft 4^{1}/4in (19.92m)
Height:	11ft 9in (3.58m)	11ft 9in (3.58m)
Width:	9ft 3in (2.82m)	9ft 3in (2.82m)
Seating:	Total: 231S	Total: 228S
	DMSO - 74S	DMSO - 74S
	PTSO - 83S	PTSO - 80S
	BDMSO - 74S	BDMSO - 74S
Internal layout:	2+2/2+3 high density	2+2/2+3 high density
Gangway:	Within set, emergency end doors	Within set, emergency end doors
Toilets:	Not fitted	Not fitted
Weight:	Total - 104.5 tonnes	Total - 104.5 tonnes
	DMSO - 36 tonnes	DMSO - 36 tonnes
	PTSO - 31 tonnes	PTSO - 31 tonnes
	BDMSO - 37.5 tonnes	BDMSO - 37.5 tonnes
Brake type:	Air (Westcode), rheostatic	Air (Westcode), rheostatic
Bogie type:	BX1	BX1
Power collection:	25kV ac overhead &	25kV ac overhead &
	750V dc third rail	750V dc third rail
Traction motor type:	8 x GEC G310AZ	8 x GEC G310AZ
Horsepower:	880hp (656kW)	880hp (656kW)
Max speed:	75mph (121km/h)	75mph (121km/h)
Coupling type:	Outer - Tightlock	Outer - Tightlock
	Inner - bar	Inner - bar
Multiple restriction:	Within class only	Within class only
Door type:	Bi-parting sliding	Bi-parting sliding
Special features:		CCTV
Total sets in traffic:	41 sets	23 sets
Construction:	Steel frame, aluminium alloy body	Steel frame, aluminium alloy body
Owner:	HSBC	HSBC
Operator:	First Capital Connect	Transport for London
Sub-class differences:	As built units (refurbished), originally for Great Northern electrification	Refurbished sets for TfL services Fitted with extra shoegear

Electric Multiple-Units

Below: *First Capital Connect presently operates a fleet of 41 Class 313/0s on the Great Northern ac/dc electrified network. The third rail power is only used on the Drayton Park-Moorgate section. Carrying the latest FCC livery, set Nos. 313062 and 313042 stand at Hornsey depot.* **Author**

Fact File

This was the first production order for 1972-design stock, devised from the prototype PEP unit. Originally all sets were used on the Great Northern electrified suburban system, but later a number of sets were transferred to the North London Line and now operate as well on the West London Line.

The largest part of the fleet - 313/0 still remain on the now First Capital Connect-operated suburban network from Kings Cross, are painted in FCC colours. TfL sets are painted in mauve and green. Dual-voltage operation is retained on all sets.

Above: *The TfL Class 313/1s presently allocated to Willesden operate on the Euston-Watford, Stratford-Richmond and Willesden Junction-Clapham Junction routes. All sets have extra shoegear to operate, carried on the inner bogie to assist in bridging gaps in some areas. Overhead power equipment is retained and fully functional, although seldom used. Due to the routes operated, internal CCTV has been fitted. Set No 313117 stops at Kensington Olympia while forming a Willesden Junction-Clapham Junction service.* **Author**

Right Middle: *Interiors of the TfL 313/1s are not in good condition; much vandalism is experienced on the routes operated and no internal refurbishment has been carried out. Seats are still of the low-back type fitted with loose cushions. Most seats are in groups and laid out in the 2+3 high-density style. Interior of No 313118 is illustrated.* **Author**

Right Bottom: *The intermediate PTSO (Pantograph Trailer Standard Open) carries the transformer, seen in this view directly below the near set of passenger doors. The wide panel of bodyside between the first set of doors and the two smaller windows allows the high-tension (25kV ac power cables) space to go from the roof to the underframe and transformer. Passenger doors are operated locally by push-buttons with a door release light (orange) located at cant rail height in the middle of the vehicle length. Car No 71229 from set 313117 is illustrated.* **Author**

Number range:	314201-314216
Introduced:	1979-1980
Built/rebuilt by:	BREL York
Formation:	DMSO+PTSO+DMSO
Vehicle numbers:	DMSO - 64583-64614
	PTSO - 71450-71465
Set length:	199ft 6in (60.83m)
Vehicle length:	DMSO - 64ft 11^{1}/$_{2}$in (19.80m)
	PTSO - 65ft 4^{1}/$_{4}$in (19.92m)
Height:	11ft 6^{1}/$_{2}$in (3.58m)
Width:	9ft 3in (2.82m)
Seating:	Total: 212S
	DMSO - 68S
	PTSO - 76S
	DMSO - 68S*
Internal layout:	2+3 high density *
Gangway:	Within set (emergency end doors)
Toilets:	Not fitted
Weight:	Total: 102.5tonnes
	DMSO - 34.5 tonnes
	PTSO - 33 tonnes
	DMSO - 34.5 tonnes
Brake type:	Air (Westcode), rheostatic
Bogie type:	BX1
Power collection:	25kV ac overhead
Traction motor type:	314201-314206 - 8 x Brush TM61-53
	314207-314216 - 8 x GEC G310AZ
Horsepower:	880hp (656kW)
Max speed:	75mph (121km/h)
Coupling type:	Outer - Tightlock, Inner - bar
Multiple restriction:	Within class only
Door type:	Bi-parting sliding
Total sets in traffic:	16
Construction:	Steel frame, aluminium alloy body
Owner:	Angel Trains
Operator:	First ScotRail
Note:	

Fact File

Built as inner-suburban stock for the Glasgow area, these are very similar to the previously covered Class 313s but are ac power pick up only. The sets were built at BREL York and were delivered between May and July 1979, entering passenger service in October the same year.

As with the Class 313s, these sets were required to operate through tunnel sections in the central Glasgow area, and to provide an emergency egress, end doors were provided.

Seating is provided in the 2+2/2+3 high-density mode with two pairs of wide double-leaf sliding doors on each vehicle, allowing rapid entry/exit of passengers at peak times.

To meet the BRB dual supply of traction equipment, the first six units of this order were equipped with Brush equipment, and the remainder GEC.

Originally the sets were painted in BR blue/grey 'Trans-Clyde' livery; this subsequently changed to Strathclyde orange and more recently carmine and cream.

All sets are now allocated to Glasgow Shields Road.

* Set 314203 has an ex-Class 507 DMSO (64426, renumbered to 64588) seating 74S and fitted with trial seating.

Below: *The 16 members of Class 314, allocated to Glasgow Shields Road depot are painted in First ScotRail carmine and cream livery and used on services principally working through the Glasgow low-level routes. Front-end emergency doors are provided. Set No 314206 is illustrated arriving at Glasgow Central. Front-end equipment conforms to the standard 1972-design style.* **Author**

Above: *The two driving cars of the Class 314 fleet classified as Driving Motor Standard Open (DMSO) are identical, seating 68 in the 2+3 high-density style using low-back seats. Passenger access is by two pairs of sliding doors, released by the conductor/driver and locally operated. Standard orange 'door release' lights are provided in the middle of each vehicle at cant rail height. As these sets are not fitted with air conditioning, opening hopper windows are provided. Set No 314209 is illustrated with car No 64599 nearest the camera.*
Bill Wilson

Right Middle: *The intermediate Class 314 vehicle is a Pantograph Trailer Standard Open (PTSO), which houses the power collection device at one end. To facilitate the down-drop of cabling associated with the pantograph a slight revision to the window layout is made to provide a solid section. This detail is shown in this view of car 71459. The small rotary valve on the close end of this vehicle at sole bar height is a local control for the first pair of doors, while the box attached to the near bogie is part of the pantograph dropping device for neutral sections.*
Bill Wilson

Right Bottom: *Class 314 interior. These are still based on the original design, but are likely to be refurbished in the near future. Seating is in the 2+3 facing style. The door vestibule areas are finished in yellow, while the rest of the saloon has cream wall panels.* **Bill Wilson**

Class 315

Number range:	315801-315861
Introduced:	1980-1981
Built/rebuilt by:	BREL York
Formation:	DMSO+TSO+PTSO+DMSO
Vehicle numbers:	DMSO - 64461-64582
	TSO - 71281-71341
	PTSO - 71389-71449
Set length:	264ft 10in (80.72m)
Vehicle length:	DMSO - 64ft 11 1/2in (19.80m)
	TSO/PTSO - 65ft 4 1/4in (19.92m)
Height:	11ft 9in (3.58m)
Width:	9ft 3in (2.82m)
Seating:	Total: 318S
	DMSO - 74S
	TSO - 86S
	PTSO - 84S
	DMSO - 74S
Internal layout:	2+2/2+3 high density
Gangway:	Within set, end emergency door
Toilets:	Not fitted
Weight:	Total: 127.5 tonnes
	DMSO - 35 tonnes
	TSO - 25.5 tonnes
	PTSO - 32 tonnes
	DMSO - 35 tonnes
Brake type:	Air (Westcode), rheostatic
Bogie type:	BX1
Power collection:	25kV ac overhead
Traction motor type:	315801-315841 - 8 x Brush TM61-53
	315842-315861 - 8 x GEC G310AZ
Horsepower:	880hp (656kW)
Max speed:	75mph (121km/h)
Coupling type:	Outer - Tightlock, Inner - Bar
Multiple restriction:	Within class
Door type:	Bi-parting sliding
Total sets in traffic:	61
Construction:	Steel frame, aluminium alloy body
Owner:	HSBC
Operator	'one' Railway

Fact File

The modernisation of the Liverpool Street suburban lines from 1980 saw a fleet of 61 four-car high-density sets built to 1972 design at BREL York.

The sets with accommodation for 320, plus an equal number standing replaced the Class 306 sliding door sets firstly on the Shenfield route and then other inner-suburban lines.

Designed for ac only operation, the sets were delivered in BR blue/grey livery, this later gave way to Network South East colours and following privatisation the colours of Great Eastern and more recently 'one' Railway. All sets are allocated to Ilford depot, with the first 43 deployed 'on paper' on Great Eastern services and the remainder on West Anglia duties.

Below: *The massive depot facility at Ilford is the base for all 61 Class 315s, but due to space limitations, out-basing is needed for many sets. Painted in 'one' Railway turquoise and striped livery, set No 315817 is seen inside the shed. The front ends of these sets include the emergency door with horns above, lights on the front end and the Tightlock coupler below providing physical, air and electrical connections.* **Author**

Electric Multiple-Units

Right Above: *Although the base livery for Class 315 sets is 'one' Railway turquoise a number of one-off and display liveries are to be found, with some sets in early 2007 sporting white base paint with no branding, as shown on set No 315851 at Seven Kings. It is expected that full refurbishment of the 315s will commence in the 2007-08 budget.* **Author**

Right Middle: *The seating on the Class 315s is the original style low-back seat set out in the 2+2 and 2+3 high-density style. Refurbishment will likely see new seats with higher backs fitted (perhaps like the Class 455s), but the same high-density configuration will be retained.* **Author**

Below: *Class 315 Pantograph Trailer Standard Open (PTSO), viewed from the non-pantograph end. The main transformer can be seen under the far end door opening, with the pantograph on the roof above. Other underframe equipment consists of switch gear, brake, heat and lighting units. This vehicle displays the latest 'one' Railway turquoise and black livery, off-set both ends by pink, yellow, turquoise, green and blue horizontal bands. Doors are finished in light blue; these are unlocked by the driver, opened by the passenger by door-side push buttons and closed and locked by the driver. A standard orange door release light is located at cant rail height in the middle of the vehicle.* **Author**

	317/1	317/5	317/6
Sub class:	317/1	317/5	317/6
Number range:	317337-317348	317501-317515	317649-317672
			317349-317372
Previous numbers:	-	From 317301-317320	
Introduced:	1981-1982	1981-1982	1985-1986
Refurbished:	-	from 2005	1999-2000
Built by:	DTSO, MSO - BREL York TCO - BREL Derby	DTSO, MSO - BREL York TCO - BREL Derby	BREL York
Refurbished by:	-	Ilford	Railcare Wolverton
Formation:	DTSO(A)+MSO+ TCO+DTSO(B)	DTSO(A)+MSO+ TCO+DTSO(B)	DTS+MSO+TSO+DTCO
Vehicle numbers:	DTSO(A) - 77036-77047 MSO - 62671-62708 TCO - 71613-71624 DTSO(B) - 77084-77095	DTSO(A) - 77001-77024 MSO - 62661-62680 TCO - 71577-71596 DTO(B) - 77048-77067	DTSO - 77200-77219, 77280-77283 MSO - 62846 - 62865, 62886-62889 TSO - 71734 - 71753, 71762-71765 DTCO- 77220 - 77239, 77284-77287
Set length:	265ft 6in (80.94m)	265ft 6in (80.94m)	265ft 6in (80.94m)
Vehicle length:	DTSO(A)- 65ft ^{3}/$_4$in (19.83m) MSO - 65ft 4^1/$_4$in (19.92m) TCO - 65ft 4^1/$_4$in (19.92m) DTSO(B) 65ft ^{3}/$_4$in (19.83m)	DTSO(A)- 65ft ^{3}/$_4$in (19.83m) MSO - 65ft 4^1/$_4$in (19.92m) TCO - 65ft 4^1/$_4$in (19.92m) DTSO(B) 65ft ^{3}/$_4$in (19.83m)	DTSO(A)- 65ft ^{3}/$_4$in (19.83m) MSO - 65ft 4^1/$_4$in (19.92m) TCO - 65ft 4^1/$_4$in (19.92m) DTSO(B) 65ft ^{3}/$_4$in (19.83m)
Height:	12ft 1^1/$_2$in (3.70m)	12ft 1^1/$_2$in (3.70m)	12ft 1^1/$_2$in (3.70m)
Width:	9ft 3in (2.82m)	9ft 3in (2.82m)	9ft 3in (2.82m)
Seating:	Total - 22F/269S DTSO(A) - 74S MSO - 79S TCO - 22F/46S DTSO(B) - 70S	Total - 291S DTSO(A) - 74S MSO - 79S TCO - 68S (declass) DTSO(B) - 70S	Total - 24F/200S DTSO - 64S MSO - 70S TSO - 62S DTCO - 24F/48S
Internal layout:	2+2F/2+3S	2+2/2+3	2+2F/2+2S
Gangway:	Throughout	Throughout	Throughout
Toilets:	TCO - 2	TCO - 2	TSO - 2
Weight:	Total - 137 tonnes DTSO(A) - 29.5 tonnes MSO - 49 tonnes TCO - 29 tonnes DTSO(B) - 29.5 tonnes	Total - 137 tonnes DTSO(A) - 29.5 tonnes MSO - 49 tonnes TCO - 29 tonnes DTSO(B) - 29.5 tonnes	Total - 137 tonnes DTSO - 29.5 tonnes MSO - 49 tonnes TSO - 29 tonnes DTCO - 29.5 tonnes
Brake type:	Air	Air	Air
Bogie type:	Powered - BREL BP20 Trailer - BREL BT13	Powered - BREL BP20 Trailer - BREL BT13	Powered - BREL BP20 Trailer - BREL BT13
Power collection:	25kV ac overhead	25kV ac overhead	25kV ac overhead
Traction motor type:	4 x GEC G315BZ	4 x GEC G315BZ	4 x GEC G315BZ
Horsepower:	1,000hp (746kW)	1,000hp (746kW)	1,000hp (746kW)
Max speed:	100mph (161km/h)	100mph (161km/h)	100mph (161km/h)
Coupling type:	Outer - Tightlock Inner – Bar	Outer - Tightlock Inner – Bar	Outer - Tightlock Inner – Bar
Multiple restriction:	Within class	Within class	Within class
Door type:	Bi-parting sliding	Bi-parting sliding	Bi-parting sliding
Special fittings:	Pressure ventilated	Pressure ventilated	Convection heating
Total sets in traffic:	12	15	24
Construction:	Steel	Steel	Steel
Owner:	Angel Trains	Angel Trains	Angel Trains
Operator:	FCC	'one' Railway	'one' Railway
Sub Class detail:	Phase 1 sets	Phase 1 sets	Phase 2 refurbished

Left: *A small number of Class 317s are named, these being applied in standard cast format. The plate of No 317892 Ilford Depot is shown. This was applied in September 2006 to mark the achievement of Ilford depot taking over the entire '317' maintenance.* **Author**

Electric Multiple-Units

317/7	317/8
317708-317732 (9 units)	317881-317892
317308-317332 (random)	317321-317336
1981-82	1981-82
2000	2006-2007
BREL York	DTSO, MSO - BREL York
	TCO - BREL Derby
Railcare Wolverton	Ilford
DTSO+MSO+TSO+DTCO	DTSO+MSO+TCO+DTSO
DTSO - 77007-77031 series	DTSO - 77020-77035
MSO - 62668-62692 series	MSO - 62681-62696
TSO - 71584-71608 series	TCO - 71597-71612
DTCO - 77055-77079 series	DTSO - 77068-77083

265ft 6in (80.94m)	265ft 6in (80.94m)
DTSO(A)- 65ft ^{3}/$_4$in (19.83m)	DTSO(A)- 65ft ^{3}/$_4$in (19.83m)
MSO - 65ft 4^1/$_4$in (19.92m)	MSO - 65ft 4^1/$_4$in (19.92m)
TSO - 65ft 4^1/$_4$in (19.92m)	TCO - 65ft 4^1/$_4$in (19.92m)
DTCO 65ft ^{3}/$_4$in (19.83m)	DTSO(B) 65ft ^{3}/$_4$in (19.83m)
12ft 1^1/$_2$in (3.70m)	12ft 1^1/$_2$in (3.70m)
9ft 3in (2.82m)	9ft 3in (2.82m)
Total - 22F/172S	Total - 20F/265S
DTS0(A) - 52S	DTSO(A) - 74S
MSO - 62S	MSO - 79S
TSO - 42S	TCO - 20F/42S
DTCO - 22F/16S	DTSO(B) - 70S
2+1F/2+2S	2+2F/2+3S
Throughout	Throughout
TSO- 2	TCO - 2
Total - 144.5	Total - 137 tonnes
DTS - 31.4 tonnes	DTSO(A) - 29.5 tonnes
MSO - 51.3 tonnes	MSO - 49 tonnes
TSO - 30.2 tonnes	TCO - 29 tonnes
DTC - 31.6 tonnes	DTSO(B) - 29.5 tonnes
Air	Air
Powered - BREL BP20	Powered - BREL BP20
Trailer - BREL BT13	Trailer - BREL BT13
25kV ac overhead	25kV ac overhead
4 x GEC G315BZ	4 x GEC G315BZ
1,000hp (746kW)	1,000hp (746kW)
100mph (161km/h)	100mph (161km/h)
Outer - Tightlock	Outer - Tightlock
Inner – Bar	Inner – Bar
Within class	Within class
Bi-parting sliding	Bi-parting sliding
Pressure ventilated	Pressure ventilated
9	12
Steel	Steel
Angel Trains	Angel Trains
'one' Railway	'one' Railway
Stansted Express units	Stansted Express 'standard' units

Right: *Class 317 front end detail: A-warning horns, B-route/destination display, C-marker light, D-tail light, E-headlight, F-cab ventilation, G-Tightlock coupler with electric and pneumatic box below, H-drum switch (controlling electrical connections of coupling. Set No 317510, renumbered from 317313 stands inside Ilford depot.* **Author**

Originally introduced as the 'Bed-Pan' electrics for the Bedford-St Pancras/Moorgate electrification, a total of 48 sets was originally built. The class saw a protracted entry into service as these were the first sets to be operated under driver-only operation.

Soon after introduction a follow-on order for 24 'phase 2' units for use on the Great Northern route was made, these were slightly different in exterior appearance.

After Class 319s were introduced on 'Thameslink' services, the '317s' transferred to the Euston-Birmingham route, but after a short time the sets were replaced by '321s' and they moved to West Anglia workings, some operating for a short time on LTS services.

The sets have now settled down to working mainly for 'one' Railway on West Anglia services and for First Capital Connect on outer suburban routes.

Nine units were rebuilt in 2000 with new front ends and revised seating to provide a 'quality' service on the developing Stansted Express service.

Today five sub-classes of '317s' are to be found.

Diesel Multiple-Units

Left Top: *First Capital Connect (FCC) operates a fleet of 12 Class 317/1 sets (317337-348) based at Hornsey. Painted in the previous TOCs purple-livery the sets work on outer-suburban duties alongside Class 365 sets. FCC livery is expected to be applied soon. These units retain first and standard class seating and are original phase 1 'Bed-Pan' units.* **Derek Porter**

Left Second: *Another adaptation of a small number of the original phase 1 units is a batch of 12 Class 317/8 sets, now operated by 'one' Railway on Stansted Airport services and painted in Stansted Airport turquoise livery. These sets have been refurbished by Ilford with revised interiors, but still retain the Class 317 phase 1 trade mark of steel-filled hopper windows. Set No 317883 is illustrated from its DTSO(A) end. The front end style of these sets, based on the proposed 'standard multiple-unit' soon fell out of favour and when the second batch of Class 317s emerged a more pleasing front end style was adopted.*
Brian Morrison

Left third: *In 1985 when the follow-on order for Class 317s were produced a more air-smoothed front end was adopted, with a rounded cab roof, the application of Group Standard light groups and the horns repositioned below draw-gear height. The vehicle redesign also saw standard opening glazed hopper windows installed and convection heating rather than pressure ventilation fitted. All phase two units are now classified as 317/6, are allocated to Ilford and operate for 'one' Railway. Set No 317666 (the original No 317366) is shown painted in full 'one' Railway livery.*
Brian Morrison

Left Bottom: *One of the most amazing rebuilds of phase 1 Class 317 stock took place at Railcare Wolverton when nine units were rebuilt as Class 317/7. The upgrade work, carried out in 2000 formed a batch of dedicated sets for use on the London Liverpool Street-Stansted Airport route. Interiors were tailored to the needs of airport travellers and catering provided. The most significant change was the replacement of the main windows with glazed hopper units and the total redesign of the front end, incorporating a rounded roof profile with a high-level marker light and revised angled light clusters in an elliptical shape. Sets were repainted in deep turquoise shown on set No 317708.*
Author

Right Top: *Class 317 standard class interior, showing the 2+3 seating layout. The interior shown is a refurbished Class 317/8 for use on the Liverpool Street to Stansted Airport route and incorporated mid blue end and vestibule panels and orange grab poles. When introduced the original batch of Class 317s had a most unusual style of hopper window; rather than being 'filled' with glass, it used metal sheet. In most cases this has been retained and offers a good recognition factor between a phase 1 and phase 2 unit. The phase 2 sets have standard glazed hopper windows.* **Author**

Right Middle: *When in 2000 nine Class 317/1s were rebuilt as Class 317/7s for Stansted Airport service. In addition to Railcare Wolverton re-styling the front ends, the interior accommodation was revised considerably, with high quality seats provided in both standard and first class. This is the first class area, complete with reclining seats, hinged armrests, curtains and new glazed hopper windows. Extra luggage stacks were fitted throughout these units and all seating was provided in the 2+2 style in standard and 2+1 in first.* **Author**

Right Bottom: *Class 317 driving cab. These quite cramped cabs are of typical 1970s-80s BR design, using a GRP moulding for the desk with switches and dials seemingly bolted on where space was available. The brake controller is on the left side of the main desk, with the master switch and power controller to the right. The two indicator dials are for speed (right) and brake pipe, bogie cylinder pressure (left). The desk switches are for frontal lights, cab lighting etc, while push buttons are for door release, door close, pantograph up/down, coupling/uncoupling, one shot sander etc. Windscreen wiper controls are on the flat desk, as are the AWS reset and horn valve. Bolted to the side of the telephone frame is the driver's reminder appliance (DRA). The AWS sunflower indicator is on the right.* **Author**

Number range:	318250-318270
Introduced:	1985-1986
Built/rebuilt by:	BREL York
Formation:	DTSOL+MSOP+DTSO
Vehicle numbers:	DTSOL - 77240-77259/77288
	MSO - 62866-62885/62890
	DTSO - 77260-77279/77289
Vehicle length:	DTSOL/DTSO - 65ft $0^3/_4$in (19.83m)
	MSO - 65ft $4^1/_4$in (19.92m)
Height:	12ft $1^1/_2$in (3.70m)
Width:	9ft 3in (2.82m)
Seating:	Total: 216S
	DTSOL - 66S
	MSO - 79S
	DTSO - 71S
Internal layout:	2+2/2+3 high density
Gangway:	Within set
Toilets:	DTSOL - 1
Weight:	Total: 107.5 tonnes
	DTSOL - 30 tonnes
	MSO - 50.9 tonnes
	DTSO - 26.6 tonnes
Brake type:	Air (Westcode)
Bogie type:	DTSOL/DTSO - BREL BT13
	MSO - BREL BP20
Power collection:	25kV ac overhead
Traction motor type:	4 x Brush TM2141
Horsepower:	1,328hp (996kW)
Max speed:	90mph (145km/h)
Coupling type:	Outer - Tightlock
	Within set - bar
Multiple restriction:	Within type only
Door type:	Bi-parting sliding
Special features:	PA, CCTV, PIS
Total sets in traffic:	21
Construction:	Steel
Owner:	HSBC Rail
Operator:	First ScotRail

Fact File

With authorisation for the electrification of the route from Paisley to Ayr in 1982, came the need in the early 1980s for extra electric stock to operate through services between Glasgow and Ayr.

A batch of 21 trains, of similar appearance to the Class 317s were ordered from BREL, being three-car outer suburban sets with high-density interiors.

The first train of the build was handed over in June 1986, more than a year before electric passenger workings commenced.

The sets have remained in the Glasgow area, but in recent years have been fully refurbished by Hunslet Barclay, Kilmarnock which has included removing the original front gangway connection, thus changing the appearance of these sets completely.

All sets are allocated to Glasgow Shields Road depot and are painted in carmine and cream livery.

Below: *Devoid of its original front end gangway connection, set No 318258 is illustrated in standard carmine and cream livery with cream passenger doors.* **Bill Wilson**

Above: *The intermediate vehicle of the Class 318 fleet is a Motor Standard Open (MSO) which incorporates the power collection pantograph at the end coupled to DTSO vehicle. These vehicles, weighing 50.9 tonnes, carry all power and control equipment in underslung boxes. Vehicles have two pairs of sliding doors which can be locally operated. Car No 62880 is illustrated from the non-pantograph end. The small button on the end of the coach closes and locks the passenger doors locally on the coach.*
Bill Wilson

Right: *When first introduced the Class 318s were fitted with end gangway connections allowing sets to operate in multiple and provide a throughway for passengers and staff. However, upon refurbishment in recent years the gangways were removed and a revised front end was fitted incorporating an extra front cab window and electronic destination and route indicator. The modification work was undertaken at Hunslet-Barclay, Kilmarnock. Front end equipment includes: A-original destination indicator, B-new electronic destination/route indicator, C-new style Group Standard headlight and joint marker/tail light unit, D-former front door position, E-warning horns, F-Tightlock coupling, G-coupling drum switch box, H-emergency manual uncoupling handle.* **Bill Wilson**

	319/0	319/2	319/3
Sub class:	319/0	319/2	319/3
Number range:	319001-319013	319214-319220	319361-319386
Former number range:	-	319014-319020	319161-319186
Introduced:	1987	1987-1988	1990
Rebuilt:	-	1996-1997	1997-1999
Built by:	BREL York	-	-
Rebuilt by:	-	Railcare Wolverton	Alstom Eastleigh
Formation:	DTSO(A)+MSO+ TSOL+DTSO(B)	DTSO+MSO+ TSOL+DTCO	DTSO(A)+MSO+ TSOL+DTSO(B)
Vehicle numbers:	DTSO(A) - 77291-77315(odd) MSO - 62891-62903 TSOL - 71772-71784 DTSO(B) - 77290-77314(even)	DTSO - 77317-77329 (odd) MSO - 62904-62910 TSOL - 71785-71791 DTCO - 77316-77328 (even)	DTSO - 77459-77497, 77973-77983 (odd) MSO - 63043-63062, 63094-63098 TSOL - 71929-71948 71979-71984 DTSO(B) - 77458-77496, 77974-77984 (evens)
Vehicle length:	DTSO(A) - 65ft $^3/_4$in (19.83m) DTSO(B) - 65ft $^3/_4$in (19.83m) MSO - 65ft $4^1/_4$in (19.92m) TSOL - 65ft $4^1/_4$in (19.92m)	DTSO - 65ft $^3/_4$in (19.83m) DTCO - 65ft $^3/_4$in (19.83m) MSO - 65ft $4^1/_4$in (19.92m) TSOL - 65ft $4^1/_4$in (19.92m)	DTSO(A) - 65ft $^3/_4$in (19.83m) DTSO(B) - 65ft $^3/_4$in (19.83m) MSO - 65ft $4^1/_4$in (19.92m) TSOL - 65ft $4^1/_4$in (19.92m)
Height:	11ft 9in (3.58m)	11ft 9in (3.58m)	11ft 9in (3.58m)
Width:	9ft 3in (2.82m)	9ft 3in (2.82m)	9ft 3in (2.82m)
Seating:	Total - 319S DTSO(A) - 82S MSO - 82S TSOL - 77S DTSO(B) - 78S	Total - 18F/212S DTSO - 64S MSO - 60S TSOL - 52S DTCO - 18F/36S	Total - 300S DTSO(A) - 70 MSO - 78S TSOL - 74S DTSO(B) - 78S
Internal layout:	2+2, 2+3	2+1F, 2+2S	2+2, 2+3
Gangway:	Within set, emergency end doors	Within set, emergency end doors	Within set, emergency end doors
Toilets:	TSOL – 2	TSOL – 2	TSOL - 2
Weight:	Total - 136.5 tonnes DTSO(A) - 28.2 tonnes MSO - 49.2 tonnes TSOL - 31 tonnes DTSO(B) - 28.1 tonnes	Total - 142 tonnes DTSO - 28.2 tonnes MSO - 49.2 tonnes TSOL - 31 tonnes DTCO - 28.1 tonnes	Total - 140.3 tonnes DTSO(A) - 29 tonnes MSO - 50.6 tonnes TSOL - 31 tonnes DTSO(B) - 29.7 tonnes
Brake type:	Air (Westcode)	Air (Westcode)	Air (Westcode)
Bogie type:	DTSO, TSOL - BREL T3-7 MSO - BREL P7-4	DTSO, DTCO, TSOL - BREL T3-7 MSO - BREL P7-4	DTSO, TSOL - BREL T3-7 MSO - BREL P7-4
Power collection:	25kV ac overhead and 750V dc third rail	25kV ac overhead and 750V dc third rail	25kV ac overhead and 750V dc third rail
Traction motor type:	4 x GEC G315BZ	4 x GEC G315BZ	4 x GEC G315BZ
Horsepower:	1,326hp (990kW)	1,326hp (990kW)	1,326hp (990kW)
Max speed:	100 mph (161km/h)	100 mph (161km/h)	100 mph (161km/h)
Coupling type:	Outer - Tightlock Inner - bar	Outer - Tightlock Inner - bar	Outer - Tightlock Inner - bar
Multiple restriction:	Within Class 319 series	Within Class 319 series	Within Class 319 series
Door type:	Bi-parting sliding	Bi-parting sliding	Bi-parting sliding
Total sets in traffic:	13	7	26
Owner:	Porterbrook	Porterbrook	Porterbrook
Operator:	Southern, First Capital C	Southern	First Capital Connect
Sub Class differences:	Original phase 1 units	'Brighton Express' sets	FCC 'Metro' units

Electric Multiple-Units

Fact File

Designed especially for the 'Thameslink' operation linking north and south London via Clerkenwell Tunnels and fitted for dual ac/dc operation, the 319s have remained on this route since introduction. Now operated by First Capital Connect, two sub-classes exist.

Southern does, however, operate a small number of sets for domestic duties on outer suburban and Brighton routes, but in the long term it is expected that these sets will be transferred to FCC to strengthen their fleet due to massive passenger growth.

Sets have 2+2 and 2+3 seating, sliding doors and end emergency doors for tunnel working.

Two batches of units were built; phase 1 sets emerged between September 1987 and October 1988, with phase 2 sets entering service between October 1990 and March 1991.

319/4
319421-319460
319021-319060
1988-1989
1997-1999
-
Railcare Wolverton
DTCO+MSO+
TSOL+DTSO
DTCO - 77331-77381
77431-77457 (odd)
MSO - 62911-62974
TSOL - 71792-71879
DTSO - 77330-77380
77430-77456 (evens)

DTCO - 65ft $^3/_4$in (19.83m)
DTSO - 65ft $^3/_4$in (19.83m)
MSO - 65ft $4^1/_4$in (19.92m)
TSOL - 65ft $4^1/_4$in (19.92m)
11ft 9in (3.58m)
9ft 3in (2.82m)
Total: 12F/277S
DTCO - 12F/54S
MSO - 77S
TSOL - 72S
DTSO - 74S
2+2
Within set,
emergency end doors
TSOL - 2
Total - 136.5 tonnes
DTSO(A) - 28.2 tonnes
MSO - 49.2 tonnes
TSOL - 31 tonnes
DTSO(B) - 28.1 tonnes
Air (Westcode)
DTSO, DTCO, TSOL - BREL T3-7
MSO - BREL P7-4

25kV ac overhead and
750V dc third rail
4 x GEC G315BZ
1,326hp (990kW)
100 mph (161km/h)
Outer - Tightlock
Inner - bar
Within Class 319 series
Bi-parting sliding
40
Porterbrook
First Capital Connect
FCC 'CityFlier' units

Right: *Painted in Thameslink
grey and blue livery, Class 319/4
No 319455 passes Flitwick in March
2006. The DTSO vehicle leading has
seating for 74 in the 2+2 low-density
style. This livery is quickly giving
way to the new First Capital Connect
colours.* **John Wills**

Above: *Class 319 front-end layout, showing first phase design. Equipment
positions are the same on second phase. A-group standard light cluster, marker,
head and tail light, B-end emergency door, C-destination and route indicator,
D-warning horn, E-Tightlock coupling, incorporating physical, air and electrical
connections, F-emergency air connection. The front end of No 319455 is
illustrated.* **Author**

Above: *The present fleet of First Capital Connect Class 319/3 units were modified from phase 2 Class 319/2 sets which incorporated a slightly revised front end, with a glass-reinforced plastic surround to the below-drawgear-height front panel; otherwise, these sets were identical in exterior appearance to the earlier 319/0 sets. Painted in a mix of Thameslink and FCC livery, set No 319365 is illustrated from its DTSO(B) end.* **Brian Morrison**

Below: *The first totally refurbished Class 319/4 under the First Capital Connect banner was No 319425, unveiled at Bedford on 26 October 2006. The set has new interiors, revised seating and looks a far cry from the original design. Set No 319425 with its DTSO leading is shown.* **Brian Morrison**

Right Top: *An area of 12 first class seats in the 2+1 low-density layout is provided in the DTCO of FCC refurbished vehicles directly behind the driving cab. All seats have tables and fixed armrests. The internal decor consists of FirstGroup light blue, mauve mottled moquette and pink grab rails and handles. No curtains are provided. Luggage accommodation consists of above seat racks, and between seats. The door at the coach end is into the driving compartment.* **Brian Morrison**

Right Middle & Bottom: *In 2007 a batch of 12 Class 319s was still operated by Southern on domestic services from London Victoria / London Bridge, where the sets' 25kV ac overhead equipment was not used. As First Capital Connect are short of units owing to growth in passenger demand, all Southern '319s' will be transferred to FCC within 12 months when the same number of additional Class 377s are delivered. The Southern sets are painted in green and white livery and are laid out for standard class-only occupation, offering a total of 319 seats per set. On the right is a TSOL vehicle with the toilet at the far end, while below set No 319011 is seen. The Southern Class 319/0 and 319/2 units are allocated to Selhurst. The Class 319/2 sets incorporate 18 first-class seats in one driving car. Some units carry names, applied to the TSOL vehicle. Both:* **Author**

Number range:	320301-320322
Introduced:	1990
Built/rebuilt by:	BREL York
Formation:	DTSO(A)+MSO+DTSO(B)
Vehicle numbers:	DTSO(A) - 77899-77920
	MSO - 63021-63042
	DTSO(B) -77921-77942
Vehicle length:	DTSO(A) - 65ft $^3/_4$in (19.83m)
	MSO - 65ft $4^1/_4$in (19.92m)
	DTSO(B) - 65ft $^3/_4$in (19.83m)
Height:	12ft $4^3/_4$in (3.78m)
Width:	9ft 3in (2.82m)
Seating:	Total: 227S
	DTSO(A) - 76S
	MSO - 76S
	DTSO(B) - 75S
Internal layout:	2+3 high density
Gangway:	Within set
Toilets:	Not fitted
Weight:	Total -114.5 tonnes
	DTSO (A) - 30.7 tonnes
	MSO - 52.1 tonnes
	DTSO(B) - 31.7 tonnes
Brake type:	Air (Westcode)
Bogie type:	DTSO(A), DTSO(B) - BREL T3-7
	MSO - BREL P7-4
Power collection:	25kV ac overhead
Traction motor type:	4 x Brush TM2141B
Horsepower:	1,328hp (996kW)
Max speed:	75mph (121km/h)
Coupling type:	Outer - Tightlock, Inner - bar
Multiple restriction:	Within class
Door type:	Bi-parting sliding
Total sets in traffic:	22
Construction:	Steel
Owner:	HSBC Rail
Operator:	First ScotRail

Fact File

Just at the time the first Class 321 units emerged from BREL York, the BRB sanctioned an order for Scotrail to have 22 three-car sets of similar exterior design but laid out for all-standard-class patronage. The sets were for use on the North Clyde routes.

Assembly followed the phase 1 Class 321s through the works, with the first sets being tested on the East Coast Main Line in the York area in May 1990. Units were allocated to Yoker depot, entering service from August.

The sets are formed with two near identical DTSOs (the 'A' vehicle having wheelchair space and presently identified by a yellow band on the front end). With a MSO with pantograph in the middle, all seating is in 2+3.

When delivered, sets were painted in Strathclyde orange; this has more recently given way to Carmine and cream.

Below: *Viewed from its DTSO(A) end with a yellow band indicating wheelchair space, set No 320308 is seen at Glasgow Central. All equipment on these sets is the same as on Class 321 and 322 units.* **Author**

Above: *The 22 outer-suburban members of the Class 320 fleet are formed with a central power/pantograph vehicle and two Driving Trailer Standard Open (DTSO) vehicles at each end. The sets are not gangwayed, have a full-width driving cab and provide a good quality travelling experience. The sets are allocated to Glasgow Shields Road depot and operate mainly on Ayrshire line services from Glasgow. Sporting a FirstGroup roundel on the front end, set No 320305 is seen at Glasgow Central.* **Bill Wilson**

Right Middle: *The intermediate vehicle is classified Motor Standard Open (MSO) and contained all power, transformer and control equipment in underslung boxes. The vehicle also carries the power collection pantograph. Since the illustration right was taken all vehicles now have contrasting colour (cream) passenger doors to meet the Disability Discrimination Act.* **Author**

Right Bottom: *The interior of the 320 fleet is set out in the high-density 2+3 style, using turquoise seat moquette. The ends of vehicles have murals depicting local Scottish scenes. As no air conditioning is fitted, opening hopper windows are provided in all main windows. Passenger access is by two pairs of sliding doors, with cab access via a single sliding plug door.* **Bill Wilson**

Electric Multiple-Units

	321/3	321/4	321/9
Sub class:	321/3	321/4	321/9
Number range:	321301-321366	321401-321448	321901-321903
Introduced:	1988-1990	1989-1990	1991
Built by:	BREL York	BREL York	BREL York
Facelifted by:	Ilford	Ilford	Ilford
Formation:	DTCO+MSO+TSOL+DTSO	DTCO+MSO+TSOL+DTSO	DTSO(A)+MSO+TSOL+DTSO(B)
Vehicle numbers:	DTCO - 78049-78094, 78131-78150	DTCO - 78095-78130, 78151-78162	DTSO(A) - 77990-77992
	MSO - 62975-63020, 63105-63124	MSO - 63063-63092, 63099-63104, 63125-63136	MSO - 63153-63155
	TSOL - 71880-71925, 71991-72010	TSOL - 71949-71978, 71985-71990, 72011-72022	TSOL - 72128-72130
	DTSO - 77853-77898, 78280-78299	DTSO - 77943-77972, 78274-78279, 78300-78311	DTSO(B) - 77993-77995
Vehicle length:	DTCO - 65ft $^3/_4$in (19.83m)	DTCO - 65ft $^3/_4$in (19.83m)	DTSO - 65ft $^3/_4$in (19.83m)
	MSO - 65ft $4^1/_4$in (19.92m)	MSO - 65ft $4^1/_4$in (19.92m)	MSO - 65ft $4^1/_4$in (19.92m)
	TSOL - 65ft $4^1/_4$in (19.92m)	TSOL - 65ft $4^1/_4$in (19.92m)	TSOL - 65ft $4^1/_4$in (19.92m)
	DTSO - 65ft $^3/_4$in (19.83m)	DTSO - 65ft $^3/_4$in (19.83m)	DTSO - 65ft $^3/_4$in (19.83m)
Height:	12ft $4^3/_4$in (3.78m)	12ft $4^3/_4$in (3.78m)	12ft $4^3/_4$in (3.78m)
Width:	9ft 3in (2.82m)	9ft 3in (2.82m)	9ft 3in (2.82m)
Seating:	Total - 16F/292S	321401-321437 Silverlink	Total - 307S
	DTCO - 16F/57S	Total - 28F/271S	DTSO(A) - 77S
	MSO - 82S	DTCO - 28F/40S	MSO - 79S
	TSOL - 75S	MSO - 79S	TSOL - 74S
	DTSO - 78S	TSOL - 74S	DTSO(B)- 77S
		DTSO - 78S	
		321438-321448 'One' Rly	
		Total - 16F/283S	
		DTCO - 16F/52S	
		MSO - 79S	
		TSOL - 74S	
		DTSO - 78S	
Internal layout:	2+2F/2+3S	2+2F/2+3S	2+3S
Gangway:	Within unit only	Within unit only	Within unit only
Toilets:	TSOL - 2	TSOL - 2	TSOL - 2
Weight:	Total - 137.9 tonnes	Total - 140.4 tonnes	Total - 138 tonnes
	DTCO - 29.7 tonnes	DTCO - 29.8 tonnes	DTCO - 29 tonnes
	MSO - 51.5 tonnes	MSO - 51.6 tonnes	MSO - 51 tonnes
	TSOL - 29.1 tonnes	TSOL - 29.2 tonnes	TSOL - 29 tonnes
	DTSO - 29.7 tonnes	DTSO - 29.8 tonnes	DTSO - 29 tonnes
Brake type:	Air (Westcode)	Air (Westcode)	Air (Westcode)
Bogie type:	MSO - BREL P7-4	MSO - BREL P7-4	MSO - BREL P7-4
	DTCO, DTSO, TSOL - BREL T3-7	DTCO, DTSO, TSOL - BREL T3-7	DTSO, TSOL - BREL T3-7
Power collection:	25kV ac overhead	25kV ac overhead	25kV ac overhead
Traction motor:	4 x Brush TM2141C	4 x Brush TM2141C	4 x Brush TM2141C
Horsepower:	1,328hp (996kW)	1,328hp (996kW)	1,328hp (996kW)
Max speed:	100mph (161km/h)	100mph (161km/h)	100mph (161km/h)
Coupling type:	Outer - Tightlock	Outer - Tightlock	Outer - Tightlock
	Inner - bar	Inner - bar	Inner - bar
Multiple working:	Classes 317-323	Classes 317-323	Classes 317-323
Door type:	Bi-parting sliding	Bi-parting sliding	Bi-parting sliding
Total sets in traffic:	66	48	3
Construction:	Steel	Steel	Steel
Special features:	PIS - dot matrix type		
Owner:	HSBC Rail	HSBC Rail	HSBC Rail
Operator:	'one' Railway	London Midland	Northern Railway
Notes:			

Fact File

Three batches of Class 321 four-car outer-suburban EMU were built by BREL Crewe. The first 66 units were designated to replace aging stock on the Liverpool Street routes, which emerged from 1988 under a Network SouthEast modernisation order.

The second batch of 48 nearly identical sets with slightly more first class accommodation emerged from 1989 for use on the Euston-Northampton/Birmingham route, displacing Class 317s. All these sets emerged in NSE livery.

In 1991, West Yorkshire PTE funded three units for its Metro service between Doncaster and Leeds, replacing aged ex-NSE sets which were used on the rapidly expanding commuter service.

The NSE sets were set out with 2+2 and 2+3 standard class and 2+2 first class seating, the WTPTE sets, classified 321/9 were standard class only.

After a few years 11 of the Euston line sets were transferred to Ilford for Liverpool Street line use.

Most 'one' Railway sets have been refurbished.

Right Top: *'one' Railway-operated Class 321/3s are allocated to Ilford depot and used on outer suburban routes, No 321361, with its DTCO leading, passes Stratford. All sets still retain the former Great Eastern livery applied under First ownership, but refurbishing will soon see these sets painted in 'one' Railway turquoise livery.* **Author**

Right Middle: *Class 321 intermediate Motor Standard Open (MSO); this is the 'works' car of the train housing the pantograph, transformer and traction equipment. This view is shown from the DTCO end, the pantograph end is always coupled to the TSOL. The MSO cars are quite heavy at 51.5 tonnes, giving an axle load of 12.87 tonnes.* **Author**

Right Bottom: *Class 321/3 interior, showing the refurbished green moquette. Seats are set out in the 2+3 high-density style, mainly in groups providing good legroom. Luggage space is provided by above seat racks and between seats. Unlike the Silverlink sets which have carpets, the 'one' units have lino floors.* **Author**

Electric Multiple-Units

Above: *The London Midland units allocated to Bletchley depot operate on Euston local services as far as Northampton and Birmingham, sharing longer-distance runs with Class 350 stock. The 321/4s are all painted in mauve, green and yellow. Viewed from its DTSO end, set No 321437 is seen at Milton Keynes. The 'P' after the number indicated parcels area. Front end equipment is minimal: A-light cluster (marker, rail and headlight), B-Tightlock coupling providing physical, electrical and pneumatic connections. This front end is also applicable to Class 320 and 322 units.* **Author**

Left Middle: *The intermediate TSOL has seating in the 2+3 style for 74, with two toilet compartments (one either side) at the end adjacent to the MSO. These sets are not air conditioned and have hinged 'hopper' quarter lights. Equipment on the TSO vehicles consists of brake equipment.* **Author**

Left Bottom: *From November 2007 the London Midland franchise took over from Silverlink Railways. The company announced that the '321' fleet will be replaced by extra Class 350s. The long-term future of this batch of '321' is unclear. Sets 321418 and 321425 are seen at Bletchley depot with their DTSO vehicles nearest the camera.* **Author**

Above: *The Class 321 interiors are principally laid out in the 2+3 style. The London Midland sets, maintained by Bletchley depot have carpets and blue fleck moquette, as shown here on the MSO vehicle. Grab poles and seat handles are finished in yellow. The Class 321s allocated to Bletchley are deemed as the most reliable EMUs operating in the UK.* **Author**

Below: *Right at the end of the Class 321 build programme, three sets were ordered for West Yorkshire PTE to operate on the Leeds-Doncaster route, replacing some aged ex-Network SouthEast units. The sets became Class 321/9 and are four-car all-standard class sets, providing accommodation for 307 passengers. Allocated to Leeds Neville Hill, the units sport Northern/Metrotrain maroon and blue livery with full yellow ends. The sets were refurbished in 2006-07.* **John Wills**

Number range:	322481-322485
Introduced:	1990
Refurbished:	2006
Built by:	BREL York
Refurbished by:	Hunslet Barclay, Kilmarnock
Formation:	DTSO(A)+TSOL+MSO+DTSO(B)
Vehicle numbers:	DTSO(A) - 78163-78167
	TSOL - 72023-72027
	MSO - 63137-63141
	DTSO(B) - 77985-77989
Vehicle length:	DTSO - 65ft ^{3}/$_4$in (19.83m)
	MSO/TSOL - 65ft 4^1/$_4$in (19.92m)
Height:	12ft 4^3/$_4$in (3.78m)
Width:	9ft 3in (2.82m)
Seating:	Total: 291S
	DTSO - 74S
	TSOL - 76S
	MSO - 83S
	DTSO - 58S
Internal layout:	2+3 high density
Gangway:	Within unit
Toilets:	TSOL - 2
Weight:	Total - 138.2 tonnes
	DTSO(A) - 29.3 tonnes
	TSOL - 28.8 tonnes
	MSO - 51.5 tonnes
	DTSO(B) - 29.1 tonnes
Brake type:	Air (Westcode)
Bogie type:	MSO - BREL P7-4
	DTSO, TSOL - BREL T3-7
Power collection:	25kV ac overhead
Traction motor type:	4 x Brush TM2141C
Horsepower:	1,328hp (996kW)
Max speed:	100mph (161km/h)
Coupling type:	Outer - Tightlock, Inner - bar
Multiple restriction:	Within Class, Class 317-323
Door type:	Bi-parting, sliding
Total sets in traffic:	5
Construction:	Steel
Owner:	HSBC
Operator:	First ScotRail

Fact File

Built under a Network SouthEast order to an identical body design as the Class 321s, these five units, designated Class 322, were intended for use on the new London Liverpool Street - Stansted Airport service. They were built with 2+2 seating and extra luggage space, finished in a grey and green livery and allocated to Ilford depot.

By 1998 the sets were taken off the dedicated airport service and under the privatised railway commenced work for First North Western, operating Euston-Manchester 'domestic' services. After a short time here the sets were taken off lease to FNW and leased to Anglia Railways to provide extra capacity on the Ipswich-London Liverpool Street route. After a brief period in Scotland the sets were again used from Ilford on West Anglia duties.

By 2005 the sets returned to Scotrail for use on the Edinburgh-North Berwick route and have subsequently been refurbished by Hunslet Barclay of Kilmarnock. All sets are now painted in First Scotrail 'Barbie' livery and interiors have been fitted out with 3+2 high-density seating, bringing them totally in line with the Class 321 configuration.

Below: *The five Class 322 sets operated by First ScotRail are allocated to Glasgow Shields Road depot and operate on the Edinburgh to North Berwick branch. The sets have all been refurbished by Hunslet Barclay, Kilmarnock and now sport 2+3 high-density seating, a bicycle stowage area and First ScotRail 'Barbie' livery. Set No 322481 is seen on the outskirts of Edinburgh, with its DTSO(A) on the left. This unit carries a 'stick-on' nameplate* North Berwick Flyer 1850-2000 *under the ScotRail branding on the leading vehicle.* **James Young**

Above: *Viewed from its Driving Trailer Standard Open (A) end, set No 322483 departs from Glasgow Central with a service bound for Edinburgh. The refurbishment of these sets has seen full First ScotRail livery applied, complete with First branding on the front end.* **Nathan Williamson**

Right Middle: *The interiors of the Class 322 are a far cry from the original low-density layout. When built for the Liverpool Street - Stansted Airport service these sets had 2+2 seating with large luggage stacks. The Hunslet-Barclay refurbishment has brought the interiors in line with the demands of the Edinburgh-North Berwick route and now 3+2 high-density seating, using high-back seats is provided. The vestibule areas are finished in pink (in keeping with FirstGroup's colours), while the seat moquette is in deep purple/blue. The interior of set 322481 is illustrated.* **Bill Wilson**

Right Bottom: *The main technical 'hub' of the Class 322 is the intermediate Motor Standard Open (MSO), this includes all power and transformer equipment in underslung boxes, together with the pantograph mounted at the TSOL end. As these sets are not fitted with air conditioning only forced air ventilation, opening hopper windows are provided.* **Bill Wilson**

Electric Multiple-Units

Number range:	323201-323243
Introduced:	1992-1993
Built/rebuilt by:	Hunslet TPL Leeds
Formation:	DMSO(A)+PTSOL+DMSO(B)
Vehicle numbers:	DMSO(A) - 64001-64043
	PTSOL - 72201-72243
	DMSO (B) 65001-65043
Vehicle length:	DMSO - 76ft 8³/₄in (23.37m)
	PTSOL - 76ft 10³/₄in (23.44m)
Height:	12ft 4³/₄in (3.78m)
Width:	9ft 2¹/₄in (2.80m)
Seating:	All except 323223-323225 - Total - 284S
	DMSO(A) - 98S
	PTSOL - 88S
	DMSO(B) - 98S
	Sets 323223-323225 - Total - 244S
	DMSO(A) - 82S
	PTSOL - 80S
	DMSO(B) - 82S
Internal layout:	2+3 high density
	Sets 323223-225 - 2+2
Gangway:	Within unit only
Toilets:	PTSOL - 1
Weight:	Total - 114.7 tonnes
	DMSO(A) - 39.1 tonnes
	PTSOL - 36.5 tonnes
	DMSO(B) - 39.1 tonnes
Brake type:	Air (Westcode)
Bogie type:	Powered - RFS BP62
	Trailer - RFS BT52
Power collection:	25kV ac overhead
Traction motor type:	4 x Holec DMKT 52/24
Horsepower:	1,565hp (1,168kW)
Max speed:	90mph (121km/h)
Coupling type:	Outer - Tightlock, Inner - bar
Multiple restriction:	Class 317-323
Door type:	Bi-parting sliding plug
Total sets in traffic:	43
Construction:	Welded aluminium alloy
Owner:	Porterbrook
Operator:	London Midland, Northern

Fact File

One of the more problematic classes during delivery and commissioning were the Class 323s, ordered by the BR Regional Sector for Birmingham Cross-City and Manchester area use, these sets were built by Hunslet TPL in 1992-93 but it was not until 1996 that the sets entered full service.

These are true high-density inner suburban sets and feature 2+3 seating with a three-car set accommodating 284 passengers.

Three sets were built with a modified 2+2 interior and extra luggage space for the Manchester Piccadilly to Manchester Airport service.

Sets are allocated to London Midlan at Soho, Birmingham and Northern Rail at Longsight, Manchester.

When built these units sported bodyside digital destination displays but these have now been plated over on most sets.

Below: *Painted in the former Central Trains/Centro grey, green, blue and white livery with a full yellow end, Class 323 No 323203 departs from Birmingham New Street on a Cross-City service, the prime operating area for these trains in the Midlands. Note the yellow upper door panels to meet Disability Discrimination Act requirements.* **Author**

Right Top: *At nearly 77ft long, the Class 323 vehicles are some of the longest in daily traffic. Here the Pantograph Trailer Standard Open Lavatory (PTSOL) is seen from the pantograph end. Underslung equipment on this vehicle consists of the main transformer and control boxes. Passenger seating is laid out in a mix of airline and group, with a (small) toilet compartment housed at the far end.* **Author**

Right Middle: *Class 323 interior showing the grey/green London Midland seat moquette, green grab handles and lino floors. Seating is in a mix of airline and group. Luggage racks are provided above seats. Note the television screen to the right of the end car communicating door, which can show the CCTV images.* **Author**

Below: *In early 2007, 17 Class 323s were operating with Northern Rail, based at Longsight and could be found in the Manchester, Liverpool local area, numerically the first three sets of NR's allocation (323223-225) are fitted with low-density seating for use on the Manchester Airport route. Set No 323234 is illustrated at Manchester Piccadilly painted in 'modified' First North Western' livery.* **John Wills**

Number range:	325001-325016 (set 325017 is a hybrid)
Introduced:	1995-1996
Built by:	Adtranz Derby
Formation:	DTPMV(A)+MPMV+TPMV+DTPMV(B)
Vehicle numbers:	DTPMV(A) - 68300-68330 (even numbers)
	MPMV - 68340-68355
	TPMV - 68360-68375
	DTPMV(B) - 68301-68331 (odd numbers)
Vehicle length:	DTPMV - 65ft 0³/₄in (19.83m)
	MPMV/TPMV - 65ft 4¹/₄in (19.92m)
Height:	12ft 4¹/₄in (3.78m)
Width:	9ft 3in (2.82m)
Seating:	None - Parcel/Mail space
Internal layout:	Open
Gangway:	Not fitted
Toilets:	Not fitted
Weight:	Total - 138.4 tonnes
	DTPMV(A) - 29.1 tonnes
	MPMV - 49.5 tonnes
	TPMV - 30.7 tonnes
	DTPMV(B) - 29.1 tonnes
Brake type:	Air (EP/auto)
Bogie type:	Powered - Adtranz P7-4
	Trailer - Adtranz T3-7
Power collection:	25kV ac overhead and 750V dc third rail
Traction motor type:	4 x GEC G315BZ
Horsepower:	1,287hp (990kW)
Max speed:	100mph (160km/h)
Coupling type:	Drophead buck-eye/screw
Multiple restriction:	Within type, TDM wired
Door type:	Roller shutter
Total sets in traffic:	16 (not all operational)
Construction:	Steel
Special features:	Retractable buffers, intruder alarm
Owner:	Royal Mail
Operator:	Royal Mail/GBRf

Fact File

In the mid-1990s Royal Mail made a considerable investment into new mail-carrying trains with the funding for 16 four-car units, built by Adtranz. The fleet can operate from 25kV ac overhead power supply or 750V dc third rail supply as well as operating with locomotives fitted with TDM-style jumpers.

Painted in classic Royal Mail red livery, the coaches have no end connections, with all access being through two roller shutter doors on each side. The cabs are separate modules and have sliding access doors.

Following Royal Mail's decision to end the Mail by Rail contract with operator EWS, the Class 325s were stored. However in recent times First/GBRF have taken on the operation of the sets and jointly with Royal Mail operate a daily service between London and Scotland.

Below: *Viewed from its DTPMV(A) car, set No 325016 is seen inside the Princess Royal Distribution Centre at Willesden. Based on Class 319 technology these units use the standard 'Networker' cab end.* **Author**

Right Top: *Class 325 front end equipment positions. A-Group Standard light cluster - marker, head and tail light, B-buck-eye coupling, C-retractable buffer, D-main reservoir pipe (yellow), brake pipe (red), E-electric train supply jumper socket, F-electric train supply jumper cable, G-TDM jumper cables, H-air horns. Unit illustrated is 325007. Note the ABB logo carried on the front of all sets.* **Author**

Right Middle: *Side detail of MPMV vehicle, showing the pantograph position at the far end, equipment boxes below and two key-locked roller shutter doors giving access to the main mail compartment. Special fixings are provided to take the latest Royal Mail trolley equipment. On the sides of most modern passenger vehicles an orange light indicates the doors are unlocked. On the Class 325 the light is blue and is a tamper or emergency light; when on, it indicates the vehicle doors have been touched. On the near end of the coach a 750V power supply jumper cable can be seen for operating the train inside a 750V dc equipped depot with 'trolley connections'.* **Author**

Right Bottom: *The Class 325 driving cab is based on the 'Networker' family, it incorporates a single power/brake controller on the left side, with other controls mounted on the main fascia panel, screen side panel or stand on the driver's right side. This incorporates the NRN radio, telephone handsets and horn valve. The driver's safety device (DSD), incorporating a vigilance device is foot-pedal-operated.* **Author**

Electric Multiple-Units

Number range:	332001-332004, 332010-332014	332005-332009
Introduced:	1997-1998, 2002	1997-1998, 2002
Built by:	Siemens Germany, CAF Spain	Siemens Germany, CAF Spain
Formation:	332001-332004, DMFO+TSO+PTSO+DMSO 332010-332014 DMSO+TSO+PTSO+DMFLO	332005-333007 DMFO+TSO+PTSO+TSO+DMSO 332008-333009 DMSO+TSO+PTSO+TSO+DMFLO
Vehicle numbers:	332001-332004 DMFO - 78400-78406 (even numbers) TSO - 72405-72412 (random) PTSO - 63400-63403 DMSO - 78401-78407 (odd numbers) 332010-332014 DMSO - 78418-78426 (even numbers) TSO - 72402-72408 (random) PTSO - 63409-63413 DMFLO - 78419-78427 (odd numbers)	DMFO - 78408-78417 (even numbers) TSO - 72400-72413 (random) PTSO - 63404-63408 TSO - 72414-72418 DMFLO - 78409-78417 (odd numbers)
Vehicle length:	Driving cars - 77ft 10³/₄in (23,74m) Intermediate cars - 75ft 11in (23.14m)	Driving cars - 77ft 10³/₄in (23.74m) Intermediate cars - 75ft 11in (23.14m)
Height:	12ft 1¹/₂in (3.70m)	12ft 1¹/₂in (3.70m)
Width:	9ft 1in (2.75m)	9ft 1in (2.75m)
Seating:	332001-332004 - Total - 26F/148S DMFO - 26F TSO - 56S PTSO - 44S DMSO - 48S 332010-332014 - Total - 14F/148S DMSO - 48S TSO - 56S PTSO - 44S DMFLO - 14F	332005-332007 - Total - 26F/204S DMFO - 26F TSO - 56S PTSO - 44S TSO - 56S DMSO - 48S 332008-332009 - Total - 14F/204S DMSO - 48S TSO - 56S PTSO - 44S TSO - 56S DMFLO - 14F
Internal layout:	2+1F/2+2S	2+1F/2+2S
Gangway:	Within set	Within set
Toilets:	PTSO + DMFLO - 1	PTSO + DMFLO - 1
Weight:	Total - 179 tonnes (all types) DMFO - 48.8 tonnes TSO - 35.8 tonnes PTSO - 45.6 tonnes DMSO - 48.8 tonnes DMFLO - 48.8 tonnes	Total - 214.8 tonnes DMSO - 48.8 tonnes TSO - 35.8 tonnes PTSO - 45.6 tonnes TSO - 35.8 tonnes DMFLO - 48.8 tonnes
Brake type:	Air (regenerative)	Air (regenerative)
Bogie type:	CAF	CAF
Power collection:	25kV ac overhead	25kV ac overhead
Traction motor type:	4 x Siemens	4 x Siemens
Horsepower:	1,876hp (1,400kW)	1,876hp (1,400kW)
Max speed:	100mph (161km/h)	100mph (161km/h)
Coupling type:	Outer - Scharfenberg, Inner - semi auto	Outer - Scharfenberg, Inner - semi auto
Multiple restriction:	Within Class and 333	Within Class and 333
Door type:	Bi-parting sliding plug	Bi-parting sliding plug
Owner:	BAA	BAA
Operator:	Heathrow Express	Heathrow Express

Designed and purchased by British Airports Authority for use on the new London Paddington - Heathrow Airport 'Heathrow Express' service, these 14 sets were ordered and equipped by Siemens with bodyshells assembled by CAF in Spain.

Originally sets were delivered as three-car units; later reformations saw nine four-car and five five-car sets formed.

Both standard and first class seating is provided and originally hold luggage could be checked in at Paddington and taken 'bonded' in modified DMFLO vehicles to the airport, but after various terrorist attacks the Paddington check-in was abolished and the vehicles may be converted to provide extra seating.

Sets are finished in Heathrow Express silver with advertising applied to some driving cars.

Above: *Displaying the Royal Bank of Scotland advertising livery, applied to some Class 332 driving cars, set No 332010 is seen in one of the two dedicated Heathrow Express platforms at London Paddington. The driving cars are very streamlined and only carry a minimal Group Standard-size high-visibility yellow warning end. Passenger seating is set out in 2+1 for first and 2+2 for standard class travellers with copious amounts of luggage space. All sets are allocated to a purpose-built Heathrow Express maintenance facility at Old Oak Common in West London.* **Author**

Right Middle: *First class seating area; this is set out in the 2+1 style and offers a high quality journey experience for the 15min-duration run between London Paddington and Heathrow Airport. Seats are a mix of leather and fabric in charcoal grey. All Heathrow Express vehicles are fully air conditioned.* **Author**

Right Bottom: *The driving cab layout of the Class 332 is basically the same as on the Class 333. It uses the standard left side position for power and brake with other controls fitted around a half width cab area. As these sets operate over the First Great Western route from Paddington, which is fitted with automatic train protection, these sets are so equipped; controls are seen below the speedometer.* **Author**

Electric Multiple-Units

Number range:	333001-333016
Introduced:	2000, TSO added 2002-03
Built by:	Siemens Germany and CAF Spain
Formation:	DMSO(A)+PTSO+TSO+DMSO(B)
Vehicle numbers:	DMSO(A) - 78451-78481 (odd Nos.)
	PTSO - 74461-74476
	TSO - 74477-74492
	DMSO(B) - 78452-78482 (even Nos.)
Vehicle length:	DMSO - 77ft $10^3/4$in (23.74m)
	PTSO/TSO - 75ft 11in (23.14m)
Height:	12ft $1^1/2$in (3.70m)
Width:	9ft $0^1/4$in (2.75m)
Seating:	Total - 360S
	DMSO(A) - 90S
	PTSO - 73S
	TSO - 100S
	DMSO(B) - 90S
Internal layout:	2+3 high density
Gangway:	Within set
Toilets:	PTSO - 1
Weight:	Total - 186.4 tonnes
	DMS(A) - 50.6 tonnes
	PTS - 46.7 tonnes
	TS - 38.5 tonnes
	DMS(B) - 50.6 tonnes
Brake type:	Air
Bogie type:	CAF
Power collection:	25kV ac overhead
Traction motor type:	4 x Siemens
Horsepower:	1,877hp (1,400kW)
Max speed:	100mph (161km/h)
Coupling type:	Outer - Scharfenberg, Inner - bar
Multiple restriction:	Within Class and 332
Door type:	Bi-parting sliding plug
Total sets in traffic:	16
Construction:	Steel
Owner:	Angel Trains
Operator:	Northern Railway (WYPTE)

Fact File

When authorisation was given for new EMUs in the West Yorkshire PTE area, the Siemens suburban EMU was selected, being an almost identical product to the Heathrow Express Class 332 fleet, except these were set out for high-density standard class occupancy.

Originally 16 three-car sets were ordered, but due to growth on the Aire Valley routes a fourth car was subsequently added.

Livery when delivered was a mix of Northern Spirit (the then franchise operator) and WYPTE, in recent times refurbishment has been undertaken and sets are now in Northern Railways / WYPTE colours.

Passenger information displays are fitted both inside and outside on this fleet, which are all based at Leeds Neville Hill depot.

These sets do not have Automatic Train Protection (ATP).

Below: *Painted in the original Northern Spirit livery, set No 333016 arrives at Leeds. All underslung equipment is housed in air-smoothed boxes. Note the passenger information display above the first side window behind the driving cab.* **John Wills**

Above: *The main area to observe Class 333 activity is Leeds. With 15 out of the 16 sets used every day, all services pass through, so it would not take long for an observer to see most of the fleet. When formed as a three-car set, No 333002 stands in one of the now replaced bay platforms at Leeds, soon after introduction to service. Although the motor cars for these sets are the driving cars, power is collected from the intermediate Pantograph Trailer Standard Open (PTSO).* **Author**

Right Middle: *Class 333 front end, also applicable to Class 332. On the roof line is the high level marker light, while marker, head and tail lights are at waist height in the yellow panel, mounted on both sides of the bodywork. The only item of draw gear is the Scharfenberg coupler, which incorporates physical, electrical and pneumatic connections. Hidden behind the two square buffer blocks on the front are anti-climbers, which are teeth bars that would interlock in case of impact and reduce the effects of over riding.* **Author**

Right Bottom: *Class 333 interior, showing the high-backed 3+2 seating layout and roof mounted passenger information displays, giving riders route and next stop information. No opening windows are provided as all vehicles are fully air conditioned. Passenger luggage racks are provided only above seats, as these units principally operate on commuter routes where large quantities of luggage are seldom carried. The interior of set No 332002 is shown.* **Author**

Class 334 'Juniper'

Number range:	334001-334040
Introduced:	1999-2002
Built by:	Alstom, Washwood Heath
Formation:	DMSO(A)+PTSO+DMSO(B)
Vehicle numbers:	DMSO(A) - 64101-64140
	PTSO - 74301-74340
	DMSO(B) - 65101-65140
Vehicle length:	DMSO(A) - 69ft 0³/4in (21.04m)
	PTSO - 65ft 4¹/2in (19.93m)
	DMSO(B) - 69ft 0³/4in (21.04m)
Height:	12ft 3in (3.77m)
Width:	9ft 2³/4in (2.80m)
Seating:	Total - 183S
	DMSO(A) - 64S
	PTSO - 55S
	DMSO(B) - 64S
Internal layout:	DMSO 2+2, PTSO 2+3
Gangway:	Within set
Toilets:	PTSO - 1
Weight:	Total - 124.72 tonnes
	DMSO(A) - 42.64 tonnes
	PTSO - 39.44 tonnes
	DMSO(B) - 42.64 tonnes
Brake type:	Air (regenerative)
Bogie type:	Alstom DMSO - LTB3, PTSO - TBP3
Power collection:	25kV ac overhead
Traction motor type:	4 x Alstom Onix
Horsepower:	1,448hp (1,080kW)
Max speed:	90mph (145km/h)
Coupling type:	Outer - Tightlock, Inner - bar
Multiple restriction:	Within Class only
Door type:	Bi-parting sliding plug
Total sets in traffic:	40
Construction:	Steel
Owner:	HSBC Rail
Operator:	First ScotRail

Fact File

When Scotland's privatised railway invested in the network in the late 1990s, they went for the Alstom 'Juniper' product range, ordering a three-car medium density standard class train with seating for 183.

A protracted introduction took place between 1999 and 2002 due to numerous technical problems. The 'Juniper' or Class 334 fleet is allocated to Glasgow Shields Road Depot and operates exclusively on the Ayrshire routes.

To save additional construction costs, these sets were fitted with pressure ventilation rather than full air conditioning and thus retain opening hopper windows.

All sets were delivered in the latest Glasgow SPT carmine and cream livery; they are non-gangwayed and fitted with Tightlock couplers to allow some compatibility with other ScotRail EMUs, although this is restricted to emergency rescue.

Below: *The Class 334 'Juniper' is basically an ac version of the South West Trains Class 458, and shows the full cab width - no gangway option which was originally offered to SWT. Front end equipment consists of cant rail level marker light, light clusters at waist height with tail, head and marker lights and a Tightlock coupler with electric/air connections, warning horns are mounted at roof height behind grilles. Set No 334026 is seen at Glasgow Central.* **Author**

Above: *The three-car Class 334 sets are used exclusively on the Ayrshire route from Glasgow and provide good accommodation on this busy and expanding route. All sets are painted in Strathclyde/ScotRail carmine & cream livery, offset by a blue band at waist height. Viewed from its DMOS(A) vehicle set, No 334006 is seen at Ayr.* **Author**

Right Middle: *The internal layout of the Class 334 fleet uses a mix of 3+2 and 2+2 seating, all in the standard class mode, with seating a mix of airline and groups. The DMSO vehicles are both set out using the 2+2 layout providing seats for 64 in each vehicle. The intermediate PTSO, which also accommodates a toilet, uses the 3+2 seating layout, providing accommodation for 55 passengers.* **Author**

Right Bottom: *The intermediate Pantograph Trailer Standard Open (PTSO) has a single arm pantograph facing inwards from the end coupled to the DMSO(A) vehicle. These coaches usually have bodyside branding applied between the two pairs of sliding plug doors, reading 'Strathclyde Passenger Transport'. These vehicles have a disabled person's wheelchair space, adjacent to the toilet area. Passenger doors are identified by being all-over cream, with angled full-height carmine frames extending from the waist height colour. The external power supply socket is visible on the end of the coach illustrated.* **Bill Wilson**

Electric Multiple-Units

Class 350 'Desiro'

Number range:	350101 - 350130
Introduced:	2004-2005
Built by:	Siemens Transportation - Vienna, Austria and Duewag, Germany
Formation:	DMSO(A)+TCO+PTSO+DMSO(B)
Vehicle numbers:	DMSO(A) - 63761-63790
	TCO - 66811-66840
	PTSO - 66861-66890
	DMSO(B) - 63711-63740
Vehicle length:	66ft 9in (20.4m)
Height:	12ft 1^{1}/$_{2}$in (3.7m)
Width:	9ft 2in (2.7m)
Seating:	Total - 183S
	DMSO(A) - 60S
	TCO - 24F/32S
	PTSO - 57S
	DMSO(B) - 60S
Internal layout:	2+2
Gangway:	Throughout
Toilets:	TCO, PTSO - 1
Weight:	Total - 179.3 tonnes
	DMSO(A) - 48.7 tonnes
	TCO -36.2 tonnes
	PTSO - 45.2 tonnes
	DMSO(B) - 49.2 tonnes
Brake type:	Air (regenerative)
Bogie type:	SGP SF5000
Power collection:	25kV ac overhead or 750V dc third rail
Traction motor type:	4 x Siemens 1TB2016-0GB02
Horsepower:	1,341hp (1,000kW)
Max speed:	100mph (160km/h)
Coupling type:	Outer - Dellner 12, Inner - bar
Multiple restriction:	Within class
Door type:	Bi-parting sliding plug
Total number in fleet:	30
Construction:	Aluminium
Owner:	Angel Trains
Operator:	London Midland
Special features:	Air conditioned

Fact File

The 30-strong fleet of Class 350 'Desiro' sets were formed of the vehicles originally ordered by Angel Trains as Class 450/2 for SWT and subsequently cancelled.

The four-car sets are operated by London Midland and used on the Euston-Birmingham and North West services as far north at Preston/Liverpool.

Until the franchise changes at the end of 2007 the units were painted in mid-grey with blue doors, but are now being re-painted in Govia style grey, green and graphite. Sets are allocated to a new purpose-built depot at Northampton and maintained under contract by Siemens.

Interiors are set out in the 2+2 low-density style in a mix of facing and airline; tables are provided at the facing positions in standard and first class.

In terms of equipment and body these sets are the same as South West Trains' Class 450s.

■ A further 30 Class 350s have been ordered by Porterbrook Leasing for the London Midland franchise to replace Class 321 stock.

Below: *Showing the new Govia - London Midland grey, green and graphite livery, set No 350102 is illustrated at Birmingham International. Sets will be progressively re-liveried through 2008. The follow-on order will be delivered in the new house colours.* **David Adams**

Above: *Standard class interior of Class 350 'Desiro'. Seats are set out in the 2+2 low-density style, with a wide central gangway and good leg room. The mix of airline and group seating seems to be well accepted by West Coast passengers. Each vehicle is fitted with passenger information displays, giving line of route and next station call, the system can also display emergency and disruption announcements. Automated station call announcements are also made. Vehicles are carpeted throughout. In first class, power sockets are provided by seats.* **Author**

Note: These units are fitted for dual ac/dc operation, but at the time of writing the dc power system was not in use. Tests have been carried out on third rail power collection and sets are certified for dual operation.

Right: *Class 350 'Desiro' equipment positions, also applicable to Class 444 and 450 stock. A-high level marker light, B-marker light, C-tail light, D-headlight, E-route indicator, F-front gangway folding door, G-Dellner 12 coupler incorporating physical, electrical and pneumatic connections, H-anti-climber grooves, I-warning horn, J-obstacle deflector plate.* **Author**

	357/0	357/2
Sub class:	357/0	357/2
Number range:	357001-357046	357201-357228
Introduced:	1999-2001	2001-2002
Built by:	Adtranz Derby	Adtranz/Bombardier Derby
Formation:	DMSO(A)+MSO+PTSO+DMSO(B)	DMSO(A)+MSO+PTSO+DMSO(B)
Vehicle numbers:	DMSO(A) - 67651-67696	DMSO(A) - 68601-68628
	MSO - 74151-74196	MSO - 74701-74728
	PTSO - 74051-74096	PTSO - 74601-74628
	DMSO(B) - 67751-67796	DMSO(B) - 68701-68728
Vehicle length:	DMSO(A), DMSO(B) - 68ft 1in (20.75m)	DMSO(A), DMSO(B) - 68ft 1in (20.75m)
	PTSO, MSO - 65ft 11^1/$_2$in (20.10m)	PTSO, MSO - 65ft 11^1/$_2$in (20.10m)
Height:	12ft 4^1/$_2$in (3.78m)	12ft 4^1/$_2$in (3.78m)
Width:	9ft 2^1/$_4$in (2.80m)	9ft 2^1/$_4$in (2.80m)
Seating:	Total - 282S	Total - 282S
	DMSO(A) - 71S	DMSO(A) - 71S
	MSO - 78S	MSO - 78S
	PTSO - 62S	PTSO - 62S
	DMSO(B) - 71S	DMSO(B) - 71S
Internal layout:	2+3	2+3
Gangway:	Within set	Within set
Toilets:	PTSO - 1	PTSOL - 1
Weight:	Total - 157.6 tonnes	Total - 157.6 tonnes
	DMSO(A) - 40.7 tonnes	DMSO(A) - 40.7 tonnes
	MSO - 36.7 tonnes	MSO - 36.7 tonnes
	PTSO - 39.5 tonnes	PTSO - 39.5 tonnes
	DMSO(B) - 40.7 tonnes	DMSO(B) - 40.7 tonnes
Brake type:	Air (rheostatic/regen)	Air (rheostatic/regen)
Bogie type:	Power - Adtranz P3-25	Power - Adtranz P3-25
	Trailer - Adtranz T3-25	Trailer - Adtranz T3-25
Power collection:	25kV ac overhead (750v dc equipped)	25kV ac overhead (750v dc equipped)
Traction motor type:	6 x Adtranz	6 x Adtranz
Output:	2,011hp (1,500kW)	2,011hp (1,500kW)
Max speed:	100mph (161km/h)	100mph (161km/h)
Coupling type:	Outer - Tightlock, Inner - bar	Outer - Tightlock, Inner - bar
Total sets in service:	46	28
Multiple restriction:	Within class only	Within class only
Door type:	Bi-parting sliding plug	Bi-parting sliding plug
Owner:	Porterbrook	Angel Trains
Operator:	c2c	c2c
Special features:	Air Conditioning	Air Conditioning

Under terms of the original franchise to operate the London, Tilbury and Southend route, new trains were stipulated. These were ordered from Adtranz (now Bombardier) who supplied the 'Electrostar' in its non-gangway form. Originally 46 units owned by Porterbrook were deployed from 1999, being supplemented by 28 identical sets owned by Angel Trains in 2001-02.

All sets are now painted in the c2c mauve livery, off-set by grey doors, and all are allocated to East Ham depot.

Seating is provided in the 2+3 high-density style and no provision is made for first class.

Power is collected by an intermediate PTSO feeding traction power to the two outer DMSO vehicles. Provision is made for 750V dc operation.

Below: *Showing the c2c mauve livery with grey doors and a stark resemblance to the Class 170 'Turbostar' DMU fleet, set No 357044 is seen from its DMSO(A) end at Stratford. These sets are fully air-conditioned.* **Author**

Above: *The 74-strong Class 357 fleet, operating solely on c2c services with high-quality dedicated maintenance facilities at East Ham, have become some of the most reliable EMUs in the UK. The sets replaced some very old and unreliable units used on the Fenchurch Street suburban routes and were a culture change for passengers. All sets are applied with vinyl in company blue and pink, after being delivered in white offset by green. Set No 357001 is seen from its DMSO(B) end, passing Ripple Lane en route to Fenchurch Street.* **Author**

Right Middle: *The 46 sets originally ordered and funded by Porterbrook were insufficient as a total route replacement, so to address route demands, a second batch of 28 sets was subsequently ordered, funded by Angel Trains. These were classified as 357/2 to keep the two owned groups separate. In terms of design, construction, and fitting out the sets are all identical. Angel Trains set No 357223 is seen at Barking.* **Nathan Williamson**

Right Bottom: *High-density 2+3 seating is fitted throughout with the two intermediate vehicles being an MSO and a PTSO fitted with the power collection pantograph and underslung transformer. To meet the Disability Discrimination Act, contrasting grey passenger doors are fitted throughout, as shown on PTSO No 74625.* **Brian Morrison**

Class 360 'Desiro'

	360/0	360/2
Class:	360/0	360/2
Number range:	360101-360121	360201-360205
Introduced:	2002-03	2004-06
Built by:	Siemens Transportation - Vienna, Austria and Duewag, Germany	Siemens Transportation - Duewag, Germany
Formation:	DMCO(A)+PTSO+TSO+DMCO(B)	DMSO(A)+PTSO+TSO(A)+TSO(B)+DMSO(B)
Vehicle numbers:	DMCO(A) - 65551-65571 PTSO - 72551-72571 TSO - 74551-74571 DMCO(A)- 68551-68571	DMSO(A) - 78431-78435 PTSO - 63421-63425 TSO(A) - 72421-72425 TSO(B) - 72431-72435 DMSO(B)- 78441-78445
Vehicle length:	66ft 9in (20.4m)	66ft 9in (20.4m)
Height:	12ft 1¹/₂in (3.7m)	12ft 1¹/₂in (3.7m)
Width:	9ft 2in (2.7m)	9ft 2in (2.7m)
Seating:	16F/265S DMCO(A) - 8F/59S PTSO - 69S TSO - 78S DMCO(A) 8F/59S	264S DMSO(A) - 63S PTSO - 66S TSO(A) - 74S TSO(B) - 74S DMSO(B) 63S
Internal layout:	2+2F/2+2 & 2+3S	2+3
Gangway:	Within set only	Within set only
Toilets:	PTOS - 1	PTOS - 1
Weight:	179.3 tonnes DMCO(A) - 45.0 tonnes PTSO - 43 tonnes TSO - 35 tonnes DMCO(B) - 45 tonnes	214.4 tonnes DMSO(A) - 44.8 tonnes PTSO - 44.2 tonnes TSO(A) - 34.8 tonnes TSO(B) - 34.8 tonnes DMSO(B) - 44.4tonnes
Brake type:	Air regenerative	Air regenerative
Bogie type:	SGP SF5000	SGP SF5000
Power collection:	25kV ac overhead	25kV ac overhead
Traction motor type:	1TB2016 - 0GB02 three phase	1TB2016 - 0GB02 three phase
Output:	1,341hp (1,000kW)	1,341hp (1,000kW)
Max speed:	100mph (161km/h)	100mph (161km/h)
Coupling type:	Outer - Dellner 12, Inner - semi-auto	Outer - Dellner 12, Inner - semi-auto
Multiple restriction:	Within Class	Within Class
Door type:	Bi-parting sliding plug	Bi-parting sliding plug
Number in traffic:	21	5
Construction:	Aluminium	Aluminium
Owner:	Angel Trains	British Airports Authority
Operator:	'one' Railway	Heathrow Connect
Special features:	Air conditioning, PIS	Air conditioning, PIS
Notes:		360201-204 were original demonstrator 'Desiro' sets. Rebuilt without end gangways for Heathrow Connect. Additional TSO(B) cars added in 2006-07, 360205 delivered as 5-car

New stock was sought for the First Great Eastern franchise of local lines out of London Liverpool Street. A contract was awarded to Siemens Transportation for 21 four-car outer suburban sets, using an aluminium body structure. This marked the first UK order for the Desiro product and also saw four demonstration sets produced.

The sets, now classified as 360/0, were built at the Duewag plant in Germany (driving cars) and the plant in Vienna, Austria (intermediate vehicles). All cars were then brought together and tested on the Siemens test track at Wildenrath, Germany before delivery to the UK.

The 21 FGE, now 'one' Railway sets have a small first class area in each driving car set out in the 2+2 style, with standard-class seating in the 2+3 mode.

British Airports Authority and FirstGroup sought new trains in 2006 for its stopping service between Paddington and Heathrow Airport marketed as 'Heathrow Connect'. The Desiro train was selected and the four pre-delivery prototype sets were rebuilt for this role. An additional TSO was built for each and one totally new five-car set was built to provide a fleet of five 5-car sets.

The BAA sets are set out for all standard class travel in the 2+3 mode; these sets are fitted with FGW-style ATP. Livery is all-over grey with a blue window band and orange doors.

Above: *The Class 360 represents the non-gangway fitted version of the electric Desiro product, and comparison should be made with the Class 350 and 450 designs to see how much the end gangway connection has changed the appearance of these sets. Viewed from its DTCO(A) end, set No 360115 departs from Colchester, bound for Clacton. These sets are fully air-conditioned, the modules for which are mounted in the roof.* **Author**

Right Middle: *Although power is collected from a roof-mounted pantograph on the PTSO vehicle, which also houses the main transformer in an underslung box; power is then transferred to the end driving vehicles which carry the propulsion equipment. A PTSO vehicle is illustrated, painted in Great Eastern livery. These cars seat 69 standard-class passengers, have two wheelchair spaces and one disabled access toilet. No opening exterior windows are provided due to air conditioning.* **Author**

Right Bottom: *To cater for first-class travellers on the Great Eastern outer-suburban routes, eight first-class seats in two bays are provided between the driving cab and first set of sliding plug doors in both driving cars. Small tables are provided by the group seats but are two small to allow much en route work. Seating is finished in deep mauve in both standard and first class. Hinged armrests are provided and a full passenger information system (PIS) is fitted inside and outside each vehicle.* **Author**

Left Top: *The four original four-car prototype 'Desiro' units which were extensively tested in Germany and the UK were spare when the Heathrow Connect order was placed. These sets were used, the shells being taken back to raw aluminium and totally reassembled, work which included removing the original gangway connections from the cab ends. Set No 360203 is illustrated, from its DMSO(A) end. Structurally these are the same as the Class 360/0 sets used on 'one' Railway. The 360/2s are jointly operated by Heathrow Express and First Great Western.* **Author**

Left Middle: *The interior of the Heathrow Connect 'Desiro' fleet is set out in high-density 2+3, using high-back seats and above seat luggage racks. Interior passenger information displays are provided in each coach and pre-recorded passenger information is played en route. The sets only operate on the Paddington-Heathrow Airport stopping services and are allocated to Old Oak Common depot.* **Author**

Below: *PTSO of Class 360/2 showing the power collection pantograph at the far end. Passenger doors are unlocked by the driver/conductor and then locally opened by passengers using a single push button attached to the door. Doors automatically close after a pre-determined time and are shut and locked by train staff. Orange door-release lights are provided at cant rail height.* **Author**

Right: *Class 360 front end equipment. A-high level marker light, B- marker light, C-tail light, D-headlight, E-route indicator, F-warning horn, G-air supply, H-Dellner 12 coupling assembly, including physical, electrical and pneumatic connections, I-obstacle deflector plate.* **Author**

Below: *Class 360 cab layout, applicable to 360/2 'Heathrow Connect' units fitted with ATP. A-TPWS switches, B-Windscreen controls - wiper, washer and heater, C-driver's master key and direction switch, D-combined power and brake controller, E-horn valve, F-speedometer with ATP controls below, G-brake demand, H-joint main reservoir and brake cylinder pressure gauge, I-Safety system isolated and passenger alarm lights, J-Emergency brake plunger, K-line light and doors locked indicator, L-driver's reminder appliance (DRA), M-AWS reset button and sunflower indicator, N-door release and close buttons right side, O-switch panel including cab heat and light, tail light indicator, pantograph up/down controls, P-cab radio system.* **Author**

Electric Multiple-Units

Class 365 'Networker Express'

Number range: 365501-365541
Introduced: 1994-1995
Built by: ABB/Adtranz York
Formation: DMCO(A)+TSO+PTSO+DMSO(B)
Vehicle numbers: DMCO(A) - 65894-65934
TSOL - 72241-72321 (odd numbers)
PTSOL - 72240-72320 (even numbers)
DMCO(B) - 65935-65975
Vehicle length: DMCO - 68ft 6^1/2in (20.89m)
TSO/PTSO - 65ft 9^3/4in (20.06m)
Height: 12ft 4^1/2in (3.77m)
Width: 9ft 2^1/2in (2.81m)
Seating: Total: 24F/239S
DMCO(A) - 12F/56S
TSO - 59S
PTSO - 68S
DMCO - 12F/56S
Internal layout: 2+2F, 2+2, 2+3S
Gangway: Within unit only
Toilets: TSO, PTSO - 1 (1 disabled use)
Weight: Total: 150.9 tonnes
DMCO(A) - 41.7 tonnes
TSOL - 32.9 tonnes
PTSOL - 34.6 tonnes
DMCO(B) - 41.7 tonnes
Brake type: Air (rheostatic/regenerative)
Bogie type: Powered: Adtranz P3-16
Trailer: Adtranz T3-16
Power collection: 25Kv ac overhead*
Traction motor type: 4 x GEC G354CX induction
Horsepower: 1,684hp (1,256kW)
Max speed: 100mph (161km/h)
Coupling type: Outer - Tightlock, Inner - semi auto
Multiple restriction: Within class only
Door type: Bi-parting sliding plug
Total sets in traffic: 40 (one out of use)
Construction: Aluminium alloy
Owner: HSBC
Operator: First Capital Connect
Special features: Modified front ends
Notes: * Wired for 750V dc operation

Fact File

Deemed as 'Networker Express' units, these four-car outer-suburban sets were introduced under the Network SouthEast banner and originally used on the South Eastern Division (16 sets) and the remainder on West Anglia Great Northern.

Following privatisation and new rolling stock deliveries it was agreed to move this entire fleet to West Anglia duties and now all are operated by First Capital Connect from Hornsey Depot.

In recent years the traditional 'Networker' front end has been revised following installation of a new cab ventilation system. Internally, sets are set out in 2+2 and 2+3 with carpeted floors and good quality seats.

From summer 2007 a major 'in house' upgrade to the '365' fleet commenced at Hornsey depot, with most sets now sporting FCC livery.

These sets could be returned to dc operation if required.

Below: *By late 2007, 36 of the 40 operational Class 365s were painted in full FCC livery. Set No 365529 is seen inside Hornsey depot, the depot responsible for the entire fleet's maintenance. Both driving cars are classified as DMCO with the area behind the cab to the first set of doors dedicated to first class use.* **Author**

Above: *Many people think the revised front end on the Class 365 gives a 'happy face' style; whatever people think, the sets are pleasing to the eye. Painted in First Capital Connect colours, set No 365539 is seen at Peterborough. When carrying FCC livery no yellow first class band is applied, just a silver '1' on the bodyside. In keeping with all 'Networker' breeds, all underslung equipment is housed behind panelling giving a pleasing side style.* **Author**

Right Middle: *Class 365 TSO, these coaches are set out in a mix of 2+2 and 2+3 with seating for 59. The layout is a mix of airline and group, with small wall-mounted tables at group positions. In FCC livery, coach numbers are applied at the bottom right and again in the middle at cant rail height, adjacent to the door-release light. To meet the Disability Discrimination Act the passenger doors are a contrasting colour, in this case FirstGroup bright pink.* **Author**

Right Bottom: *Class 365 front end equipment. A-Destination indicator, B-tail light, C-marker light, D-headlight, E-ventilation grille, F-horn, G-Tightlock coupling, incorporating physical, electrical and pneumatic connections. Although these sets are technically able to interconnect with Networkers, as these sets are now designated ac only, multiple operation with dc South Eastern Trains sets would not be authorised.* **Author**

Sub class:	373/1	373/2
Number range:	373001-022/373101-108/373201-232 3999 (spare PC)	373301-373314
Introduced:	1992-1996	1996
Built by:	GEC Alsthom	GEC Alsthom
Formation:	DM+MS+TS+TS+TS+TS+TBK+TF+TF+TBF	DM+MS+TS+TS+TS+TBK+TF+TBF
Set length:	1,291ft 8in (393.72m)	1,046ft 4in (318.92m)
Vehicle length:	DM - 72ft 8in (22.15m)	DM - 72ft 8in (22.15m)
	MS - 71ft 8in (21.84m)	MS - 71ft 8in (21.84m)
	TS, TBK, TF, TBF - 61ft 4in (18.70m)	TS, TBK, TF, TBF - 61ft 4in (18.70m)
Height:	12ft 4^1/$_2$in (3.77m)	12ft 4^1/$_2$in (3.77m)
Width:	9ft 3in (2.81m)	9ft 3in (2.81m)
Seating:	Total - 103F/272S (half train)	Total - 66F/232S
	DM - 0	DM - 0
	MS - 48S	MS - 48S
	TS - 56S	TS - 58S
	TS - 56S	TS - 58S
	TS - 56S	TS - 58S
	TS - 56S	TBK - 0
	TBK - 0	TF - 39F
	TF - 39F	TBF - 18F
	TF - 39F	
	TBF - 25F	
Internal layout:	2+1F, 2+2S	2+1F, 2+2S
Gangway:	Within set and at half set end	Within set and at half set end
Toilets:	MS - 2, TBF - 1, TF - 1, TS - 1 or 2	MS - 1, TBF - 1, TF - 1, TS - 1 or 2
Weight:	Total - 816.1 tonnes	Total - 682.2 tonnes
	DM - 68.5 tonnes	DM - 68.5 tonnes
	MS - 44.6 tonnes	MS - 44.6 tonnes
	TS - 28.1-29.7 tonnes	TS - 28.1-29.7 tonnes
	TBK - 31.1 tonnes	TBK - 31.1 tonnes
	TF - 29.6 tonnes	TF - 29.6 tonnes
	TBF - 39.4 tonnes	TBF - 39.4 tonnes
Brake type:	Air	Air
Power collection:	25kV ac overhead, 750V dc third rail, ‡ 3kV dc overhead*	25kV ac overhead, 750V dc third rail ‡
Horsepower:	25kV ac operation - 16,400hp (12,240kW) 3kV dc operation - 7,368hp (5,000kW)	25kV ac operation - 16,400hp (12,240kW)
Max speed:	25kV ac operation 186mph (300km/h) 750V dc operation 100mph (161km/h) ‡	25kV ac operation 186mph (300km/h) 750V dc operation 100mph (161km/h) ‡
Coupling type:	Outer - Scharfenberg, Inner - bar	Outer - Scharfenberg, Inner - bar
Multiple restriction:	Not permitted	Not permitted
Door type:	Single leaf sliding plug	Single leaf sliding plug
Special features:	TVM430, CT equipment	TVM430, CT equipment
Total sets in traffic:	62 half sets	14 half sets (now in mainland Europe)
Construction:	Steel	Steel
Owner:	Eurostar UK, SNCF, SNCB	Eurostar UK
Operator:	Eurostar UK, SNCF, SNCB	-
Notes:		

* Sets 3201-04/07-10/15/16/23-30 are fitted with French 1,500 V overhead equipment to allow south of France running.

+ Sets 373203/04/25/26/27/28 modified for domestic French operation only and not part of Eurostar fleet.

‡ 750v dc equipment now removed folowing opening of HS1 in November 2007.

For operations through the Channel Tunnel consisting of through services from the UK to France and Belgium, this most impressive fleet of scaled-down French-style TGV sets was built in the early 1990s.

62 half train 'three-capitals' sets were originally built, owned by the UK (Eurostar UK), SNCB (Belgian Railways) and SNCF (French Railways). Since original introduction, some scaling-down of the fleet has taken place with some sets stored and others transferred to French domestic services on the Paris-Lille and South of France routes.

Originally it was planned to operate North of London to Europe services and for this 14 short-length half sets were built; however, this service was abandoned and the sets stored, being used for testing and hire to GNER, the UK East Coast operator on the London-York/Leeds route.

All operational three-capitals sets are now refurbished, and the short sets have commenced work on domestic French services.

Electric Multiple-Units

Fact File

Above: *One of the most stylish trains to operate in the UK are the Eurostar formations, which until November 2007 used Waterloo as their UK terminus. After that the London base became St Pancras International. With the change, servicing moved from North Pole in West London to Temple Mills and the trains all lost their dc third rail power equipment. Running over the third rail network, but taking overhead power, set No 373106 arrives at Ashford (Kent) with a service bound for Paris.* **Author**

Right Middle: *The intermediate Eurostar vehicles are articulated, sharing a bogie. The two 'end' vehicles of each half train have a full bogie at the outer end. Standard and first class Eurostar vehicles share a common body structure, the MS, TBK and TBF all having unique structures. Externally the buffet car (TBK) has revised livery and is thus recognisable from a distance. A TS vehicle is shown in this view. All vehicles are numbered in the international series.* **Author**

Right Bottom: *By 2003 a major refurbishment project commenced with revised seats and decorations. In first class grand plans were unveiled for novel interiors but these were later abandoned in favour of a simple refurbishment of the existing layout. The view right shows the standard class seating, using the airline 2+2 style covered in a grey and brown moquette. Luggage racks are provided at vehicle ends and above seats.* **Author**

Sub class:	375/3	375/6
Number range:	375301-375310	375601-375630
Introduced:	2001-2002	1999-2001
Built by:	Bombardier Derby	Adtranz/Bombardier Derby
Formation:	DMCO (A)+TSO+DMCO(B)	DMCO(A)+MSO+PTSO+DMCO(B)
Vehicle numbers:	DMCO(A) - 67921-67930	DMCO(A) - 67801-67830
	TSO - 74351-74360	MSO - 74251-74280
	DMCO(B) - 67931-67940	PTSO - 74201-74230
		DMCO(B) - 67851-67880
Vehicle length:	DMCO - 66ft 9in (20.4m)	DMCO - 66ft 9in (20.4m)
	TSO - 65ft 6in (19.99m)	MSO, PTSO - 65ft 6in (19.99m)
Height:	12ft 4in (3.78m)	12ft 4in (3.78m)
Width:	9ft 2in (2.80m)	9ft 2in (2.80m)
Seating:	Total - 24F/152S	Total - 24F/218S
	DMCO(A) - 12F/48S	DMCO(A) - 12F/48S
	TSO - 56S	MSO - 66S
	DMS(B) - 12F/48S	PTSO - 56S
		DMCO(B) - 12F/48S
Internal layout:	2+2	2+2
Gangway:	Throughout	Throughout
Toilets:	TSO - 1	PTSO, MSO - 1
Weight:	Total - 124.1 tonnes	Total - 173.6 tonnes
	DMCO(A) - 43.8 tonnes	DMCO(A) - 46.2 tonnes
	TSO - 36.5 tonnes	MSO - 40.5 tonnes
	DMCO(B) - 43.8 tonnes	PTSO - 40.7 tonnes
		DMCO(B) - 46.2 tonnes
Brake type:	Air, regenerative	Air, regenerative
Bogie type:	Power - Adtranz P3-25	Power - Adtranz P3-25
	Trailer - Adtranz T3-25	Trailer - Adtranz T3-25
Power collection:	750V dc third rail	750V dc third rail, and
		25kV ac overhead
Traction motor type:	4 x Adtranz	6 x Adtranz
Output:	1,341hp (1,000kW)	2,012hp (1,500kW)
Max speed:	100mph (161km/h)	100mph (161km/h)
Coupling type:	Outer - Dellner 12, Inner - bar	Outer - Dellner 12, Inner - bar
Multiple restriction:	Class 375 - 377	Class 375 - 377
Door type:	Bi-parting, sliding plug	Bi-parting, sliding plug
Total sets in traffic:	10	30
Construction:	Aluminium, steel cabs	Aluminium, steel cabs
Owner:	HSBC	HSBC
Operator:	SouthEastern	SouthEastern

Fact File

The lucrative contract to replace the rolling stock on the former Southern Region Central and Eastern sections under privatisation was awarded to Adtranz/Bombardier, using its 'Electrostar' product range.

Sets were constructed from 1999 at the rate of more than one per week, with 'add-on' orders increasing the Class 375 fleet to 112 sets in various configurations.

The 375/3s are three-car sets, the 375/6s four-car dual voltage sets, while 375/7 and 375/8 are four-car dc-only sets and 375/9s are high-density units. 375/2-375/8 are officially 'express' stock and 375/9 'outer-suburban'.

Interior layouts are of a high standard with quality seats with armrests and carpeted floors. All sets are fully air conditioned.

When delivered to Connex, sets were in unbranded white with grey band. South Eastern Trains livery is now applied.

All sets are allocated to Ramsgate and maintained under a SET/Bombardier contract.

Left: *The South Eastern Trains livery of white and grey, offset by the company name and logo looks very smart, shown here on MSO 74252 from 375/6 No 375602. Underslung equipment consists of electrical units, brake and lighting modules. Air conditioning is housed in roof boxes. Note the yellow doors to meet the Disability Discrimination Act.* **Author**

375/7	375/8	375/9
375701-375715	375801-375830	375901-375927
2001-2002	2003-2004	2003-2004
Bombardier Derby	Bombardier Derby	Bombardier Derby
DMCO(A)+MSO+TSO+DMCO(B)	DMCO(A)+MSO+TSO+DMCO(B)	DMCO(A)+MSO+TSO+DMCO(B)
DMCO(A) - 67831-67845	DMCO(A) - 73301-73330	DMCO(A) - 73331-73357
MSO - 74281-74295	MSO - 79001-79030	MSO - 79031-79057
TSO - 74231-74245	TSO - 78201-78230	TSO - 79061-79087
DMCO(B) - 67881-67895	DMCO(B) - 73701-73730	DMCO(B) - 73731-73757
DMCO - 66ft 9in (20.4m)	DMCO - 66ft 9in (20.4m)	DMCO - 66ft 9in (20.4m)
MSO, TSO - 65ft 6in (19.99m)	MSO, TSO - 65ft 6in (19.99m)	MSO, TSO - 65ft 6in (19.99m)
12ft 4in (3.78m)	12ft 4in (3.78m)	12ft 4in (3.78m)
9ft 2in (2.80m)	9ft 2in (2.80m)	9ft 2in (2.80m)
Total - 24F/218S	Total - 24F/218S	Total - 24F/250S
DMCO(A) - 12F/48S	DMCO(A) - 12F/48S	DMCO(A) - 12F/59S
MSO - 66S	MSO - 66S	MSO - 73S
TSO - 56S	TSO - 52S	TSO - 59S
DMCO(B) - 12F/48S	DMCO(B) - 12F/52S	DMCO(B) - 12F/59S
2+2	2+2	2+2, 2+3
Throughout	Throughout	Throughout
TSO, MSO - 1	TSO, MSO - 1	TSO, MSO - 1
Total - 173.6 tonnes	Total - 163.3 tonnes	Total - 162.9 tonnes
DMCO(A) - 46.2 tonnes	DMCO(A) - 43.3 tonnes	DMCO(A) - 43.4 tonnes
MSO - 40.5 tonnes	MSO - 39.8 tonnes	MSO - 39.3 tonnes
TSO - 40.7 tonnes	TSO - 35.9 tonnes	TSO - 35.8 tonnes
DMCO(B) - 46.2 tonnes	DMCO(B) - 43.3 tonnes	DMCO(B) - 43.4 tonnes
Air, regenerative	Air, regenerative	Air, regenerative
Power - Adtranz P3-25	Power - Bombardier P3-25	Power - Bombardier P3-25
Trailer - Adtranz T3-25	Trailer - Bombardier T3-25	Trailer - Bombardier T3-25
750V dc third rail	750V dc third rail	750V dc third rail
6 x Adtranz	6 x Adtranz	6 x Adtranz
2,012hp (1,500kW)	2,012hp (1,500kW)	2,012hp (1,500kW)
100mph (161km/h)	100mph (161km/h)	100mph (161km/h)
Outer - Dellner 12, Inner - bar	Outer - Dellner 12, Inner - bar	Outer - Dellner 12, Inner - bar
Class 375 - 377	Class 375 - 377	Class 375 - 377
Bi-parting, sliding plug	Bi-parting, sliding plug	Bi-parting, sliding plug
15	30	27
Aluminium, steel cabs	Aluminium, steel cabs	Aluminium, steel cabs
HSBC	HSBC	HSBC
SouthEastern	SouthEastern	SouthEastern

Below: *Class 375 painted in full standard South Eastern Trains livery. Class 375/8 No 375808 is viewed from its DMCO(A) end. Two slightly different front end designs can be found on the 375 fleet, members of the 375/3, 375/6 and 375/7 sub-classes having the older style three piece marker, rail and headlight group, while 375/8s and 375/9s have two-piece units with a joint tail/marker light, as shown here.* **Author**

Electric Multiple-Units

Above: *The 30 members of Class 375/6 are fitted for dual ac/dc operation and thus have an operational pantograph on the roof of the PTSO vehicle, illustrated on vehicle 74202 of set 375602. These vehicles also have the main ac/dc transformer mounted on the underframe. All Class 375s are 'wired' for dual-voltage operation. The PTSO cars also house the disabled access area, identified by the blue downward-pointing chevron above the doors and the disabled sign on the doors.* **Author**

Left Middle: *A total of 15 sets make up the Class 375/7 sub-class. Numbered 375701-375715, these are identified by SET as dc-only express units. Set No 375713 illustrated shows the original front-end style with a Tightlock coupling; all sets fitted with Tightlocks have been modified to have Dellner 12 couplers, but unlike the Southern-allocated sets retained their Class 375 classification. Set No 375713 is seen at Wandsworth Road.* **John Wills**

Left Bottom: *The 30 members of Class 375/8, numbered 375801-375830, are identified by SET as dc-only express units fitted with modified shoe gear. These sets, together with members of Class 375/9, were delivered with modified front ends incorporating just two lights on either side, the smaller light being a joint marker/tail light assembly. Set No 375811 is illustrated near Dover from its DMCO(B) vehicle.* **Brian Morrison**

Above: *The final 27 South Eastern Trains Class 375s of sub-class 375/9 are high-density sets used for outer-suburban duties. 3+2 seats are fitted in standard areas, while first class is retained in the driving cars for 12 passengers. The external appearance of the sets is the same as previous sub-classes. All have the later style two section head and marker/tail light group. Set No 375915 is viewed at Ashford, Kent on a stopping service from London Charing Cross.* **Author**

Right Middle: *The high-density layout of the Class 375/9 does look a little cramped especially with the use of high-back seats. The walk space between the seats is very limited and the 'larger' passenger can find it difficult to walk the length of a vehicle. Seats are covered in either a maroon/red or blue moquette.*
Brian Morrison

Right Bottom: *The number of first-class ticket holders using South Eastern services justified the retention of first-class seating on all Class 375s. This is provided in driving vehicles and uses the high-density 2+2 style with a higher-quality seat and extra space compared to a standard-class seat. Limited tables are provided and no refinements such as curtains or a power supply are fitted.*
Brian Morrison

Number range:	376001-376036
Introduced:	2004-2005
Built by:	Bombardier Derby
Formation:	DMSO(A)+MSO+TSO+MSO+DMSO(B)
Vehicle numbers:	DMSO(A) - 61101-61136
	MSO - 63301-63336
	TSO - 64301-64336
	MSO - 63501-63536
	DMS)(B) - 61601-61636
Vehicle length:	DMSO - 66ft 9in (20.4m)
	TSO, MSO - 65ft 6in (19.99m)
Height:	12ft 4in (3.78m)
Width:	9ft 2in (2.80m)
Seating:	Total - 344S (216 seat, 12 tip, 116 perch)
	DMSO(A) - 36S, 6 Tip, 22 Perch
	MSO - 48S, 24 Perch
	TSO - 48S, 24 Perch
	MSO - 48S, 24 Perch
	DMSO(B) - 36S, 6 Tip, 22 Perch
Internal layout:	2+2 low density with standing room
Gangway:	Within set
Toilets:	Not fitted
Weight:	Total - 197.4 tonnes
	DMSO(A) - 42.1 tonnes
	MSO - 36.2 tonnes
	TSO - 36.3 tonnes
	MSO - 36.2 tonnes
	DMSO(B) - 42.1 tonnes
Brake type:	Air rheostatic
Bogie type:	Power - Bombardier P3-25
	Trailer - Bombardier T3-25
Power collection:	750V dc third rail
Traction motor type:	8 x Bombardier
Output:	2,000kW (2,662hp)
Max speed:	75mph (121km/h)
Coupling type:	Outer - Dellner 12, Inner - bar
Multiple restriction:	Class 375-377
Door type:	Bi-parting, sliding
Total sets in traffic:	36
Construction:	Aluminium with steel cabs
Owner:	HSBC Rail
Operator:	SouthEastern

Note: 44 trains of this design in four- and five-car formation are on order (as Class 378) for TfL for its 'Overground' network.

Fact File

To cater for inner-suburban needs on South Eastern Trains, this fleet of five-car tram-like trains was built in 2004-05. The layout is very basic, with 2+2 seating supplemented by a large number of perch seats in each carriage, answering an alleged need to provide more standing room for short-haul passengers in peak periods.

Externally the sets were also very basic, with traditional bi-parting sliding doors and no gangway connection between units, thus the cab end in recent times is unusual in having three front windows. Apart from no gangway, front-end equipment is standard 'Electrostar'.

These sets are finished in South Eastern Trains white and grey livery with yellow doors; they are allocated to Slade Green and operate on the high-density routes in South East London and Kent, especially the routes between London and Dartford.

Below: With its unusual front-end design incorporating three windows, Class 376 'Electrostar' No 376002 approaches London Bridge with a service bound for Cannon Street. With four powered vehicles on these sets developing 2,662hp, acceleration is rapid and the ride is very good.
Author

Above: *Although these sets are part of the Electrostar product range offered by Bombardier, there are few common factors between these and the Class 375 and 377 fleets. The most noticeable exterior difference are the sliding doors, which are slightly recessed and give a messy effect to the shape of the vehicles. The cab door is of the sliding plug type Set No 376004 at London Bridge is heading for Dartford.* **Author**

Right Middle: *Intermediate MSO car No 63504 from set No 376004. Passenger doors are controlled overall by the driver, but local open and close buttons are provided (body mounted). A door-release light (yellow) is located in the middle of each vehicle at cant rail height. The Class 376s are only fitted with pressure heating and ventilation rather than full air conditioning and thus have opening hopper windows.* **Author**

Right Bottom: *Class 376 door vestibule and perch area. It is quite amazing how the travelling public in South East London and Kent accept this form of accommodation, which in UK terms is more in keeping with a tram than a train. This shows a standard door position, with many grab poles for standees, perches for passengers and limited 2+2 seating towards the gangway connection to the next vehicle. Passenger door open/close buttons are seen adjacent to the door and a step light shines on the train-platform interface.* **Author**

Electric Multiple-Units

Sub class:	377/1	377/2	377/3
Number range:	377101-377164	377201-377215	377301-377328
Original numbers:	-	-	375311-375338
Introduced:	2002-2004	2002-2003	2002-2004
Built by:	Bombardier Derby	Bombardier Derby	Bombardier Derby
Formation:	DMCO(A)+MSO+TSO+DMCO(B)	DMCO(A)+MSO+TSO+DMCO(B)	DMCO(A)+TSO+DMCO(B)
Vehicle numbers:	DMCO(A) - 78501-78564	DMCO(A) - 78571-78585	DMCO(A) - 68201-68228
	MSO - 77101-77164	MSO - 77171-77185	TSO - 74801-74828
	TSO - 78901-78964	PTSO - 78971-78985	DMCO(B) - 68401-68428
	DMCO(B) - 78701-78764	DMCO(B) - 78771-78785	
Vehicle length:	DMCO - 66ft 9in (20.4m)	DMCO - 66ft 9in (20.4m)	DMCO - 66ft 9in (20.4m)
	MSO, TSO - 65ft 6in (19.99m)	MSO, TSO - 65ft 6in (19.99m)	TSO - 65ft 6in (19.99m)
Height:	12ft 4in (3.78m)	12ft 4in (3.78m)	12ft 4in (3.78m)
Width:	9ft 2in (2.80m)	9ft 2in (2.80m)	9ft 2in (2.80m)
Seating:	Total - 242S	Total - 24F/222S	Total - 176S
	DMCO(A) - 12F/48S - 12F/56S	DMCO(A) - 12F/48S	DMCO(A) - 12F/48S
	MSO - 62S - 70S	MSO - 69S	TSO - 56S
	TSO - 52S - 62S	PTSO - 57S	DMCO(B) - 12F/48S
	DMCO(B) - 12F/48S - 12F/56S	DMCO(B) - 12F/48S	
Internal layout:	2+2, and 2+3 various	2+2, and 2+3	2+2, and 2+3
Gangway:	Throughout	Throughout	Throughout
Toilets:	MSO, TSO - 1	MSO, PTSO - 1	TSO - 1
Weight:	Total - 161.2 tonnes	Total - 168.3 tonnes	Total - 122.4 tonnes
	DMCO(A) - 43.4 tonnes	DMCO(A) - 44.2 tonnes	DMCO(A) - 43.5 tonnes
	MSO - 39 tonnes	MSO - 39.8 tonnes	TSO - 35.4 tonnes
	TSO - 35.4 tonnes	PTSO - 40.1 tonnes	DMCO(B) - 43.5 tonnes
	DMCO(B) - 43.4 tonnes	DMCO(B) - 44.2 tonnes	
Brake type:	Air regenerative	Air regenerative	Air regenerative
Bogie type:	Power - Bombardier P3-25	Power - Bombardier P3-25	Power - Bombardier P3-25
	Trailer - Bombardier T3-25	Trailer - Bombardier T3-25	Trailer - Bombardier T3-25
Power collection:	750V dc third rail	750V dc third rail, and	750V dc third rail
		25kV ac overhead	
Traction motor type:	6 x Bombardier	6 x Bombardier	4 x Bombardier
Output:	2,012hp (1,500kW)	2,012hp (1,500kW)	1,341hp (1,000kW)
Max speed:	100mph (161km/h)	100mph (161km/h)	100mph (161km/h)
Coupling type:	Outer - Dellner 12, Inner - bar	Outer - Dellner 12, Inner - bar	Outer - Dellner 12, Inner - bar
Multiple restriction:	Class 375 - 377	Class 375 - 377	Class 375 - 377
Door type:	Bi-parting, sliding plug	Bi-parting, sliding plug	Bi-parting, sliding plug
Total number of sets:	64	15	28
Body structure:	Aluminium, steel ends	Aluminium, steel ends	Aluminium, steel ends
Special features:	PIS	PIS	PIS
	Provision for ac fitting		Provision for ac fitting

When delivered the original sets were classified as Class 375 and fitted with Tightlock couplers, changed to 377

■ Porterbrook have ordered a further 12 four-car Class 377s for use on the Southern franchise, to replace Class 319s which will be transferred to the First Capital Connect franchise.

Below: *Class 377 DMCO side detail, showing the first-class area behind the driving cab. Underslung equipment is for traction; note the two line voltage shoe fuse boxes in light grey on the underframe close to the passenger doors.* **Author**

Fact File

A total of 182 Class 377 'Electrostar' sets in various sub-classes were introduced to replace slam-door stock on South Central, later Southern. Sets come in either three- or four-car form and the 15 members of 377/2 are dual ac/dc sets.

Structurally the same as the Class 375s, these sets have a high quality 2+2/2+3 interior with a small first class area behind the driving cab on all driving cars.

Sets are finished in Southern green and white livery and allocated to either Brighton or Selhurst depots.

377/4
377401-377475

-

2003-2004
Bombardier Derby
DMCO(A)+MSO+TSO+DMCO(B)
DMCO(A) - 73401-73475
MSO - 78801-78875
TSO - 78601-78675
DMCO(B) - 73801-73875
DMCO(A) - 66ft 9in (20.4m)
MSO, TSO - 65ft 6in (19.99m)
12ft 4in (3.78m)
9ft 2in (2.80m)
Total - 20F/221S
DMCO(A) - 10F/48S
MSO - 69S
TSO - 56S
DMCO(B) - 10F/48S
2+2, and 2+3
Throughout
MOS, TSO - 1
Total - 160.8 tonnes
DMCO(A) - 43.1 tonnes
MOS - 39.3 tonnes
TSO - 35.3 tonnes
DMCO(B) - 43.1 tonnes
Air
Power - Bombardier P3-25
Trailer - Bombardier T3-25
750V dc third rail

6 x Bombardier
1,500kW
100mph (161km/h)
Outer - Dellner 12, Inner - bar
Class 375 - 377
Bi-parting, sliding plug
75
Aluminium, steel ends
PIS
Provision for ac fitting

Above: *Class 377 PTO vehicle 78974 (only found in 377/2 units). The pantograph is at the far end. The red vertical bands on the near passenger doors indicate the disabled area and location for stowage of bicycles. Underslung equipment consists of a main transformer and electrical control equipment. On the coach on the right the bodyside camera is shown, giving the driver a view along the side of the train for driver-only operation.* **Author**

Above: *Class 377 interior, showing the 2+2 seating layout in groups with tables. Luggage racks are provided above and between seats.* **Author**

Below: *Class 377/1 No 377108 is viewed from the DMCO(B) end inside Brighton depot, which is responsible for maintaining the majority of the fleet. A total of 64 members of this sub-class exist.* **Author**

Above: *During the course of the Class 377 build, Bombardier revised the front-end design of the Electrostar product range, changing from the use of three separate lights for head, marker and tail to two units with the marker/tail light being able to display either a white or a red light. The modification changed the front end appearance slightly. Units numbered up to 377139 had the three-light arrangement, while 377140 onwards have the two-light display. Members of classes 377/2 and 377/4 all have the two-light display, while all members of class 377/3 have three lights. Nos 377117 and 377161 are seen at Brighton.* **Author**

Below: *The 15 members of Class 377/2 are fitted for dual ac/dc operation and are deployed on the Brighton/Gatwick to Watford service, changing over from dc to ac operation on the West London Line near North Pole. Externally the sets are the same as the others except for the pantograph on the PTSO vehicle. The sets are used on other domestic Southern services when not needed for Watford duties. Set No 377204 is illustrated at London Bridge.* **Author**

Right Top: *The 28 members of the Class 377/3 sub class are usually deployed in formations of two, three or four on the fast Victoria-Brighton services. To cater for the line's business travellers, wi-fi equipment has recently been installed. Storming through Clapham Junction in July 2006, set No 377310 (with numbers applied on both sides of the front), heads for Brighton.* **Author**

Right Middle: *The largest sub-class within Class 377 is 377/4 with 74 four-car sets. All allocated to Brighton, these units share main-line operations and can be found throughout the Southern system. Seating in these sets is 2+2 facing and two longitudinal in first class and 2+2 and 2+3 facing and airline style in standard class. Total accommodation per unit is for 20 first and 221 standard. Viewed inside Brighton depot set, No 377409 shows the blister above the driver's cab side window protecting the vehicle-length camera.* **Author**

Right Bottom: *The standard Electrostar driving cab is fitted to the Class 377. It incorporates the now standard combined power and brake controller on the left side with master switch to the rear. All indicators and switches are mounted on the angular desk, with a screen for train observation and train diagnostics on the left and right side. The driver's visibility in these units is very restricted owing to the presence of the front-end gangway, especially when compared with full width cab Electrostars such as the Class 357.* **Author**

Class 390 'Pendolino'

Number range:	390001-390053
Introduced:	2001-2005
Assembled by:	Alstom, Washwood Heath; body shells from Italy
Formation:	DMRF+MF+PTF+MF+TS+MS+PTSRMB+MS+DMSO
	DMRF - 69101-69153
	MF - 69401-69453
	PTF - 69501-69553
	MF - 69601-69653
	TS - 68801-68853
	MS - 69701-69753
	PTSRMB - 69801-69853
	MS - 69901-69953
	DMSO - 69201-69253
Vehicle length:	DMRF, DMSO - 75ft 6in (23.05m)
	MF, PTF, TS, MS, PTSRMB - 78ft 4in (23.90m)
Height:	11ft 6in (3.56m)
Width:	8ft 11in (2.73m)
Seating:	Total - 147F/300S
	DMRF - 18F, MF - 39F, PTF - 44F, MF - 46F, TS - 76S,
	MS - 66S, PTSRMB - 48S, MS - 64S, DMSO - 46S
Internal layout:	2+1F/2+2S
Gangway:	Within set
Toilets:	MF, PTF, TS, MF, MSO, TS, MF(D) - 1
Weight:	Total - 459.7 tonnes
	DMRF - 55.6 tonnes
	MF - 52 tonnes
	PTF - 50.1 tonnes
	MF - 51.8 tonnes
	TS - 45.5 tonnes
	MS - 50 tonnes
	PTSRMB - 52 tonnes
	MS - 51.7 tonnes
	DMSO - 51 tonnes
Brake type:	Air (regenerative)
Bogie type:	Fiat/SIG tilting
Power collection:	25kV ac overhead
Traction motor type:	12 x Alstom Onix 800
Output:	5,100 kW (6,840hp)
Max speed:	140mph (Restricted to 125mph)
Coupling type:	Outer - Dellner, Inner - bar
Multiple restriction:	No multiple facility, operable with Class 57/3
Door type:	Single-leaf sliding plug
Total sets in traffic:	53
Construction:	Aluminium
Special features:	Tilt
Owner:	Angel Trains
Operator:	Virgin Trains

Below: *A full nine-car Pendolino set arrives at Manchester Piccadilly. The trains are usually operated with the first class end towards London. Each vehicle on the train is slightly different in terms of technical equipment. The two driving cars, while looking identical, have different seating and internal layouts. All Pendolino stock is finished in Virgin silver and red livery.* **Author**

Left Above: *Front end view of Pendolino set, demonstrating a full tilt (9 deg). Normally Pendolino stock does not tilt when stationary; this was staged as a demonstration of the system.* **Author**

Top Right: *Although Pendolino sets do not operate in multiple, end Dellner couplers are provided for attachment to Class 57/3 locomotives or another Pendolino set in the case of emergency. The coupler is retractable and kept behind the hinged front panel. In addition to the Dellner, which provides electrical and physical connections, shore supply and ETS jumper cables are provided. Set No 390010 shows the equipment behind the nose door. The coupling is shown in its retracted position.* **Author**

Middle Right: *Standard-class accommodation throughout the Pendolino sets is provided in the 2+2 layout, using a mix of red and blue moquette. All seats have hinged armrests to ease getting to the inner or window seats. Seating is arranged in a mix of airline and group, with the predominance for the airline style. All aisle seats have 'Mickey Mouse' hand grips in a contrasting colour. First class seating is in the 2+1 style.* **Author**

Right Bottom: *The Pendolino driving cab is a very complex affair. A combined power and brake controller is located on the left side, with all instrumentation and displays on an angled desk, including the on-board computer system. The large empty space on the front panel is where ERTMS will eventually be fitted.* **Author**

Electric Multiple-Units

Class 395 'Javelin'

Number range:	395001 - 395029
Introduced:	2007-2009
Built by:	Hitachi Industries, Kasado, Japan
Formation:	DTSO1+MS1+MS2+MS3+MS4+DTSO2
Vehicle numbers:	DTSO1 - 39011 - 39291
	MS1 - 39012 - 39292
	MS2 - 39013 - 39293
	MS3 - 39014 - 39294
	MS4 - 39015 - 39295
	DTSO2 - 39016 - 39296
Vehicle length:	DTSO - 67ft 7in (20.65m)
	MS - 65ft 6in (20m)
Height:	12ft 6in (3.81m)
Width:	9ft 2in (2.81m)
Seating:	Total: 348S
	DTSO1 - 28S
	MS1 - 68S
	MS2 - 68S
	MS3 - 68S
	MS4 - 68S
	DTSO2 - 48S
Internal layout:	2+2
Gangway:	Within unit only
Toilets:	1 in each DTSO
Weight:	Total: 268.5 tonnes
Brake type:	Air (Rheostatic/regen)
Bogie type:	Hitachi
Power collection:	25kV ac overhead & 750V dc third rail
Traction motor type:	IGBT Converter, three-phase
Max speed:	HS1 - 140mph (225km/h)
	Normal - 100mph (160km/h)
Coupling type:	Outer: Scharfenberg, Inner - Bar
Multiple restriction:	Within Class only (2-unit max)
Door type:	Single leaf sliding
Total number in traffic:	29 (on delivery)
Construction:	Aluminium
Owner:	HSBC
Operator:	South Eastern Trains
Special features:	PIS, CCTV, TVM430/KVB, GPS
	Air conditioned, SDO

Fact File

With the building of High Speed 1 (HS1) linking London with the Channel Tunnel, came the option to operate a fast domestic service between Kent and London St Pancras International using spare capacity on the dedicated route.

A fleet of 29 six-car 140mph top speed electric multiple-units was therefore ordered from Hitachi Industries in Japan for delivery from late 2007 through to mid-2009 for a service introduction in late 2009.

The sets, the first Japanese trains to operate in the UK, are being assembled at the Kasado and Mito factories and when *Traction Recognition* went to press the first set had arrived in the UK for type test approval.

The sets, with all one class of seating, will be able to operate from 750V dc third rail or 25kV ac overhead and use conventional signalling or TVM430 for operation over HS1.

Sets will be allocated to new purpose-built depot facilities at Ashford, Kent as well as using modified existing depot facilities at Ramsgate.

In addition to operating domestic services over HS1, the sets, named 'Bullet' or 'Javelin', will also be used to transport participants and spectators to the 2012 Olympic Games which is to be held near Stratford (East London), operating a 7min duration link service from St Pancras International to Stratford International.

Set No 395001 operated under power in the UK for the first time on 1 October 2007.

Left: *The interior of the Class 395 looks a little spartan, with hard covered floors and only basic fittings - heating, luggage racks and safety features. Seats are in the 2+2 mode, set out in both airline and group styles. All seats have hinged armrests. In defence of such a suburban tram-like interior on what will be a premium-fare service, the journey times will only be very short, London-Ashford taking just 37 minutes and London-Margate via Rochester 98 minutes.* **Author**

Above: *The external livery for the 'Javelin' or Hitachi 'Bullet' train sets is mid-blue, off-set by light blue passenger doors and a UK Group Standard yellow end. The air-smoothed nose end includes two hinged access doors which cover a Scharfenberg auto coupler for attaching two units together, or a rescue locomotive in the case of on-line failure. Other front end equipment consists of a cant rail marker light and two light clusters, each containing a headlight and a joint marker/tail light. Complete with its www.hitachi-rail.com bodyside and front end branding, set No 395001 is seen inside the new Ashford depot.* **Author**

Below: *The Class 395 driving cab is a complex affair, being able to operate from both 750V dc third rail and 25kV ac overhead and deal with standard, TVM and KVB signalling systems. The desk style incorporates the now standard use of a single power and brake controller located on the driver's left side. Fault display screens are located on the main driving desk and external CCTV panels on the right side. Space on the desk is allocated for the eventual installation of ERTMS. The cab of set No 395001 is illustrated.* **Author**

Sub class:	421/7
Number range:	(42)1497-(42)1498
Former number range:	(42)1883 & (42)1888
Alpha code:	3-CIG (3 Corridor Intermediate Guards)
Built:	1971
Modified as 3-CIG:	2004
Built by:	BR/BREL York
Modified by:	SWT Wimbledon
Formation:	DTCOL(A)+MBS+DTSOL(B)
Vehicle numbers:	DTCOL(A) - 76764 & 76773
	MBS - 62402 & 62411
	DTSOL(B) - 76835 & 76844
Vehicle length:	64ft 9½in (19.75m)
Height:	12ft 9¼in (3.89m)
Width:	9ft 3in (2.81m)
Seating:	Total - 170S
	DTCOL(A) - 18F/36S
	MBS - 56S
	DTSOL - 54S
Internal layout:	6-seat compartments F/2+2S
Gangway:	Throughout
Toilets:	DTSOL - 2
Weight:	Total - 119.5 tonnes
	DTCOL - 35.5 tonnes
	MBS - 49 tonnes
	DTCOL - 35 tonnes
Brake type:	Air (Auto/EP)
Bogie type:	Power - Mk6
	Trailer - B5 (SR)
Power collection:	750V dc third rail
Traction motor type:	4 x EE507
Horsepower:	1,000hp (740kW)
Max speed:	90mph (145km/h)
Coupling type:	Buck-eye
Multiple restriction:	1951-1966 stock, 73/1, 33/1
Door type:	Slam (CDL fitted)
Total sets in traffic:	2
Construction:	Steel
Owner/Operator:	South West Trains
	for Brockenhurst-Lymington Pier shuttle

Fact File

Originally introduced in the 1960s as replacement stock for the Brighton and later Portsmouth main lines, the CIG units were some of the most popular EMUs operated by the Southern Region, sporting very comfortable interiors, with all seats lining up with windows.

The slam-door units were low-density and frequently worked at speeds up to 90mph on main-line services on the Central and Western divisions of the Southern Region.

When slam-door stock was being phased out of service, two sets were sold to South West Trains for operation on the Community line between Lymington Pier and Brockenhurst. The sets were refurbished at Wimbledon depot, fitted with simple central door locking (CDL) and restored to earlier liveries, one set receiving 1950s BR green and the other 1970s BR blue and grey. Both were given local area names.

Below/Inset: *Blue and grey-liveried No 1497* Freshwater *departs from Eastleigh bound for Lymington Pier. These sets retain their original features, plus the additional fitting of a headlight and central door locking. Both:* **John Wills**

Above: *The second of the restored CIG units for the Community Partnership Brockenhurst-Lymington line is green-liveried No 1498, displaying as near as possible with current Group Standards the original BR Multiple Unit green livery applied when the first phase 1 sets were delivered in 1963. However, today a half yellow warning end and headlight are applied. No 1498 is seen at Brockenhurst.* **Brian Morrison**

Below: *The interior layout of the CIG design is based on the low-density 2+2 style with first class and standard class compartments in driving cars directly behind the driving position. The seating in a DTC car is shown, looking towards the compartment area. Note the underseat heaters, proper grab handles and wide spacing between seat groups.* **Brian Morrison**

Electric Multiple-Units

Traction Recognition

221

Number range:	442401-442424
Alpha code:	Original - 5-WES (WESsex electric)
Introduced:	1988-1989
Built by:	BREL Derby
Formation:	DTFL+TSOL(A)+MBRSM+TSOL(B)+DTSL
Vehicle numbers:	DTFL - 77382-77405
	TSOL(A) - 71818-71841
	MBRSM - 62937-62960
	TSOL(B) - 71842-71865
	DFSL - 77406-77429
Vehicle length:	DTFL/DFSL - 75ft 11 ^{1}/$_2$in (23.15m)
	TSOL(A)/TSOL(B)/MBRSM - 75ft 5 ^{1}/$_2$in (23m)
Height:	12ft 6in (3.81m)
Width:	8ft 11^3/$_4$in (2.74m)
Seating:	Total - 50F/290S
	DFTL - 50F
	TSOL(A) - 82S
	MBRSB - 52S
	TSOL(B) - 78S
	DTSL - 78S
Internal layout:	First 2+2 and compartment, 2+2S
Gangway:	Throughout
Toilets:	DTFL - 1, TSOL(A) - 2, TSOL(B) - 2, DTSOL - 1
Weight:	Total - 202.84 tonnes
	DTFL - 39.06 tonnes
	TSOL(A) - 35.26 tonnes
	MBRSM - 54.10 tonnes
	TSOL(B) - 35.36 tonnes
	DTSL - 39.06 tonnes
Brake type:	Air (EP/auto)
Bogie type:	Power - BR Mk6
	Trailer - BREL T4
Power collection:	750V dc third rail
Traction motor type:	4 x EE546
Horsepower:	1,608hp (1,200kW)
Max speed:	100mph (160km/h)
Coupling type:	Outer - buck-eye
	Inner - bar
Multiple restriction:	421, 423, 73/1, 33/1
Door type:	Single-leaf sliding plug
Owner:	Angel Trains
Operator:	Until 2007 - South West Trains, then off-lease
	Re-lease to Southern/Gatwick Express

Fact File

In the mid-1980s the need arose to replace the REP/TC stock in use on the Waterloo-Bournemouth/Weymouth line, and at the same time investment was authorised to electrify the line from Bournemouth on to Weymouth. To cover this need a fleet of 24 high-specification five-car EMUs, based on Mk3 rolling stock design, were ordered from BREL.

In many ways these were the pinnacle of electric multiple-unit design and incorporated swing-plug passenger doors.

The sets, formed with a central powercar, emerged from May 1988, with the final set commissioned in February 1989.

The first 13 sets were built with luggage cages either side of the guard's office, the remaining sets being built with a seating 'snug' adjacent to the buffer, and earlier sets were retro-fitted.

Allocated to Bournemouth, the sets settled down to operating on the Waterloo-Weymouth route and later took over some express services on the Waterloo-Portsmouth line.

With the mass replacement of slam-door stock and the introduction of Desiro units of Class 444 and 450 from 2001, the Class 442s fell from favour as non-standard and from early 2007 all 24 sets were withdrawn from service and stored.

Owners Angel Trains sought new operators and when we closed for press a handful of sets were being taken over by Southern/Gatwick Express for a revised London Victoria - Gatwick Airport/Brighton service from early 2008.

Left: *Displaying South West Trains 'white' or main line livery, a Class 442 departs from Southampton bound for Weymouth. On this example the front-end air pipe and multiple-control jumper cable covers are missing. Marker and headlights are located behind the curved glass front screens. Conventional buck-eye couplers and retractable buffers are fitted.*
Author

Above: *After withdrawal of the REP/TC formations, the Class 442s, or 'Plastic Pigs' as the sets became known, formed the backbone of London-Bournemouth services. They proved very popular with the travelling public, the five-car sets offering high-quality accommodation with a buffet counter and easy accessibility throughout the train. Painted in the final SWT 'refurbished' livery with orange cab doors, set No 2409 passes Vauxhall.* **Author**

Right Middle: *Standard class seating was provided in the 2+2 low-density style throughout, with a mix of spacious airline and group layouts. All vehicles were carpeted throughout and above-seat luggage racks were fitted. Standard class seat moquette was in deep red.* **Author**

Right Bottom: *First class accommodation, provided in one driving car, was laid out as an open two bay directly behind the driving cab cross-walkway followed by compartments fed from a side corridor, a method of seating much favoured by many travellers. The first class open area was set out in the 2+2 style, while the compartments seated six.* **Author**

■ It is expected that many interior changes will be made to the Class 442s for their new operators Southern; full details are awaited.

Electric Multiple-Units

Class 444 'Desiro'

Class:	444
Number range:	444001-444045
Alpha code:	Not issued
Introduced:	2003-2005
Built by:	Siemens Transportation SGP, Austria
Formation:	DMSO+TSO(A)+TSO(B)+TSRMB+DMCO
Vehicle numbers:	DMSO - 63801-63845
	TSO(A) - 67101-67145
	TSO(B) - 67151-67195
	TSRMB - 67201-67245
	DMCO - 63851-63895
Vehicle length:	77ft 3in (23.57m)
Height:	12ft 1¹/₂in (3.7m)
Width:	8ft 9in (2.74)
Seating:	Total: 35F/299S
	DMSO - 76S
	TSO(A) - 76S
	TSO(B) - 76S
	TSRMB - 47S
	DMCO 35F/24S
Internal layout:	2+2, 2+1F
Gangway:	Throughout
Toilets:	TSO, TSRMB - 1
Weight:	Total: 227 tonnes
	DMSO - 52 tonnes
	TSO(A) - 41 tonnes
	TSO(B) - 37 tonnes
	TSRMB - 42 tonnes
	DMCO - 52 tonnes
Brake type:	Air, regenerative
Bogie type:	Siemens SGB5000
Power collection:	750V dc third rail
Traction motor type:	1TB2016 three phase
Output:	2,682hp (2,000kW)
Max speed:	100mph (161km/h)
Coupling type:	Outer - Dellner 12, Inner - semi auto
Multiple restriction:	444 and 450
Door type:	Single leaf sliding plug
Total number in traffic:	45
Construction:	Aluminium
Special features:	Air conditioned, PIS
Owner:	Angel Trains
Operator:	South West Trains

Fact File

As part of the replacement order for South West Trains to rid itself of slam-door units, a fleet of 45 Desiro express five-car sets was ordered.

Painted in SWT 'white' main line livery, these are the Rolls-Royces of the Desiro fleet, fitted with low density 2+2 seating and with single-leaf sliding plug doors feeding cross vestibules at coach ends, rather than opening into passenger saloons.

Sets are fully air-conditioned, with a small buffet counter at one end on the TSRMB attached to the DTCO vehicle.

Originally sets were deployed on fast Waterloo-Portsmouth line duties as well as some Waterloo-Bournemouth-Weymouth route services; however, following withdrawal of the Class 442s in early 2007, the Class 444s have become the mainstay of traction for the Waterloo-Weymouth line.

All sets are based at the purpose-built Siemens maintenance facility at Northam, Southampton.

Below: *Viewed from its DTSO vehicle, set No 444009 passes Clapham Junction. The front ends of the 444s are similar to the 450 fleet but have several detail differences, including vestibule supports and a cut-out in the vestibule for the top marker light.* **Author**

Left: *The most interesting coach in a '444' is the TSRMB, viewed here from the disabled toilet end, where one bay of seats is located at the coach end, the disabled-access toilet being adjacent to the vestibule. The lower roof section is for a pantograph if fitted. The small buffet counter and guards office are at the far end attached to the DMCO. Vehicle No 67244 is illustrated.* **Author**

Right: *The driving car at the London end of Class 444 units is a Driving Motor Composite Open, with accommodation for 35 first class passengers in the 2+1 mode behind the drivers cab and vestibule. Mid-length doors separate the 2+2 standard class seating for 24. First-class seats are finished in blue moquette, while standard class is red. Three-pin power points are located on the dado panel adjacent to first class seats. Full passenger information displays are provided inside and outside each vehicle, and pre-recorded announcements are played* en route. **Author**

Left: *Standard-class TSO, showing the standard high-back 'Desiro' seats laid out in a mix of airline and group. Group seats have a full size table. All seat armrests are hinged to provide easy access to inner or window seats. Luggage racks are provided above seats with a glazed tray to assist in locating items. Dividers are provided to stop items moving along the rack shelf. Class 444s are carpeted throughout. Full air conditioning is provided and thus no opening hopper windows are fitted.* **Author**

Right: *The Class 444 driving cab is the same as fitted to the Class 450 sets. With a front gangway, space is very limited and the driver's accommodation is quite tight. A combined power and brake controller is operated by the driver's left hand, while door controls are provided on the two side panels. If this and the cab layout of the Class 360 are compared the amount of driving space lost by having the gangways is quite noticeable.* **Author**

Electric Multiple-Units

Number range:	450001-450127
Alpha code:	Not issued
Introduced:	2002-2007
Built by:	Siemens Duewag, Germany and Siemens SGP, Austria
Formation:	DMOS(A)+TCO+TSO+DMOS(B)
Vehicle numbers:	DMOS(A): 63201-300/63701-710/63901-63917
	TCO: 64201-64300/66851-66860/63921-63937
	TSO: 68101-68200/66801-66810/66901-66917
	DMOS(B): 63601-700/63751-760/66921-66937
Vehicle length:	66ft 9in (20.4m)
Height:	12ft 1^1/$_2$in (3.7m)
Width:	9ft 2in (2.7m)
Seating:	Total: 24F/246S
	DMOS(A): 70S
	TCO: 24F/36S
	TSO: 70S
	DMOS(B): 79S
Internal layout:	2+2F/2+3S
Gangway:	Throughout
Toilets:	TCO - 1, TSO - 1
Weight:	Total: 162 tonnes
	DMOS(A): 46 tonnes
	TCO: 35 tonnes
	TSO: 35 tonnes
	DMOS(B): 46 tonnes
Brake type:	Air, regenerative
Bogie type:	Siemens SGP SF5000
Power collection:	750V dc third rail
Traction motor type:	4 x 1TB2016 0GB02 three phase
Output:	2,682hp (2,000kW)
Max speed:	100mph (161km/h)
Coupling type:	Outer - Dellner 12, Inner - semi auto
Multiple restriction:	444 and 450
Door type:	Bi-parting sliding plug
Total number in traffic:	127
Construction:	Aluminium
Owner:	Angel Trains
Operator:	South West Trains
Special features:	Air conditioned, CCTV, PIS

Fact File

The replacement outer-suburban stock for South West Trains, ordered to replace slam-door VEP and CIG stock consists of a batch of 127 four-car Siemens-built 'Desiro' units.

These bi-parting sliding door sets, with doors opening into the main seating area, are set out for 2+3 high-density occupation but to a high standard. Carpeting is fitted throughout and first-class accommodation is provided in the 2+2 mode in the intermediate TCO vehicle, separated from the remainder of the coach by end sliding doors.

Sets operate throughout the SWT area and are allocated to purpose-built depot facilities at Northam, Southampton.

All units are finished in SWT blue livery.

Originally a fleet of five-car Class 450s were to be built, but this order was cancelled with the vehicles going to the Class 350 fleet.

Below: *The '450s' painted in outer-suburban SWT blue livery look impressive, with the body colour offset by red passenger doors in a yellow frame. Viewed from the DMSO(B), set No 450078 approaches Clapham Junction. (For front-end equipment see Class 350).* **Author**

Electric Multiple-Units

Right Top: *The Class 450 Intermediate Trailer Composite Open (TCO) vehicle has standard-class seating at the vehicle ends and first class between the two bi-parting door vestibules. The first class area is identified by a row of blue dots at cant rail height, rather than the time-honoured yellow band. The area directly to the right of the first pair of doors in this view shows the conductor's office. The blip in the smooth roof in the middle of the coach is the air conditioning equipment.* **Author**

Right Middle: *Standard class 'Desiro' seating, set out in the 2+3 style with high-back seats in a mix of group and airline styles. Vehicles are carpeted throughout with vestibule areas in sky blue. SWT orange grab poles and handles are provided.* **Author**

Below: *Class 450 sets can be found on all South West Trains routes except the London commuter network, which is operated by Class 455s. Here an eight-car formation led by No 450012 departs from Woking with an Alton-Waterloo semi-fast service. The DTSO(A) coach is leading. Power collection is by shoes on both DTSO bogies.* **Author**

	455/7	455/8
Sub class:	455/7	455/8
Number range:	455701-455742/50	455801-455874
Introduced:	1984-1985	1982-1984
Refurbished:	2003-2007	2003-2008
Built by:	BREL York	BREL York
Refurbished by:	Bombardier Chart Leacon	(Southern) Alstom Eastleigh (SWT) Bombardier Chart Leacon
Formation:	DTSO(A)+MSO+TSO+DTSO(B)	DTSO(A)+MSO+TSO+DTSO(B)
Vehicle numbers:	DTSO(A) - 77727-77811 (odds)	DTSO(A) - 77579-77725 (odds)
	MSO - 62783-62825	MSO - 62709-62782
	TSO - 71526-71568	TSO - 71637-71710
	DTSO(B) - 77728-77812 (evens)	DTSO(B) - 77580-77726 (evens)
Vehicle length:	DTSO - 65ft $1/2$in (19.83m)	DTSO - 65ft $1/2$in (19.83m)
	MSO/TSO - 65ft $41/2$in (19.92m)	MSO/TSO - 65ft $41/2$in (19.92m)
Height:	DTSO/MSO - 12ft $11/2$in (3.7m)	12ft $11/2$in (3.7m)
	TSO - 11ft $61/2$in (3.58m) (ex-Class 508)	
Width:	9ft $31/4$in (2.82m)	9ft $31/4$in (2.82m)
Seating:	Total: 244S	Total: Southern 310S, SWT 316S
	DTSO(A) - 54S	DTSO(A) - Southern 74S, SWT 74S
	MSO - 68S	MSO - Southern 78S, SWT 84S
	TSO - 68S	TSO - Southern 84S, SWT 84S
	DTSO - 54S	DTSO(B) - Southern 74S, SWT 74S
Internal layout:	2+2	2+3
Gangway:	Throughout	Southern - Within set, SWT -Throughout
Toilets:	Not fitted	Not fitted
Weight:	Total: 130 tonnes	Total: 137.1 tonnes
	DTSO - 29.5 tonnes	DTSO - 29.5 tonnes
	MSO - 45.5 tonnes	MSO - 50 tonnes
	TSO - 25.5 tonnes	TSO - 28.1 tonnes
	DTSO - 29.5 tonnes	DTSO - 29.5 tonnes
Brake type:	Air (Westcode)	Air (Westcode)
Bogie type:	DTSO - BREL BT13	DTSO - BREL BT13
	MSO - BREL BP27	MSO - BREL BP20
	TSO - BREL BX1	TSO - BREL BT13
Power collection:	750V dc third rail	750V dc third rail
Traction motor type:	4 x EE507	4 x EE507
Horsepower:	1,000hp (746kW)	1,000hp (746kW)
Max speed:	75mph (121km/h)	75mph (121km/h)
Coupling type:	Outer: Tightlock, Inner: bar	Outer: Tightlock, Inner: bar
Multiple restriction:	Class 455 and 456	Class 455 and 456
Special features:	CCTV	CCTV
Door type:	Bi-parting sliding	Bi-parting sliding
Total sets in traffic:	43	74
Construction:	Steel (TSO - Aluminium)	Steel
Owner:	Porterbrook	HSBC, Porterbrook
Operator:	South West Trains	Southern, South West Trains

Left: *Numerically the first of the Class 455 fleets are the 455/7s, comprising 43 units built as three-car sets and augmented to four by the insertion of a TSO from a Class 508 unit. Thus these units have two different vehicle profiles, as seen here on refurbished 455/7 No (45)5725 at Clapham Junction, the ex-508 vehicle being the third coach. Refurbishment of these sets has also seen the former marker light removed from the light cluster and a joint marker/tail light fitted. All Class 455s are fitted with Tightlock couplers but use separate main reservoir air and multiple control cables.* **Author**

455/9
455901-455920
1985
2004-2007
BREL York
Bombardier Chart Leacon

DTSO(A+MSO+TSO+DTSO(B)
DTSO(A) - 77813-77852 (odds)
MSO - 62826-62845
TSO - 71714-71733
DTSO(B) - 77814-77852 (evens)
DTSO - 65ft 1/2in (19.83m)
MSO/TSO - 65ft 41/2in (19.92m)
12ft 11/2in (3.7m)

9ft 31/4in (2.82m)
Total: 244S
DTSO(A) - 54S
MSO - 68S
TSO - 68S
DTSO(B) - 54S
2+2
Throughout
Not fitted
Total: 128.1 tonnes
DTSO - 29 tonnes
MSO - 45.5 tonnes
TSO - 27.1 tonnes
DTSO - 26.5 tonnes
Air (Westcode)
DTSO - BREL BT13
MSO - BREL BP20
TSO - BREL BT13
750V dc third rail
4 x EE507
1,000hp (746kW)
75mph (121km/h)
Outer: Tightlock, Inner: bar
Class 455 and 456
CCTV
Bi-parting sliding
20
Steel
Porterbrook
South West Trains

Introduced from 1982 as inner suburban stock on the Southern Region, the '455s' were originally used on the Western section; later, a batch was transferred to the Central section to replace older stock.

Three batches of Class 455s were built. The first 74 (4558xx) units have a rugged front end while the later 43 and 20 (4557xx and 4559xx) units have a rounded front end top design.

The 43 members of 455/7 were built as three-car sets and were augmented to four by the addition of the TSO vehicles originally formed in the Class 508 units which operated on the Southern when first built.

Upon privatisation the 455s were split between HSBC and Porterbrook and all sets are now either refurbished or in the process of refurbishment.

The Porterbrook sets operated by South West Trains have had one of the most radical refurbishments which has produced what many think is a brand new train.

Sets are allocated to Selhurst (Southern) and Wimbledon (SWT).

Above: *The South West Trains-operated Class 455/8 units still retain the original front end gangway-fitted design. Refurbishment and application of SWT suburban red livery was completed in December 2007. To show the previous SWT colours, sets Nos (45)5867 and (45)5874 are seen at Vauxhall.* **Author**

Below: *The 20 members of the third generation, the '455/9s', are all allocated to SWT and now refurbished. Set No (45)5904 is illustrated at Waterloo, showing an early application of 'red livery' in the cab area, with the yellow slightly wrapped around the cab side. The 455/9 fleet can be distinguished from the 455/7 batch by all vehicles having the same roof profile.* **Brian Morrison**

Left: *The refurbishment at Alstom Eastleigh of the 46 Class 455/8s operated by Southern made a number of significant changes to the DTSO vehicles. The original gangway door was sealed up as part of a cab improvement package which included the fitting of air conditioning, while the original light clusters are replaced with new style units. Front end equipment: A-warning horns, B-route/destination indicator, C-former gangway door now housing air conditioning, D-main reservoir pipe (yellow), E-multiple control jumper cable, F-multiple control jumper socket, G-cab air vent, H-marker/tail light, I-headlight, J-tightlock coupling, K-drumswitch box (controls multiple working).* **Author**

Below: *Southern Class 455 No 455804, led by its DTSO(A) vehicle is seen arriving at London Bridge. All these sets are allocated to Selhurst and together with the Class 456s form the backbone of inner suburban Southern services. This illustration serves as a good comparison between the newer 'Electrostar' front end and the 1980s-built '455s'. The Southern refurbishment did not include saloon air conditioning and thus the opening hopper windows have been retained. Two pairs of bi-parting sliding doors, locally controlled are provided on either side of all vehicles. The cab area is fed from a single sliding door, feeding a cross vestibule.* **Author**

Above: *The Bombardier Chart Leacon refurbishment of the South West Trains Class 455s has produced what many regular travellers think is a new train. The entire interior has been gutted and a new design installed, using 2+2 seating, wide vestibules with stand-back areas and 'perch' seats. Walls are finished in light blue, lino is provided on the floors and orange grab poles provided. This view depicts a TSO vehicle looking through a vestibule position showing the stand-back and new rubbish bins.* **Author**

Right Middle: *As part of the refurbishment, recording CCTV has been fitted to add to passenger safety and a full passenger information display is inside every carriage, giving line of route, next stopping point and travel information.* **Author**

Right Bottom: *The South West Trains refurbished sets have emerged in inner-suburban red livery, offset by blue passenger doors in a yellow frame. An ex-Class 508 TSO is illustrated, showing the lower roof profile of these vehicles. All vehicles have a centrally-mounted cant rail height orange door-release light.* **Author**

Electric Multiple-Units

Number range:	456001-456024
Introduced:	1990-1991
Built/rebuilt by:	BREL York
Formation:	DMSO+DTSO
Vehicle numbers:	DMSO - 64735-64758
	DTSO - 78250-78273
Vehicle length:	65ft 3 ^{1}/$_4$in (19.83m)
Height:	12ft 4 ^{1}/$_2$in (3.77m)
Width:	9ft 3in (2.82m)
Seating:	Total: 152S
	DMSO - 79S
	DTSO - 73S
Internal layout:	2+3
Gangway:	Within set
Toilets:	DTSOL - 1 (out of use)
Weight:	Total: 72.5 tonnes
	DMSO - 41.1 tonnes
	DTSO - 31.4 Tonnes
Brake type:	Air (Westcode)
Bogie type:	Powered: BREL P7
	Trailer: BREL T3
Power collection:	750V dc third rail
Traction motor type:	2 x GEC507-20J
Horsepower:	500hp (370kW)
Max speed:	75mph (121km/h)
Coupling type:	Outer - Tightlock, Inner - Bar
Multiple restriction:	Class 455 and 456
Door type:	Bi-parting sliding
Total sets in traffic:	24
Construction:	Aluminium
Owner:	Porterbrook
Operator:	Southern

Fact File

To allow the operation of two, six or ten-car formations, Network SouthEast ordered a fleet of 2-car Class 456 sets from York Works which were delivered in 1990-91.

As these sets were to operate alongside the Class 455s on SouthCentral services it was surprising that end gangways were not fitted, however this omission did allow a full width driving cab to be installed, in many ways resembling the Class 319.

With accommodation for 152 standard class passengers in the 2+3 facing mode, these sets have always been allocated to Selhurst and deployed on their own, in pairs or to augment '455' stock on suburban routes, their longest journeys usually being on the London-Tattenham Corner service.

Originally painted in NSE livery, a major refurbishment was carried out at Wolverton Works in 2006-07 with an application of Southern green and white livery.

Below: *Showing the previous Network SouthEast livery, Class 456 No 456018 approaches Clapham Junction on a service for West Croydon. As will be seen the front end of these sets, while fully compatible with the Class 455s, looks a mess, especially with a rather novel jumper cover arrangement with pull-down handles on a cover plate, a feature not progressed on any other unit type. Standard Tightlock couplers are fitted. Sets are fitted with pressure ventilation and thus have opening hopper windows. The DMSO coach is leading in this view.* **Author**

Above: *In late 2006 a start was made on refurbishing the 24 Class 456 units. A contract was let to Alstom Engineering at Wolverton, with sets loco-hauled between Selhurst and Wolverton Works. The overhaul has seen a more modern interior fitted, much in keeping with the Class 455s which the fleet operate alongside. Externally the sets are finished in Southern white and green livery. No changes have been made to the rugged end styling, but refurbishment has seen CCTV equipment fitted throughout. Sporting Southern livery, set No 456017 is seen at London Bridge.* **Nathan Williamson**

Right Middle: *The use of trains as mobile 'billboards' has continued and now includes Southern, which unveiled Class 456 set No 456006 in a 'Making London Safer' wrap in February 2007, marking the continued installation of CCTV and video surveillance cameras throughout the Transport for London area. The application of such high-quality pictogram branding on this set has extended to the doors, where to provide a colour differential, the picture has been placed in relief.* **Brian Morrison**

Right Bottom: *The original interior of the Class 456 sported slightly higher back seats than those fitted to Class 455s, with Eddie Pond murals on end panels. DTSO vehicle has a very small toilet compartment (little more than a cupboard) at the inner end, shown here on set No 456003.* **Author**

Traction Recognition

Class 458 - 4JOP 'Juniper'

Number range:	458001-458030
Alpha code:	4-JOP (Juniper Outer suburban Porterbrook)
Introduced:	1999-2002
Built by:	Alstom, Washwood Heath, Birmingham
Formation:	DMCO(A)+PTSO+MSO+DMCO(B)
Vehicle numbers:	DMCO(A) - 67601-67630
	PTSO - 74001-74030
	MSO - 74101-74130
	DMCO(B) - 67701-67730
Vehicle length:	DMCO - 69ft 6in (21.16m)
	PTSO, MSO - 65ft 4in (19.94m)
Height:	12ft 3in (3.77m)
Width:	9ft 2in (2.80m)
Seating:	Total: 24F/250S
	DMCO(A) - 12F/63S
	PTSO - 49S
	MSO - 75S
	DMCO(B) - 12F/63S
Internal layout:	2+2F, 2+3S
Gangway:	Throughout
Toilets:	PTSO - 1
Weight:	Total: 164.3
	DMCO(A) - 45.2 tonnes
	PTSOL - 33.3 tonnes
	MOS - 40.6 tonnes
	DMCO(B) - 45.2 tonnes
Brake type:	Air, regenerative
Bogie type:	ACR
Power collection:	750V dc third rail
Traction motor type:	6 x Alstom
Horsepower:	2,172hp (1,620kW)
Max speed:	100mph (161km/h)
Coupling type:	Outer - Tightlock, Inner - semi auto
Multiple restriction:	Within class only
Door type:	Bi-parting sliding plug
Special features:	Air conditioned, PIS
Total number in traffic:	30
Construction:	Steel
Owner:	Porterbrook
Operator:	South West Trains

Fact File

The four-car Alstom 'Juniper' outer suburban units for South West Trains could rate as some of the most ugly ever built. If this fleet and the Class 334 or 460 are compared, it clearly shows that the demand from SWT for an end gangway has left a most un-pleasing exterior design.

Introduced from 2000, but not without problems, this fleet soon fell out of favour with the operators and by 2005 most were sidelined in favour of the 'Desiro' product range. A decision was made that the entire fleet would be returned to Porterbrook from the end of 2006. In mid-2006 a further blow befell the class when UK Government Disability Discrimination Act regulations dictated the fleet be taken out of service as the passenger information displays were 'too small'.

However, following the re-awarding of the SWT franchise to Stagecoach, all 30 sets were returned to full operational condition and brought up to the latest standards.

The fleet is allocated to Wimbledon and used on the Waterloo-Reading/Ascot and Guildford routes.

All units are painted in SWT's main-line 'white' livery.

Below: *Painted in SWT 'white' main line livery No (45)8024 is seen at Waterloo forming a Reading line service. The front-end equipment is standard for the 'Juniper' product range, with the addition of a digital route display above the door position. DMCO(A) is leading.* **Author**

Above: *The Motor Standard Open (MSO) intermediate vehicle of a Class 458 carries the same traction equipment as the two driving cars. To provide a power pick-up for this, a set of power collection shoes are attached to the bogie at the DMCO end of the car. Passenger accommodation is provided for 75 in the 3+2 style. Two pairs of passenger-operated sliding plug doors are provided on each side, opening direct into the saloon area. The air-conditioning module can be seen in the centre of the roof.* **Author**

Right Middle: *The Pantograph Trailer Standard Open (PTSO) does not actually carry a 25kV ac pantograph; one could be attached if the units were transferred to an overhead power collection area. The well for the pantograph is seen at the far end of this view of a PTSO vehicle. The underframe on these cars is very light with an all-in weight for the vehicle of just 33.3 tonnes. All vehicles have the standard door release orange light at cant rail height in the middle. Emergency door opening valves can be seen mid-way up the body just inward of the first pair of doors.* **Author**

Right Bottom: *The driving cab of the Class 458 is one of the narrowest of any electric multiple unit in the UK. Fitting in all the equipment was a major challenge to Alstom and when the sets first arrived a number of drivers complained about the space provided. They are best described as 'compact'. The standard dual power and brake controller is on the left side. Forward visibility is limited on this design.* **Author**

Class 460 8-GAT 'Juniper'

Number range: 460001-460008 (Numbered as 01-08)
Alpha code: 8 GAT (8 car GATwick)
Introduced: 1999-2001
Built by: Alstom, Birmingham
Formation: DMFL+TFO+TCO+MSO+MSO+TSO+MSO+DMSO
Vehicle numbers: DMFL - 67901-67908, TFOL - 74401-74408
TCOL - 74411-74418, MSO - 74421-74428
MSO - 74431-74438, TSOL - 74441-74448
MSO - 74451-74458, DMSO - 67911-67918
Vehicle length: DMFL, DMSO - 68ft 11 ¹/₂in (21.05m)+
TFO, TCO, MSO, TSO - 65ft 4 ³/₄in (19.94m)
Height: 12ft 4¹/₂in (3.77m)
Width: 9ft 2¹/₄in (2.80m)
Seating: Total - 48F/316S
DMFL - 10F, TFO - 28F, TCO - 9F/42S, MSO - 60S,
MSO - 60S, TSO - 38S, MSO - 60S, DMSO - 56S
Internal layout: 2+1F/2+2S
Gangway: Within set
Toilets: TFO - 1, TCO - 1, TSO - 2
Weight: Total - 317 tonnes
DMFL - 42.6 tonnes, TFO - 33.5 tonnes,
TCO - 34.9 tonnes, MSO - 42.5 tonnes
MSO - 42.5 tonnes, TSO - 35.2 tonnes,
MSO - 40.5 tonnes, DMSO - 45.3 tonnes
Brake type: Air (rheostatic)
Bogie type: Alstom ACR
Power collection: 750V dc third rail
Traction motor type: 10 x Alstom T3517 3-phase
Horsepower: 3,626hp (2,704kW)
Max speed: 100mph (161km/h)
Coupling type: Scharfenberg*
Multiple restriction: Not authorised
Door type: Bi-parting sliding plug
Total sets in traffic: 8
Construction: Steel
Owner: Porterbrook
Operator: Gatwick Express
Notes:
+ Length does not include GRP nose cone
* When delivered Tightlock couplers were fitted

Fact File

The 1990s modernisation of the Gatwick Express operation between London Victoria and Gatwick Airport introduced some of the most stylish electric multiple-units ever to operate in the UK.

Built as part of the Alstom 'Juniper' family, these eight-car sets with fully streamlined outer ends, based on the same shell fabrication as the Class 458, operate the 15min-interval dedicated airport service.

Each set has one driving car set aside for luggage, with a small coupe for 10 first class passengers at the inner end. This has a roller shutter side door. All other carriages have two pairs of sliding plug doors on each side feeding directly into the saloon areas.

In addition to the driving cars which are motored, three intermediate MSO are provided giving a top speed of 100mph and excellent acceleration.

These sets are designed as two half trains of four carriages, with the non-driving 'inner' end of each half portion powered, in addition the vehicle behind the driving motor standard (country end) is also powered. Trains are painted in Gatwick Express or advertising livery.

Left: *In normal operation, the London-end driving car is the Driving Motor First Luggage (DMFL), identifiable by its almost solid body side. Access to the luggage area is by a single roller-shutter door on either side. The inner end of the vehicle is set out for first class occupancy and is fed by a pair of sliding plug doors on either side. The front ends are very streamlined, but conform to the standard 'Juniper' equipment positions. A Scharfenberg coupling is housed behind the lower front skirting, which is hinged. With the moon shining brightly, set No 460004 is seen at Gatwick Airport ready to form an overnight service to London Victoria.* **Author**

Above: *Viewed from its DMSO end, set No 460002 (identified only by the number '02' on the front) hurries past Clapham Junction. The Gatwick Express services usually use the main lines and travel at speeds up to 100mph. Over the years a number of advertising contracts have been operated by Gatwick Express where trains have worn complete advertising liveries for limited periods. In early 2007 this was Delta Airlines, but this campaign was due to end mid-year.* **Author**

Right Middle: *First class seating is provided at the inner end of the DMFL vehicle, in one complete TFO and half the length of the TCO. First class seating is in the 2+1 layout with all seats having a table. Luggage stacks are provided, as are overhead racks.* **Author**

Right Bottom: *Standard class seating is in the low-density 2+2 style, with a mix of airline and group seats. Group seats have a small table. A number of luggage racks are provided through the train to cope with air passengers' luggage needs and the luggage van at the front of the train is available if needed. The Gatwick Express sets are fully air conditioned with no opening hopper windows and are carpeted throughout. When not in use, sets are maintained at Stewarts Lane depot located between Victoria and Clapham Junction.* **Author**

Electric Multiple-Units

	465/0	465/1
Sub class:	465/0	465/1
Number range:	465001-465050	465151-465197
Year introduced:	1991-1993	1993-1994
Year modified:	-	-
Built by:	BREL/ABB York	BREL/ABB York
Modified by:	-	-
Formation:	DMSO(A)+TSO+TSOL+DMSO(B)	DMSO(A)+TSO+TSOL+DMSO(B)
Vehicle numbers:	DMSO(A) - 64759-64808	DMSO(A) - 65800-65846
	TSO - 72028-72126 (even numbers)	TSO - 72900-72992 (even numbers)
	TSOL - 72029-72127 (odd numbers)	TSOL - 72901-72993 (odd numbers)
	DMSO(B) - 64809-64858	DMSO(B) - 65847-65893
Vehicle length:	DMSO - 68ft 6^1/$_2$in (20.89m)	DMSO - 68ft 6^1/$_2$in (20.89m)
	TSO, TSOL - 65ft 9^3/$_4$in (20.06m)	TSO, TSOL - 65ft 9^3/$_4$in (20.06m)
Height:	12ft 4^1/$_2$in (3.77m)	12ft 4^1/$_2$in (3.77m)
Width:	9ft 3in (2.81m)	9ft 3in (2.81m)
Seating:	Total: 348S*	Total: 348S
	DMSO(A) - 86S*	DMSO(A) - 86S
	TSO - 90*	TSO - 90S
	TSOL - 86S*	TSOL - 86S
	DMSO (B) - 86S*	DMSO (B) - 86S
Internal layout:	2+3 high-density	2+3 high-density
Gangway:	Within set	Within set
Toilets:	TSOL - 1	TSOL - 1
Weight:	Total - 133.6 tonnes	Total - 136 tonnes
	DMSO(A)- 39.2 tonnes	DMSO(A) - 39.2 tonnes
	TSO - 27.2 tonnes	TSO - 27.2 tonnes
	TSOL - 28 tonnes	TSOL - 28 tonnes
	DMSO(B) - 39.2 tonnes	DMSO(B) - 39.2 tonnes
Brake type:	Air (rheostatic and regenerative)	Air (rheostatic and regenerative)
Bogie type:	Powered - Adtranz P3	Powered - Adtranz P3
	Trailer - Adtranz T3	Trailer - Adtranz T3
Power collection:	750V dc third rail	750V dc third rail
Traction motor type:	8 x Brush TIM970	8 x Brush Squirrel Cage
Horsepower:	3,004hp (2,240kW)	3,004hp (2,240kW)
Max speed:	75mph (121km/h)	75mph (121km/h)
Coupling type:	Outer - Tightlock, Inner - Semi-auto	Outer - Tightlock, Inner - Semi-auto
Multiple restriction:	Class 465 and 466	Class 465 and 466
Door type:	Bi-parting sliding plug	Bi-parting sliding plug
Total sets in traffic:	50	47
Construction:	Aluminium	Aluminium
Owner:	HSBC	HSBC
Operator:	South Eastern Trains	South Eastern Trains
Sub-Class differences	BREL/ABB phase 1 train	BREL/ABB phase 2 train

Note: * Set 465014 has 2+2 seating and seats Total - 304S. DMSO(A) -74S, TSO - 80S, TSOL - 76S, DMSO(B) - 74S

465/2	465/9
465235-465250	465901-465934
1991-1993	1991-1993
-	2005
Metro-Cammell, Birmingham	Metro-Cammell, Birmingham
-	Wabtec, Doncaster
DMSO(A)+TSO+TSOL+DMSO(B)	DMCO(A)+TSOL+TSO+DMCO(B)
DMSO(A) - 65734-65749	DMC0(A) - 65700-65733
TSO - 72787-72817 (odd numbers)	TSOL - 72719-72785 (odd numbers)
TSOL - 72788-72818 (even numbers)	TSO - 72720-72786 (even numbers)
DMSO(B) - 65784-65799	DMCO(B) - 65750-65783
DMSO - 68ft 6^1/$_2$in (20.89m)	DMCO - 68ft 6^1/$_2$in (20.89m)
TSO, TSOL - 65ft 9^3/$_4$in (20.06m)	TSO, TSOL - 65ft 9^3/$_4$in (20.06m)
12ft 4^1/$_2$in (3.77m)	12ft 4^1/$_2$in (3.77m)
9ft 3in (2.81m)	9ft 3in (2.81m)
Total: 348S	Total: 24F/302S
DMSO(A) - 86S	DMCO(A) - 12F/68S
TSO - 90S	TSO - 76S
TSOL - 86S	TSOL - 90S
DMSO (B) - 86S	DMCO (B) - 12F/68S
2+3 high-density	2+2F/2+3S
Within set	Within set
TSOL - 1	TSOL - 1
Total - 136 tonnes	Total - 138.2 tonnes
DMSO(A) - 39.2 tonnes	DMCO(A) - 39.2 tonnes
TSO - 27.2 tonnes	TSOL - 30.3 tonnes
TSOL - 28 tonnes	TSO - 29.5 tonnes
DMSO(B) - 39.2 tonnes	DMCO(B) - 39.2 tonnes
Air (rheostatic and regenerative)	Air (rheostatic and regenerative)
Powered - SRP BP62	Powered - SRP BP62
Trailer - SRP BT52	Trailer - SRP BT52
750V dc third rail	750V dc third rail
8 x Alsthom G352AY	8 x Alsthom G352BY
3,004hp (2,240kW)	3,004hp (2,240kW)
75mph (121km/h)	75mph (121km/h)
Outer - Tightlock, Inner - Semi-auto	Outer - Tightlock, Inner - Semi-auto
Class 465 and 466	Class 465 and 466
Bi-parting sliding plug	Bi-parting sliding plug
16	34
Aluminium	Aluminium
Angel Trains	Angel Trains
South Eastern Trains	South Eastern Trains
Metro Cammell built train	Refurbished train with first class

Modernisation of the Kent suburban network took place in the 1990s with Network SouthEast ordering four-car EMUs from BREL; these were of the same general body style as the Class 165 DMU fleet and became known as the 'Networker' fleet.

In total 147 four-car sets were built in three batches, 97 from BREL/ABB and 50 from Metro-Cammell. The sets were very similar but with detail differences, mainly involving the original interiors.

A protracted delivery following many technical issues saw the fleet revolutionise rail travel on the Kent inner and outer suburban network, introducing driver-only operation, rapid acceleration and comfortable train interiors.

Originally all sets were painted in NSE colours, but following privatisation and operation by Connex and later South Eastern Trains these operators' liveries were also applied.

34 of the original Metro-Cammell build were extensively rebuilt in 2005 for longer-distance services. First class seating was provided in each driving car and a total refurbishment of the interior carried out, these sets being reclassified 465/9.

Members of Class 465/0, 465/1 and 465/2 are allocated to Slade Green depot, while the 465/9 batch is allocated to Gillingham. All units have pressure ventilation.

Left: *One of the original BREL-built 'Networker' units, No 465035, is seen at London Bridge. The front ends of these sets have been modified in recent years to remove the front handles and footstep above the coupling to reduce 'train surfing' problems. This set shows standard South Eastern Trains livery, with yellow passenger doors.* **Author**

Right: *BREL 'Networker' TSO No 72096. All technical equipment is behind streamlined boxes, with door-open buttons fitted on the door, with lock indicators at cant rail height adjacent. Emergency door controls are at solebar level and the door release light (orange) is at cant rail height in the middle.* **Author**

Electric Multiple-Units

Above: *When introduced, the 'Networker' fleet were finished in Network SouthEast white, blue and red livery, a colour scheme which was only removed from the last fleet members in 2007. The Class 465/1 fleet, which are identical to the 465/0s, were a follow-on order assembled at York under the ABB banner. With its DMSO(B) nearest the camera, No 465162 approaches London Bridge. This unit sports the latest 'anti-surfer' modifications.* **Author**

Left Second: *Class 465/1 TSOL No 72923 viewed from the non-toilet compartment side. These units have a chemical retention toilet, which is emptied at depots as part of routine maintenance. As no air conditioning is fitted to the 'Networker' build all main windows have an opening 'hopper'.* **Author**

Left Third: *Class 465/1 No 465161 showing the latest South Eastern Trains livery. When this was applied the front end yellow was extended downwards over the 'buffers' (which are also anti-climbers) to include the anti-surfing panel. The Networker fleet only operates on the SouthEastern inner and outer suburban routes and one of the best locations to observe the class is London Bridge, with some 95 per cent of the fleet booked to pass through in a 24-hour cycle.* **Author**

Left Bottom: *Class 465/2s No 465201 shows the original 'as built' condition with front end grab rails and steps on the upper side of the buffer beam. Due to differences with internal ventilation, the BREL/ABB sets have side grille vents at cant rail height, which are not installed on the Metro-Cammell sets. Front end connections consist of a fully automatic Tightlock coupler incorporating physical, electrical and pneumatic connections.* **Author**

Above: *In 2005, 34 of the original Metro-Cammell Class 465/2 units were extensively rebuilt by Wabtec, Doncaster for longer distance outer-suburban services. First class seating was provided in each driving car and a total refurbishment of the interior carried out, these sets being reclassified 465/9. Externally the sets are the same as Class 465/2s except for the first class branding and yellow cant rail stripe directly behind the driving cabs. Set No 465906 is illustrated.* **Author**

Above (inset): *Detail of Networker 'Tightlock' coupler, incorporating physical coupling above with pneumatic and electrical connections in the box below under the roll-open cover.* **Author**

Right Middle: *The revised interior in DMCO vehicles showing the 2+2 first class area. The behind cab seating uses high-back, arm-rest fitted seats in airline and group layout with small tables. Angled vestibule screens are provided to the door area.* **Derek Porter**

Right Bottom: *The standard class interior of the Class 465 fleet is set out in the 2+3 style, with seats laid out in a mix of airline and facing. As these are suburban units no tables are fitted. Small above-seat luggage racks are provided. All main windows have opening hoppers.* **Author**

Number range:	466001-466043
Introduced:	1992-1994
Built by:	GEC-Alsthom, Birmingham
Formation:	DMSO+DTSO
Vehicle numbers:	DMSO - 64860-64902
	DTSO - 78312-78354
Vehicle length:	68ft 6$\frac{1}{2}$in (20.89m)
Height:	12ft 4$\frac{1}{2}$in (3.77m)
Width:	9ft 3in (2.81m)
Seating:	Total - 168S+
	DMSO - 86S+
	DTSO - 82S+
Internal layout:	2+3 high density +
Gangway:	Within set
Toilets:	DTSO - 1
Weight:	Total - 72 tonnes
	DMSO - 40.6 tonnes
	DTSO - 31.4 tonnes
Brake type:	Air (rheostatic and regenerative)
Bogie type:	Powered - Adtranz P3
	Trailer - Adtranz T3
Power collection:	750V dc third rail
Traction motor type:	4 x Alstom G352AY
Horsepower:	1,502hp (1,120kW)
Max speed:	75mph (121km/h)
Coupling type:	Outer - Tightlock, Inner - Semi-auto
Multiple restriction:	Class 465 and 466
Door type:	Bi-parting sliding plug
Total sets in traffic:	43
Construction:	Aluminium
Owner:	Angel Trains
Operator:	South Eastern Trains

+ Set 466017 fitted with 2+2 seating Total -140S DMSO - 72S, DTSO - 68S

Fact File

For low-patronage branch line use and to augment formations to either six or eight cars, a batch of 43 two-car 'Networker' sets were built by GEC-Alstom at Washwood Heath, Birmingham in 1993-94. These sets are basically a two-car version of the Class 465/2 breed, except that one DMSO does not have traction equipment and is a Driving Trailer Standard Open, these vehicles also house a small toilet compartment.

All sets are allocated to Slade Green and are painted in South Eastern Trains white and beige livery. The units can be seen throughout the SET operating area; all have now had their original front handrails removed and are fitted with angled anti-surfer plates above the buffer beam.

Left: *Front end detail of Networker breed. A-cab air conditioning intake (465/2, 465/9 and 466 only), B-electronic destination and route indicator, C-cab door controls, D-Group Standard light cluster, tail, marker and headlight, E-Tightlock coupling incorporating physical, electrical and pneumatic connections. F-recently applied anti-surfer angle plate on top of original flat buffer beam.* **Author**

Above: *The fleet of 43 two-car Class 466 units, allocated to Slade Green, are painted in the latest South Eastern Trains white and grey livery, offset by SET branding and yellow/black front ends. As per the Class 465s, the front steps have recently been fitted with angular edges to stop 'train surfing'. Set No 466017 is seen at Waterloo East heading for Charing Cross.* **Author**

Right Middle: *Class 466 sets are used to either supplement train formations to 10-car length or to operate lesser-used branch lines, where the deployment of a four-car train would be wasteful of resources. It is seldom that a single two-car set would be found working on the main line. Set No 466007 approaches Bromley North with the shuttle service from Sundridge Park on 18 August 2004.* **Brian Morrison**

Right Bottom: *Here is a comparison between the 'Networker' and suburban 'Electrostar' product, both supplied by the same manufacturer, Adtranz/Bombardier. When launched many thought the 'Networker' breed was bland, but the design was distinctly stylish when compared with the later suburban 'Electrostar' product. Nos 466007 and 376002 share platform space at Bromley North.* **Brian Morrison**

Electric Multiple-Units

Class 483

Number range:	(483)002-(483)009 (last three digits carried)
Former number range:	Ex LUL 1938 stock
Introduced originally:	1938
Introduced Isle of Wight:	1989-1990
Built by:	Metro-Cammell
Rebuilt by:	BRML Eastleigh
Formation:	DMSO(A)+DMSO(B)
Vehicle numbers:	DMSO(A) - 122-129
	DMSO(B) - 224-229 (not in order)
Vehicle length:	DMSO - 52ft 4in (15.95m)
Height:	9ft 5^1/$_2$in (2.88m)
Width:	8ft 8^1/$_2$in (2.65m)
Seating:	Total - 82S
	DMSO(A) - 40S
	DMSO(B) - 42S
Internal layout:	2+2, bench
Gangway:	Within set, emergency end doors
Toilets:	Not fitted
Weight:	Total - 54.8 tonnes
	DMSO(A) - 27.4 tonnes
	DMSO(B) - 27.4 tonnes
Brake type:	Air (Auto/EP)
Bogie type:	LT
Power collection:	660V dc third rail
Traction motor type:	4 x Crompton Parkinson/GEC/BTH
Horsepower:	670hp (500kW)
Max speed:	45mph (72.5km/h)
Coupling type:	Wedgelock
Multiple restriction:	Within type only
Door type:	Bi-parting and single sliding
Total sets in available:	7 (only four in use at any time)
Construction:	Steel
Owner:	South West Trains
Operator:	South West Trains - Isle of Wight

Fact File

The railway system on the Isle of Wight has always been a little world of its own, and today the remaining railway which operates from Ryde Pier Head through to Shanklin is no exception.

Electrified by the BR Southern Region in the mid-1960s to rid steam traction from the Island, no normal railway stock could be used due to gauge clearances. To provide stock BR purchased a fleet of redundant standard 1923-25 tube stock and rebuilt this for use on the isolated network.

This stock became life-expired in the late 1980s and the then Network SouthEast purchased some more 'modern' tube stock, dating from 1938! This was rebuilt into power-car twin sets which either operate in two- or four-car formations.

Sets are allocated to Ryde St Johns depot; they have LU-style group and longitudinal seats with crew-operated sliding doors.

Livery is either blue with dinosaur pictures, mock London Transport red or Heritage.

Below: *IOW sets Nos 007 and 009 are currently painted in mock London Transport red livery with a light grey roof. To conform with National Network safety certification, small yellow warning panels are applied. Two pairs of double leaf and one single leaf sliding door (not in a contrasting colour) are provided on each side. An end emergency door is fitted. Set No 007 is seen at Ryde St Johns Road.* **Author**

Electric Multiple-Units

Above: *In 1990 one of the most radical liveries ever to be applied to a UK train emerged from the depot at Ryde St Johns Road, when a start was made on painting the Class 483 Isle of Wight units in dinosaur livery; to say that people stopped and looked is an understatement. At the same time some sets received dinosaur names, applied in the destination box on the cab ends. By 2007, following the transfer of stock to South West Trains and the merging of the Isle of Wight and SWT franchises, the IOW network is to become a Community Railway and from mid-2007 a new Heritage livery is to be applied, based on London Underground red and cream. Dinosaur-liveried set No 006 is seen at Ryde depot.* **Author**

Right Middle: *The Class 483 interiors, refurbished at Ryde, sport a mix of bench and facing seats, to much the same style as in London Transport days. Two pairs and one single locally operated sliding doors are provided on each vehicle. Modern fluorescent lighting is fitted and the passenger environment is kept very clean and tidy by local staff.* **Author**

Right Bottom: *By today's standards the driving cabs of the Class 483s are rather cramped and basic, with just a power and brake controller, speedometer and pneumatic gauges. Cabs were refurbished as part of the overhaul before these units came to the island.* **Author**

Electric Multiple-Units

Number range:	507001-507033
Introduced:	1978-1980
Built/rebuilt by:	BREL York/Alstom Eastleigh
Formation:	BDMSO+TSO+DMSO
Vehicle numbers:	BDMSO - 64367-64399
	TSO - 71342-71374
	DMSO - 64405-64437
Vehicle length:	BDMSO/DMSO - 64ft 11^1/$_2$in (19.80m)
	TSO - 65ft 4^1/$_4$in (19.92m)
Height:	11ft 6^1/$_2$in (3.58m)
Width:	9ft 3in (2.82m)
Seating:	Total: 222S
	BDMSO - 59S
	TSO - 74S
	DMSO - 57S
Internal layout:	2+2
Gangway:	Within set (emergency end doors)
Toilets:	Not fitted
Weight:	Total: 98 tonnes
	BDMSO - 37 tonnes
	TSO - 25.5 tonnes
	DMSO - 35.5 tonnes
Brake type:	Air (EP/rheostatic)
Bogie type:	BX1
Power collection:	700-750 V dc third rail
Traction motor type:	8 x GEC G310AZ
Horsepower:	880hp (657kW)
Max speed:	75mph (121km/h)
Coupling type:	Outer - Tightlock, Inner - bar
Multiple restriction:	Class 507 and 508/1 only
Door type:	Bi-parting sliding
Total number in traffic:	32 (one stored)
Construction:	Body - aluminium, Frame - steel
Special features:	CCTV
Owner:	Angel Trains
Operator:	MerseyRail

Fact File

A derivative of the BR 1972-design suburban EMU is this fleet of Class 507s.

Designed and equipped for the MerseyRail electrified network around Liverpool, the sets were originally of the high-density layout, but following refurbishment under the Merseytravel banner sets now sport 2+2 interiors.

When built, sets were painted in standard blue and grey BR colours, this giving way later to MerseyRail yellow and now MerseyTravel silver-grey and yellow.

Refurbishment at Eastleigh Works in recent years has seen revised front ends fitted with new headlight and marker lights.

All sets are allocated to Birkenhead depot and operate alongside the Class 508/1 stock.

Below: *The entire Class 507 and 508/1 fleets are refurbished and sport revised front ends with a top marker light, two large headlights and a combined marker/tail light on each side. Sets are painted in silver/yellow MerseyRail livery. A Class 507 and 508 pass at Hoylake.* **Fred Kerr**

Above: *Allocated jointly with the Class 508/1 fleet to Birkenhead North, the 60-strong fleet operates all MerseyRail services in and around Liverpool and as far as Chester. The end doors are for emergency use only and are usually kept locked. Steps are carried on board the train for end evacuation in case of accident or incident in the Central Liverpool tunnel section. Set No 507013 is seen at Southport.* **Nathan Williamson**

Right Middle: *Passenger access is via two pairs of bi-parting sliding doors; these are operated by on train staff and do not have external local controls. To meet the Disability Discrimination Act, the doors are finished in yellow, with a deep grey edge. This view shows a DMB vehicle with the underslung motor generator and the 'one-shot' sanding pipe adjacent to the wheelset.* **Fred Kerr**

Right Bottom: *The post-privatisation refurbishment of these sets at Eastleigh Works has produced a common interior for MerseyRail Class 507 and 508 sets, having a low-density 2+2 seating layout with high-back seats. Small above seat luggage racks are provided with other storage located between seat backs. As these sets are not fitted with air conditioning, opening hopper windows are provided. Internal CCTV and passenger information systems are installed.* **Nathan Williamson**

Electric Multiple-Units

Class 508

Sub class:	508/1	508/2	508/3
Number range:	508103-508143	508201-508212	508301-508303
Former number range:	508003-508043	508101/105/106/ 107/109/113/116/ 119/121/129/132/133	508102/135/142
Originally built:	1979-1980	1979-1980	1979-1980
Introduced:	As 508/1 - 1984-1985	As 508/2 - 1998	As 508/3 - 2002-03
Originally built:	BREL York	BREL York	BREL York
Refurbished by:	BRML Eastleigh	Alstom Eastleigh	Alstom Eastleigh
Formation:	DMSO+TSO+BDMSO	DMSO+TSO+BDMSO	DMSO+TSO+BDMSO
Vehicle numbers:	DMSO - 64651-64691 TSO - 71485-71525 BDMSO - 64694-64734	DMSO - 64649-64681 series TSO - 71483-71515 series BDMSO - 64692-64724 series	DMSO - 64650-64690 series TSO - 71484-71524 series BDMSO - 64693-64733 series
Vehicle length:	DMSO - 64ft 11¹/₂in (19.80m) TSO - 65ft 4¹/₂in (19.92m)	DMSO - 64ft 11¹/₂in (19.80m) TSO - 65ft 4¹/₂in (19.92m)	DMSO - 64ft 11¹/₂in (19.80m) TSO - 65ft 4¹/₂in (19.92m)
Height:	11ft 6¹/₂in (3.58m)	11ft 6¹/₂in (3.58m)	11ft 6¹/₂in (3.58m)
Width:	9ft 3in (2.82m)	9ft 3in (2.82m)	9ft 3in (2.82m)
Seating:	Total - 192S DMSO - 59S TSO - 74S BDMSO - 59S	Total - 219S DMSO - 66S TSO - 79S BDMSO - 74S	Total - 222S DMSO - 68S TSO - 86 BDMSO - 68
Internal layout:	2+2	2+3 high density	2+3 high density
Gangway:	Within set, emergency end doors	Within set, emergency end doors	Within set, emergency end doors
Toilets:	Not fitted	Not fitted	Not fitted
Weight:	Total - 99.49 tonnes DMSO - 36.16 tonnes TSO - 26.72 tonnes BDMSO - 36.61 tonnes	Total - 99.49 tonnes DMSO - 36.16 tonnes TSO - 26.72 tonnes BDMSO - 36.61 tonnes	Total - 99.49 tonnes DMSO - 36.16 tonnes TSO - 26.72 tonnes BDMSO - 36.61 tonnes
Brake type:	Air (Westcode/rheostatic)	Air (Westcode/rheostatic)	Air (Westcode/rheostatic)
Bogie type:	BX1	BX1	BX1
Power collection:	750V dc third rail	750V dc third rail	750V dc third rail
Traction motor type:	8 x GEC G310AZ	8 x GEC G310AZ	8 x GEC G310AZ
Horsepower:	880hp (657kW)	880hp (657kW)	880hp (657kW)
Max speed:	75mph (121km/h)	75mph (121km/h)	75mph (121km/h)
Coupling type:	Outer - Tightlock Inner - bar	Outer - Tightlock Inner - bar	Outer - Tightlock Inner - bar
Multiple restriction:	Class 507 and 508/1	Within sub class only	Within sub class only
Special features:	CCTV		CCTV
Door type:	Bi-parting sliding	Bi-parting sliding	Bi-parting, sliding
Total sets in traffic:	27	12 (six stored)	3
Construction:	Body - aluminium	Body - aluminium	Body - aluminium
Owner:	Angel Trains	Angel Trains	Angel Trains
Operator:	MerseyRail	South Eastern Trains	Transport for London

Below: *Sporting the latest silver and yellow MerseyRail livery Class 508/1 sets Nos 508120 and 508128 stand at Birkdale on 22 May 2007. To assist in bridging power gaps on the network, collection shows are fitted to both bogies on driving cars.* **Fred Kerr**

Fact File

These 43 sets were originally introduced on the Southern Region in 1979; they were transferred to the Liverpool area in 1984, but left one TSO vehicle on the Southern for use in Class 455 stock.

Not all 43 sets were needed for Liverpool operations and 15 sets were stored before returning to traffic; 12 on Connex South Eastern and three more recently on Transport for London.

Most sets have now been refurbished and those on MerseyRail have revised front ends.

Above: *The Class 507 and 508/1 fleets operating on the Liverpool-area MerseyRail network are fitted with end emergency doors for operating through the inner-city tunnel sections. These are not usually available for between-unit passenger use and are normally locked. The post privatisation refurbishment at Alstom Eastleigh has seen a revised front end incorporating a cant rail height marker light and large headlights and joint marker/tail lights below each front window. Set No 508117 is seen at Liverpool Central on 9 March 2006.* **Nathan Williamson**

Right: *If compared with the original interiors of the Class 508/0s when delivered for Southern Region use in the 1970s, the passenger accommodation on these sets has hugely altered, from the original 2+3 low-back seats, interiors are now furnished in low-density 2+2 seats with high backs. Pleasingly-angled grab poles are provided in the vestibule areas and internal passenger information systems are installed, as is CCTV equipment for passenger and staff security. The interior of set No 508122 is shown.* **Fred Kerr**

Electric Multiple-Units

Above: *Broadside view of Class 508 driving car, showing the bi-parting passenger doors at the one-third and two-thirds positions with a single leaf sliding cab door. No passenger door controls are provided (unlike the SET and Silverlink-operated sets). BDMSO No 64716 is illustrated.* **Fred Kerr**

Above: *In 1998 12 spare Class 508 sets were taken over by Connex South Eastern for local branch line use, where the deployment of Networker stock could not be justified. The sets were refurbished at Eastleigh and reclassified 508/2. Painted in Southeastern livery, set No 508208 is seen at London Bridge on a Tunbridge Wells service.* **Brian Morrison**

Left Second: *Today half the 508/2s now operated by South Eastern Trains are either stored or out of use, while the remaining six operational sets are being refurbished at Wabtec Doncaster in 2007-08. This view shows the intermediate TSO, with accommodation for 79 passengers and has one wheelchair space. Passenger access is by two pairs of bi-parting sliding doors feeding directly into the seating area. As no air conditioning is provided hopper windows are fitted.* **Author**

Left Bottom: *The interior of SET and Silverlink sets retain the original low-back seats, set out in the 2+3 high-density style. Lino is fitted to the floor and two banks of open-tube fluorescent lighting run longitudinally down the coach ceiling. Passenger doors are locally operated after release by the conductor.* **Author**

Above: *A major refurbishment contract for six of the Southeastern Class 508 units commenced at Wabtec Doncaster in summer 2007. New interiors were fitted, upgraded technical equipment and the most noticeable change a new livery was applied, using light and dark grey offset by white. Set No 508205, the first set to be refurbished is seen at Wabtec, Doncaster.* **Derek Porter**

Right: *Capacity issues on the Silverlink-operated North London Line from Euston to Watford and Stratford-Richmond saw the operator request extra train sets in 2002-03. As no Class 313s were available, three long-stored Class 508s were upgraded for use on the dc-operated Euston-Watford route and reclassified as 508/3. The sets were overhauled at Alstom Eastleigh and finished in Silverlink mauve and yellow livery. Set No 508302 is shown departing from Willesden Junction low level, bound for Watford Junction. These sets retain their original 3+2 high-density seating.* **Author**

Electric Multiple-Units

Departmental EMUs

Departmental EMU stock

Number	Former number	Type	Use	Set No.
975025	60755	Saloon	Inspection saloon	-
999602	62483	MT	Ultrasonic test car	901001
-	62482	MT	Ultrasonic test car (spare)	-
999606	62356	MT	Ultrasonic test car	-

Set No.	Car No.	Type	Use
(42)3905		3-COP	Depot tractor, Bombardier Chart Leacon
(42)3918		3-COP	Depot tractor, Bombardier Chart Leacon
-	72640	TSO	Make-up vehicle
-	72641	TSO	Make-up vehicle
8303	72603	TSO	Make-up vehicle
8303	72608	TSO	Make-up vehicle
8308	72614	TSO	Make-up vehicle
8308	72707	TSO	Make-up vehicle
8308	72615	TSO	Make-up vehicle
9102	68501	GLV	Sandite
9109	68508	GLV	Sandite

910001	72616+72708+72639 - Brake force runner set
910002	72612+72706+72613 - Brake force runner set
930204	977874 (65302) + 977875 (65304) - Depot Sandite SU
930206	977924 (65382) + 977925 (65379) - Depot Sandite SU

Fact File

As with DMU stock, a number of redundant EMU vehicles have passed to departmental use. In the main this has been on the tracks of the former Southern Region where sets were used for de-icing, stores and development work.

Today a fleet of ex-EMU Gatwick Express stock is used as brake force runners for test trains and three former SR dc EMU power cars have been adapted as Ultrasonic test cars.

Two former Gatwick Express DMLVs are now operated by Network Rail as de-icers.

975025, although originally a Hastings DEMU buffet vehicle, is included in this section as it conforms to EMU characteristics as a non-powered driving inspection saloon.

Left: *At first glance one would not imagine this was a former 4REP driving car. Apart from the cab door position, little remains of the original bodywork. Car 999602 is rebuilt from 62483 and operated with two ex-Class 101 driving cars as set 901001.* **Nathan Williamson**

Below: *Two ex-Class 488 Gatwick Express vehicles, Nos 76212/13 painted in NR blue livery are seen with the track test train.* **Author**

Electric Multiple-Units

Above: *At one time Railtrack and later Network Rail operated a sizeable fleet of Southern Region-style dc EMUs for de-icing operations. Based at most of the main depots, these sets would 'patrol' the network in the small hours of winter morning to ensure no ice built up on the live rail. Today no such operations take place. Selhurst Depot, operated by Southern, still has two de-icing power twins, Nos 930204 and 930206, on their books. These Railtrack-liveried sets are confined to yard use. Set No 930206 is illustrated.* **Brian Morrison**

Right Middle: *In 2005 two former Gatwick Express Luggage Vans (GLVs) Nos 9102 and 9109 were taken over by Network Rail for main line de-icing on dc tracks, being out-based at Tonbridge. The modification work saw the vehicles lose their self propelled status and traction is now provided by 'top and tail' GBRf Class 73s. The cars are painted in NR yellow with black ends. The two vehicles are seen at Ashford powered by EDs Nos 73208 and 73206.* **Brian Stephenson**

Right Bottom: *Perhaps more correctly this vehicle should be in the DMU section, as it is a rebuild from an ex-Hastings line DEMU buffet car. However, its use and operation is more in keeping with EMU stock. The saloon has a modified 1963-type driver's desk and can operate in multiple with 1951, 57, 63 and 66 SR style EMUs and Class 33/1 and 73 locomotives. Painted in mock SR green livery and usually kept at the RTC Derby, it is frequently used for route inspections, often with a Class 33/1 locomotive.* **Author**

UK Maintenance Depots

A large number of maintenance and stabling facilities exists throughout the rail system. These are mainly operated by the Train Operating Companies, but an increasing number of private sites now service and maintain UK traction.

Many of the more modern multiple-unit passenger fleets have been ordered under contracts which include lifelong maintenance deals performed by the manufacturers' staff; in some cases former railway depots have been taken over for this role but in others, new purpose-built facilities have been constructed.

Under the privatised railway the number of depots has considerably reduced, with the freight operators largely having 'paper allocations' with maintenance performed by depots closest to where locomotives are operating when attention falls due. An increased number of private maintenance providers exists, frequently performing light exams while locomotives lay over between duties.

Unlike the railway of the past under the BR banner, the UK maintenance sites are very secure locations and casual visits are not permitted. Some of the nationally recognised railway enthusiast groups operate visits to these sites; details are usually available through the railway press.

AC	Aberdeen Clayhills (NX)	HST/Stock
AD	Ashford (Hitachi)	395
AF	Ashford Chart Leacon (BT)	375
AK	Ardwick (Siemens)	185
AL	Aylesbury (Chiltern)	165, 168, 960
AN	Allerton (EWS)	08, 09
AY	Ayr (EWS)	-
BA	Crewe Basford Hall (FLT)	57, 66, 86
BB	Billingham (Enron)	08
BD	Birkenhead North (MerseyRail)	507, 508
BF	Bedford Cauldwell Walk (FCC)	319
BI	Brighton (Southern)	09, 377
BK	Barton Hill (EWS)	Stock
BM	Bournemouth (SWT)	73, 421
BN	Bounds Green (NX)	08, 91, Stock
BS	Bescot (EWS)	08 ,09
BY	Bletchley (London Midland)	150, 321
BZ	St Blazey (EWS)	Stock
CE	Crewe International (EWS)	86, 90, 92, 325
CH	Chester (Alstom/ATW)	175
CK	Corkerhill (FSR)	156
CP	Crewe Carriage Shed (LNWR)	47, Stock
CS	Carnforth (WCRC)	33, 37, 47, Stock
CZ	Central Rivers (Bombardier)	08, 220, 221, 222
DF	Derby Rail Engineering	08, 31, 37, 47, 73
DM	Dollands Moor (EWS)	21
DR	Doncaster (EWS)	08
DY	Derby Etches Park (Maintrain)	08, 09, 222, Stock
EA	Earles Sidings (EWS)	08, 20
EC	Craigentinny (NX)	08, 43, Stock
EH	Eastleigh (EWS)	-
EM	East Ham (c2c)	357
EZ	Exeter St Davids (FGW)	142, 143, 150, 153, 158
FF	Forest, Brussels (Eurostar)	373
FR	Fratton (SWT)	-
FW	Fort William (EWS)	Stock
FX	Felixstowe (FDRC)	01, 08

Below: *With the introduction of Bombardier 'Electrostar' stock on the Southern-operated routes from London Victoria to Surrey and Sussex came major development at Brighton depot where the original depot facility was rebuilt to cope with the demands of modern stock. Class 377/1 No 377119 is seen inside the main servicing and repair depot in December 2006. The Southern-operated maintenance facility at Selhurst also carries out Class 377 maintenance.* Author

Above: *A once sizeable depot with a significant allocation of locomotives and diesel mechanical multiple-units, Ayr in South West Scotland is little more than a stabling point today, looking after out-based Class 66s. A two-track, single-locomotive-length fuelling and inspection shed is provided, hosting No 66143 in this August 2002 view.* **Author**

GI	Gillingham , Kent (SET)	375, 465, 508
GL	Gloucester Horton Road (CR)	08, 31, 33, 47
GW	Glasgow Shields (FSR)	314, 318, 320, 334
HA	Haymarket (FSR)	150, 158, 170
HE	Hornsey (FCC)	313, 317, 365
HT	Heaton (NR/GCR)	43, 142, 156, 158
IL	Ilford (One)	315, 317, 321, 360
IM	Immingham (EWS)	60
IS	Inverness (FSR)	08, 158, Stock
KK	Kirkdale (MerseyRail)	507, 508
KM	Carlisle Kingmoor (DRS)	20, 37, 47, 57, 66
LA	Laira (FGW)	08, 43, Stock
LD	Leeds Midland Road (FLT)	08, 66
LE	Landore (FGW)	08, 43, 57

LG	Longsight Electric (NR)	323
LO	Longsight Diesel (NR)	08, 57
LY	Le Landy, Paris (SNCF)	373
MA	Manchester Int (WCTC)	390
MD	Merehead (Mendip)	08, 59
MG	Margam (EWS)	08, 09, 37
MN	Machynlleth (ATW)	158
ML	Motherwell (EWS)	08, 09, 37
NC	Norwich Crown Point (One)	08, 90, 150, 153, 156, 170, Stock
NH	Newton Heath (NR)	142, 150, 156, 158
NL	Neville Hill (NR/NX)	08, 43, 156, 158, 333, 321, Stock
NM	Northampton (Siemens)	350
NT	Northam (Siemens/SWT)	444, 450

Right: *The new Eurostar engineering facility opened at Temple Mills, East London in November 2007. This is the only UK depot to look after Eurostar stock used on Channel Tunnel services to Mainland Europe. One major building looks after daily maintenance as well as classified overhauls and specialist work. A half NOL Eurostar set, No 373308, is seen inside the depot.* **Author**

Traction Recognition

OC	Old Oak Common (EWS)	08, 09
OH	Old Oak Common (Siemens/ Heathrow Express)	332, 360
OM	Old Oak Common (FGW)	Stock
OO	Old Oak Common (FGW)	08, 180, Stock
OY	Oxley (WCTC)	390, Stock
PC	Polmadie (WCTC)	Stock
PM	St Philips Marsh (FGW)	08, 43, 150, 153, 158
PE	Peterborough (GBRf)	66
PZ	Penzance (FGW)	08, Stock
RG	Reading (FGW)	165, 166
RM	Ramsgate (SET)	375
RR	Doncaster Roberts Rd (Fastline)	56
RY	Ryde St Johns (SWT)	483
SA	Salisbury (SWT)	158, 159
SG	Slade Green (SET)	376, 465, 466
SI	Soho (Maintrain)	323
SL	Stewarts Lane (GatX/VSOE)	73, 460
SU	Selhurst (Southern)	171, 319, 377 455, 456
TD	Temple Mills (Eurostar)	08, 373
TE	Thornaby (EWS)	08, 60, 66
TO	Toton (EWS)	08, 09, 37, 59, 66, 67
TS	Tyseley (Maintrain)	150, 153, 156, 158, 170
WB	Wembley (WCTC)	325, Stock
WD	East Wimbledon (SWT)	455, 458
WN	Willesden (TfL)	08, 313, 508
YS	York (Siemens)	185
XW	Crofton (BT)	170, 222

Left: *The only depot operated by Silverlink Railways, for its fleets of Class 150 and 321 stock is the four-track Bletchley depot, situated on a spur line from Bletchley station. The depot was built as part of the mid-1960s electrification of the West Coast route and has been updated for its present role. Two Class 321 units share space in January 2007. The depot is electrified at 25kV ac.* **Author**

Below: *South West Trains operates Salisbury depot, located adjacent to the station, for the maintenance and housing of its entire DMU fleet of Class 158, 159 and 960 stock. This is the view of the west end of the single-ended building with Class 159 No 159021 entering the shed.* **Author**

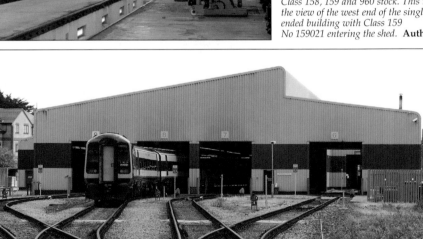

TOC abbreviations

ATW - Arriva Trains Wales
BT - Bombardier Transportation
CR - Cotswold Rail
EWS - English Welsh & Scottish Rly
FCC - First Capital Connect
FDRC - Felixstowe Dock & Railway Co

DRS - Direct Rail Services
FGW - First Great Western
FLT - Freightliner
GatX - Gatwick Express
GBRf - GB Railfreight
FSR - First ScotRail
LNWR - London North Western Rly

NR - Northern Rail
NX - National Express
SET - South Eastern Trains
SWT - South West Trains
VSOE - Venice Simplon Orient Exp
WCRC - West Coast Railway Co
WCTC - West Coast Train Care